An Encyclopedia of AUX

Linguistic Inquiry Monographs

Samuel Jay Keyser, general editor

1. Word Formation in Generative Grammar

   Mark Aronoff

2. $\bar{X}$ Syntax: A Study of Phrase Structure

   Ray Jackendoff

3. Recent Transformational Studies in European Languages

   Samuel Jay Keyser, editor

4. Studies in Abstract Phonology

   Edmund Gussmann

5. An Encyclopedia of AUX: A Study in Cross-Linguistic Equivalence

   Susan Steele

An Encyclopedia of AUX:
A Study in Cross-Linguistic Equivalence

Susan Steele

with

Adrian Akmajian

Richard Demers

Eloise Jelinek

Chisato Kitagawa

Richard Oehrle

Thomas Wasow

The MIT Press

Cambridge, Massachusetts

London, England

© 1981 by
The Massachusetts Institute of Technology

All rights reserved. No part of this book may be reproduced in any form or by any means electronic or mechanical, including photocopying, recording, or by any information storage and retrieval system, without permission in writing from the publisher.

Printed and bound in the
United States of America

Library of Congress Cataloging in Publication Data

Steele, Susan.
   An encyclopedia of AUX.

   Bibliography: p.
   Includes index.
   1. Grammar, Comparative and general. I. Title.
P201.S69   415   81-8418
ISBN 0-262-19197-0 (hard)   AACR2
ISBN 0-262-69074-8 (paper)

Publisher's Note

This format is intended to reduce the cost of publishing certain works in book form and to shorten the gap between editorial preparation and final publication. Detailed editing and composition have been avoided by photographing the text of this book directly from the author's camera-ready copy.

CONTENTS

Foreword	vi
Preface	vii
1. The Theoretical Framework	1
2. A Definition and Its Instantiations	21
3. Equivalence	141
4. Further Exploration	168
Appendix A. AUX in English	226
Appendix B. The AUX in German and the History of English	260
List of Abbreviations	303
References	304
Index	313

FOREWORD

We are pleased to present this monograph as the fifth in the series *Linguistic Inquiry Monographs*. These monographs will present new and original research beyond the scope of the article, and we hope they will benefit our field by bringing to it perspectives that will stimulate further research and insight.

Originally published in limited edition, the *Linguistic Inquiry Monograph* series is now available on a much wider scale. This change is due to the great interest engendered by the series and the needs of a growing readership. The editors wish to thank the readers for their support and welcome suggestions about future directions the series might take.

Samuel Jay Keyser
for the Editorial Board

PREFACE

This monograph was first conceived over two years ago as a more detailed investigation of the subject raised in Akmajian, Steele, and Wasow (1979): the status of the category AUX in Universal Grammar. Its rather overlong gestation is, perhaps, a natural consequence of the number of parents involved, but it was also necessitated in part by the controversy the Akmajian, Steele, and Wasow article produced. (See, for example, Pullum (1981), Kaisse (1981), and Heny and Richards, eds. (forthcoming).) The various objections--and revelations of entrenched pre-suppositions--put forward in these works led to a rethinking of some of the positions taken in that earlier article; the result of the reconsideration will be most obvious here in chapter 1.

Although this work has a relatively large number of authors, it is not an anthology of our various concepts of the category AUX. Each of us, probably, has views on this topic which diverge, even if only slightly, from those of the others; however, we attempted to put aside whatever differences do exist in order to produce a unified exposition and statement. As a technical exercise alone, this was an interesting task, since no section was written by all the authors in concert.

The work contains four chapters and two appendices. I wrote the first and third chapters. The longest chapter--chapter 2--is divided into six major sections, four of which deal with different languages. Richard Demers wrote the section on Lummi; Eloise Jelinek, the section on Egyptian Arabic; Adrian Akmajian and Chisato Kitagawa, the section on Japanese. I wrote the section on Luiseño, as well as the introduction and conclusion which tie the various language analyses together. Richard Oehrle and I are responsible for the fourth chapter. The appendices concentrate on languages which have historically been the center of the AUX controversy. Appendix A, concerning English, was written by Richard Oehrle, while appendix B, concerning German and the history of English, was written by Thomas Wasow and Adrian Akmajian.

Primary responsibility for the pieces of the work can thus be assigned. However, many of the ideas expressed in any of these chapters or sections are the result of discussion among (some subset) of the various authors, so that, while individual authors are primarily accountable for the sections with which they have been identified, the work represents a more general collaboration.

Even assuming a spirit of collaboration, someone had to be responsible for integrating the pieces. I have undertaken this task in chapter 1. In addition, someone had to edit and revise the individual sections so they fit together. This was also largely my responsibility.

The research represented in this work has been supported primarily by a grant from the National Science Foundation to Adrian Akmajian, Thomas Wasow, and myself. Research on Luiseño has been supported, at various times, by the University of California, the Phillips Fund of the American Philosophical Society, the National Science Foundation, and the University of Arizona. The University of Arizona has also been generous in its support of Richard Demer's work on Lummi. Some of the research on Egyptian Arabic by Eloise Jelinek was supported by the Wenner-Gren Foundation.

Finally, I must thank Anne Mark and Theresa A. Huard for their help in the preparation of the manuscript, and Tom Larson for preparing the index.

Susan Steele

An Encyclopedia of AUX

Chapter 1

THE THEORETICAL FRAMEWORK

1.1 Introduction

If we suppose there to be some inherent similarity among the grammars of particular languages--and there are many reasons to do so, among them the fact that the human language faculty is a species-specific property--then we must make the attempt to state precisely where that similarity lies. There is a large and ever-growing body of literature concerned with just this problem; however, the part of it which deals with syntactic categories is largely presumptive. That is, assuming that categorial distinctions are necessary to an adequate analysis of any language, it is common practice to employ similar sets of labels in making language-internal categorial distinctions and commonly presumed that the linguistic distinctions thus indicated share more in common than just the labels used to mark them. This practice is approved--and the presumption explicitly stated--by Chomsky in <u>Aspects of the Theory of Syntax</u>. (p. 65f).

"...we must ask whether the formatives and category symbols used in Phrase-markers have some language-independent characterization, or whether they are just convenient mnemonic tags, specific to a particular grammar....I shall assume that these elements...are selected from a fixed, universal inventory..."

Clearly, it is not necessary to presume some universal inventory to give an adequate analysis of some particular language in language-particular terms. Assuming that it is necessary to distinguish some set of elements from other sets of elements on various grounds, it is in principle relatively easy to do so by identifying the various sets with any arbitrary set of symbols or descriptive labels. The hypothesis of a universal inventory is intended, then, to speak directly to the supposition of inherent similarity across grammars, by precluding such language-particular analyses. However, it should be obvious that until some substance is given to the labels that are applied across languages, until the properties which a label names are given language-independent characterization, the universal inventory of categories is a dogma, not a testable hypothesis. Unless it is true--and it appears patently false--that the distinctions which the presumed labels name are identical across languages, there must be some method of determining when some category in a particular language is to be identified with a category in another. In fact, if we wish to treat the "universal inventory" as a hypothesis, rather than a dogma, there must be some method of determining when some category in a particular language is an instance of some member of the universal inventory. The fact that there is no point-by-point identity across languages suggests the necessity of formulating some such principle; it is, as yet, unspecified--even by those who presume the universal inventory and argue over its membership.

 This monograph attempts to put the question of the similarity of categories across the grammars of particular languages on a substantive empirical basis. We are concerned essentially with providing a framework--with giving a principled method of cross-linguistic comparison--in terms of which the question can be decided, rather than its answers presumed. Section 1.3 returns to the notion of a "universal inventory" as embedded in a theory of Universal Grammar. While the critical issue, as we see it, is general to a consideration of any syntactic category, the framework which we propose below will be applied in later chapters specifically to a category which we call AUX--a category which we will proceed to define and instantiate relative to a variety of language. The final section of this chapter summarizes the controversy over this category as it relates to the discussion in sections 1.2 and 1.3.

1.2 Equivalence

It is extremely unlikely that a framework for cross-linguistic comparison could provide necessary and sufficient conditions for deciding categorial status language-internally, for a very simple reason: the lack of point-by-point identity across languages alluded to above.[1] It is realistic, however, to expect a framework for cross-linguistic comparison to allow identification of a set of language-internal categories, given language-internal analyses, as _equivalent_. The judgment of equivalence across a set of language-particular categories depends on providing, first, definitions which allow identification of the language-internal categories as distinct or nondistinct and, second, tests of the linguistic interest of the identification.

The necessity of definitions to a framework of cross-linguistic comparison seems, to us, patently obvious. It is certainly true that such traditionally used and accepted categories as Noun, Verb, or Sentence have some intuitive basis; a linguist who attempts to analyze some previously unanalyzed language may, with some confidence, assign certain elements to them. Clearly, however, the identification of a category in one language with a category in another cannot depend on the labels which we have given the categories, if we have not stated what the label refers to, independent of any language-particular instantiation.[2]

Because the elements of a definition are necessarily presumed, the list of such elements should be kept as small as possible. That is, we abide here by Occam's Razor: the smaller the set of elements presumed in advance, all other things being equal, the better the definition. The empirical value of a definition, then, is inversely proportional to what is presumed in the definition. Our position here follows from the fact that ours is an empirical approach to cross-linguistic equivalence--an approach in which one wants to minimize assumptions and maximize empirical content. If, to determine the similarity across languages in terms of syntactic categories (or anything else, for that matter), we have to assume substantial similarity in other aspects of the languages in question, we have contributed little to our understanding of cross-linguistic similarity in general.

The bases for positing a category in the grammar of a particular language will typically be some clustering of semantic, syntactic, morphological, and phonological properties, although whether one or another of these is primary or even necessary may very well be a language-internal decision.[3] There is no reason to believe that definitions which are meant to apply cross-linguistically will depend on different properties. However, as we will argue in justifying the category AUX, the definitions by which a set of language-internal categories are identified require some notional criteria. We agree with Greenberg (1963,59) when he states:

"...the adequacy of a cross-linguistic definition of 'noun' would, in any case, be tested by reference to its results from the viewpoint of the semantic phenomena it was designed to explicate. If, for example, a formal definition of 'noun' resulted in equating a class containing such glosses as 'boy', 'nose', and 'house' in one language with a class containing such items as 'eat', 'drink', and 'give' in a second language, such a definition would forthwith be rejected and that on semantic grounds."

This is not to say that the definitions are limited to notional criteria; our definition of AUX is not, and we expect that definitions which attempt to accomplish what ours does cannot be purely semantic. Rather, the statement is intended to point up the essential character of semantic criteria to the enterprise.

It also distinguishes our position from another which has been taken, although there is no real correspondence between the reasons for definitions in the two. Jackendoff (1977a,253), following Chomsky (1970), proposes a set of formal features which distinguish the members of a set of categories. In Jackendoff's proposal, there are four (±Subject, ±Object, ±Comp, and ±Det); these define what he takes to be the categories of, at least, English. (1) shows Jackendoff's use of these features.

(1)

	Subj	Obj	Comp	Det
V	+	+	+	
M	+	+	−	
P	−	+	+	
Prt	−	+	−	
N	+	−	+	
Art	+	−	−	+
Q	+	−	−	−
A	−	−	+	
Deg	−	−	−	+
Adv	−	−	−	−

Jackendoff admits that his features are arbitrary,[4] and there are reasons to believe that defining categories in terms of some set of formal syntactic features does not allow the system to be extended to other languages. For example, Jackendoff's system argues that V(erb) and M(odal) have some similarity, playing on the often repeated observation that English Modals are verblike. His system is much less successful in accounting for languages in which there is no syntactic similarity between verbs and modals--and such languages clearly exist, as we will see in some detail. There is little reason to believe that the problems which arise in regard to auxiliary elements in such a system are limited to them.

   A definition, then, allows the members of a set of language-internal categories to be identified as distinct or nondistinct. This identification is necessary, but not sufficient, to establish equivalence across these categories. The framework of cross-linguistic comparison must also provide a test of the linguistic interest of the identification.

Obviously, not all conceivable definitions--even those which are equally parsimonious--are of equal interest. There is no reason to assume that any definition which might be proposed will, in fact, be instantiated when it is tested across the categories of a set of languages. Thus, the simplest test of a definition is whether or not it receives instantiation. However, even if a definition receives instantiation in a set of analyses, there is no guarantee that the identification of these categories will have interesting consequences for a theory of the properties of languages. Suppose that a definition of the following sort were given: Q occurs sentence-finally. The definition given for Q is tautological; that is, it will be instantiated without fail in every language. Therefore, the results of such an identification have no interesting consequences for an empirical study of the properties of languages and are an investigative deadend.[5]

There is, of course, no logical necessity that any properties other than the definitional one(s) hold across a set of language-internal categories. Therefore, the identification of a set of language-internal categories has interesting consequences only if the members of the set of categories share certain nondefinitional properties of the set of categories that the definition identifies. If a definition identifies a set of categories and if the members of that set share certain nondefinitional properties, we will take that set to be a linguistically significant equivalence class.[6]

It is important to make clear what we mean by a set of categories "sharing nondefinitional properties". It is not essential that language-particular instantiations of the definition exhibit identical properties--other than the definitional ones. Rather, the question is whether, taken as a whole, the set of language-particular categories which have been identified by the definition exhibits some specifiable subset of those properties which are logically possible. That is--if the identification is linguistically interesting--this set will show a cluster of properties, none of which need be common to all the language-particular instantiations, but all of which are repeated intermittently throughout the set, to the exclusion of other logical possibilities.

By requiring that a set of categories identified under some definition share nondefinitional properties, we can test the linguistic interest of the identification. However, the method also thereby generates theoretically interesting questions. Every time a nondefinitional property is found to be associated with some set of categories identified by a definition, one must ask why this should be the case. Furthermore, the questions which arise have some empirical basis. We would argue that the ability to raise further, substantive, questions about some set of equivalent elements is one of the strengths of the framework we have advocated.

In sum, the definition and the empirical tests of the identification allowed by the definition establish cross-linguistic equivalence. We have discussed the method specifically as it applies to categories; it should be clear, however, that the method applies to other linguistic properties as well--insofar as it is possible to formulate non-language-particular definitions for these properties.

1.3 Universal Grammar

We are now ready to consider the notions of "Universal Grammar" and the "fixed, universal inventory". Universal Grammar "determines the class of possible grammars and the way they operate" (Chomsky and Lasnik (1977)); that is, it (or that segment of it recently termed Core Grammar) is part of the genetic endowment of the child.[7] If one necessary aspect of a grammar is some set of categorial distinctions, the fixed, universal inventory referred to in section 1.1 is part of Universal Grammar. That is, (2) seems a fair formulation of the hypotheses inherent in the quotation from _Aspects_ in section 1.1.

(2)
a. Universal Grammar includes a list of categories.

b. The categories in a natural human language are necessarily selected from a list of categories in Universal Grammar.

As we stated earlier, there has been no attempt to give substance to the categorial labels in Universal Grammar. The framework which we specified in section 1.2 allows a language-independent characterization of a category. The set of definitional and nondefinitional properties under which an equivalence is given--and which the label of the definition names--specify a category in language-independent terms. The definitional properties are absolute properties of any language-particular instantiation of the category, while the nondefinitional properties specify the parameters, a set of possibilities, within which any language-particular instantiation will fall.

However, our proposals should not be seen simply as a method giving substance to each member of some set of categorial symbols in Universal Grammar. There are differences between the empirical approach to discovering the cross-linguistic similarity which we have advocated and the assumptions which, apparently, underlie Universal Grammar.

First, we required that definitions under which similarity can be tested should minimize assumptions. The approach fostered by assumptions concerning innateness leads one instead to want to maximize the a priori constructs. These two positions are not in any essential conflict, but they suggest different ways of evaluating proposals about cross-linguistic similarity.

Second, Universal Grammar applies from the top down. Universal Grammar specifies some set of categories, a subset of which is found in any natural human language. The primary issue, then, is to determine which of those, given any randomly chosen language, are applicable in its analysis. The framework we have proposed here takes precisely the opposite tack. We do not assume a set of categories in advance of language-internal analyses and a principled method of comparing those analyses. Rather, we give a metric by which the similarities across the categories of the analyses can be determined, and the judgment of equivalence made. Using language-specific categorial labels or descriptive terms in the analysis of any one language does not preclude the possibility of cross-language comparison; in fact, to allow specific language-internal categories is to explicitly recognize the lack of point-by-point identity which we have at times noted and which we will exemplify in detail in later chapters. However, it also avoids the dogma of assuming some set of categorial symbols in advance of a method by which they can be determined. That is, while it may turn out to be the case that there is some "universal inventory", we consider that an empirical question to be investigated; therefore, any attempt to specify a universal set of categories requires a method of determining when some element in a particular language is an instance of a particular universal category. The method advocated here attempts to place the issue of categorial comparison on grounds as factual as possible, relative to our understanding of particular languages.

In support of our position, we note that the concept of a "fixed, universal inventory" needs considerable refinement if it is in any sense to "determine" a possible grammar.

First, (2) has at least two possible interpretations: there is a universal set of categories from which languages choose, or there is a universal set of categorial systems from which languages choose one. Let us take the first interpretation and assume that the universal inventory includes the categories in (3).

(3)
X, Y, Z, P, Q, R, S, T

The inventory in (3) could represent a set of language types, as in (4), with nonintersecting categories.

(4)
a. X, Y
b. Z, P
c. Q, R
d. S, T

Alternatively, some subset of the categories in (3) could be shared--say, X and Y--and the remainder distributed among languages. This would allow the set of grammars listed in (5).

(5)
a. X, Y, Q
b. X, Y, P
c. X, Y, R
d. X, Y, S
e. X, Y, T

Finally, all languages could exhibit precisely the same set of categories. We see, then, that even only one of the two conceivable interpretations of (2) subsumes a number of alternatives, and the first of these (that is, (4)) can claim to be "universal", to determine the class of possible grammars, only in the sense that it covers all the possible cases.
   The second interpretation of (2) is implicit in theories of X-bar syntax. (See especially Jackendoff (1977b).) Under such a theory, certain categorial choices depend on certain other categorial choices. That is, it is implicitly assumed that categories are not of equal status and that a theory of Universal Grammar must stipulate their internal relationships. If we translate the letters in (3) into certain commonly used categorial labels--say, DET, ADJ, ADV, N, NP, V, VP, and PP--this theory rules out the choice of certain logically possible subsets; for example, a grammar which employed DET, VP, and ADJ and only those should be impossible. Such an addition to (2) does not, of course, decide among the three logical possibilities specified

above. Since not all categorial choices are crucially interdependent, a grammar could logically choose only those which were. For example, a grammar could contain the categories DET, N, and NP and only those. It would therefore still be possible for two languages to have totally nonintersecting categories. That is, there could logically be two types of language, one which chooses DET, N, and NP and another which chooses V, ADJ, and VP.

A second problem inherent in the notion of a "fixed, universal inventory" is this. Unless all the members of the list of categories in Universal Grammar are found in every natural human language, the "universal inventory" is simply a catalogue of the properties which can be found in natural human languages. The universal inventory cannot be fixed in advance of knowing what the possible categories are; whenever we come upon a language with a new category, even a totally idiosyncratic one, the category can always be added to the list of categories in Universal Grammar. Thus, in effect, the notion of a fixed, universal vocabulary places no limits on the grammars of particular languages, although this is precisely what it is intended to do.

The second problem is not obviously resolvable. The first problem has been addressed, although somewhat indirectly, in more recent statements of the form of Universal Grammar; however, its resolution raises certain other issues, which (at least) need clarification. According to Chomsky and Lasnik (1977,430), Universal Grammar is composed of two parts: Core Grammar and Non-Core Grammar.

"...there is a theory of core grammar with highly restricted options, limited expressive power, and a few parameters. Systems that fall within core grammar constitute 'the unmarked case'; we may think of them as optimal in terms of the evaluation metric. An actual language is determined by fixing the parameters of core grammar and then adding rules or rule conditions, using much richer resources.... These added properties of grammars we may think of as the syntactic analogue of irregular verbs."

Koster (1978) accepts the division which Chomsky and Lasnik propose, although he does not use the term Universal Grammar, and seems to believe that the two parts make up a whole (that is, that they determine the class of possible grammars).

"Core grammar ... is responsible for the most rigid part of language. Its rules and conditions are either invariant across languages, or fall within a very limited range....Beyond this, languages may have rules in different degrees of markedness. On the periphery of language, anything learnable (in whatever way) is possible....Plasticity increases towards the periphery, but at no level is there unlimited choice." (pp. 566-567)

Neither discussion includes specification of categories, but there is no reason to think, in either case, that it cannot be included in the formulation of Universal Grammar.[8] The distinction drawn in these discussions between Core and Non-Core Grammar can be interpreted as requiring that some one of the three possibilities sketched above be chosen.

The framework proposed here could allow us to determine whether a given category falls within the core or not; assuming some criteria by which we can identify a language-internal category and some test of these criteria, we can determine whether categories meeting them are found in all languages or only some. Furthermore, the results of our framework of cross-linguistic comparison--that is, that, language-independently, a categorial symbol must be the label of a set of properties, some of which are essential to any instantiation of the category and some of which are options within which instantiations will vary--appear consistent, in an interesting fashion, with the distinction between core and noncore properties. However, if we take Koster's hypothesis of invariance across languages in terms of the core seriously, Core Grammar should include only the essential properties of a given category (also in the core), those properties which any instantiation will necessarily exhibit. But this decision has the undesirable consequence of leaving a significant amount of what can be specified about a category outside the core--all the properties within which languages can vary but which can be specified within certain parameters. The alternative, of course, is to allow these last properties to be included in Core Grammar as well. However, that solution requires that the claim of "essential invariance" for the structure of Core Grammar be given much more precise characterization than it has received to date.

In short, our proposals should not be viewed simply as giving substance to the notion of "category" in these theories of Universal Grammar as it is presently conceived--although it will allow language-independent specification of the properties of some category. Our framework is a method by which equivalence across the categories of language-particular grammars can be decided; it provides an empirical test of the assumption of similarity across grammars, rather than presuming it in advance. Furthermore, it explicitly recognizes the lack of absolute point-by-point identity among the grammars of languages and systematically exploits this very fact.

1.4   The AUX Controversy[9]

We have presented a framework in which categories can be systematically compared across languages. In its specifics, this work analyzes the role of the cross-linguistically identifiable category AUX in the grammar of various natural languages. The controversy over this category is a case study in the problems raised by accepting, uncritically, the dogma of Universal Grammar. In this section, then, we will outline the AUX controversy. Our discussion makes concrete the general criticisms of Universal Grammar mentioned in the immediately preceding section.

In <u>Syntactic Structures</u>, Chomsky proposed an analysis of English which included the following phrase structure rule:

(6)
Aux ⟶ Tense (Modal) (have+en) (be+ing)

Two fundamental features of the analysis are that (a) a syntactic category Aux is proposed, which appears as a syntactic node in phrase markers, and (b) this category consists of a collection of elements (which in (6) can be characterized notionally as Tense, Modality, and Aspect) whose relative distribution (i.e. linear position in a string) is directly specified and constrained by the phrase structure rule. (Transformations, of course, could affect the relative distribution.) The fundamental features of this analysis have been accepted in such works as Chomsky (1965), Jackendoff (1972), Emonds (1976), Culicover (1976), Akmajian and Wasow (1975), and others, although these authors have discussed in considerable detail the character of the analysis which depends on these premises. That is, (6) has not gone unmodified.

There is another school of thought which denies the validity of the premises upon which the analysis in (6) is based. Ross (1967) does not posit a syntactic category Aux; rather, he considers its purported members to be main verbs that take full sentential complements. The complex deep structures required by this analysis undergo certain transformations (notably, raising and/or equi rules) that collapse the complex embeddings into simple surface structures. Furthermore, the distribution of the auxiliary elements is said to be governed not by a phrase structure rule, but rather by supposedly independently necessary constraints holding between main verbs and their sentential complements. This analysis has also been modified by various researchers, the most complete treatment of this view being Pullum and Wilson (1977).

Gazdar, Pullum, and Sag (1980) is, in part, a continuation of the main verb analysis; however, it is distinctive in that it recognizes in the phrase structure a category which is distinct from other categories, namely, V_n. That is, what Chomsky analyzed as the category Aux is really an instance of Verb, but Gazdar, Pullum, and Sag introduce a symbol V_n, where $\underline{V}$ is meant to specify the category as such and the subscript $\underline{n}$ specifies rule-defined subcategories of V.

Since all the analyses of English in this literature distinguish among three classes of elements--illustrated, for example, by <u>can</u>, <u>have</u> or <u>be</u>, and <u>run</u>--this particular aspect of the AUX controversy makes sense only in the context of assumptions about the "fixed, universal inventory". With his analysis, Chomsky adds an element to that inventory, a move which, as we pointed out above, is consistent with assuming such an inventory in advance of knowing its members. Proponents of the other view have taken the position that eliminating the category Aux from the grammar of English constitutes a simplification and is, hence, a priori desirable. It is not simply the case that eliminating the category Aux from the grammar of English constitutes a simplification of English grammar; its elimination is also taken to be a reduction in the members of the set of categories in Universal Grammar, although the argument in these works turns on analyses of English. If Chomsky's position is consistent with the notion of Universal Grammar, the opposing view has misconstrued Universal Grammar to be a much more powerful notion than it is. If the inventory of categories in Universal Grammar is a catalogue, there is no argument in the theory of an inventory against the addition of new categories.

Equally important, none of the works mentioned give any substance to the categorial symbol AUX--or any other symbol for that matter--outside the English analysis which is its only instantiation in this part of the literature. This omission gives the debate a somewhat metaphysical character. Akmajian, Steele, and Wasow (1979) confront this issue directly by showing that there is reason to argue for a category in other languages having essentially the features exhibited by the English Aux. That is, they propose a definition of a category which they label AUX and then test analyses of two languages--English and Luiseño--against that definition. The categories in either language which meet the definition are taken to be instantiations of AUX. Further, Akmajian, Steele, and Wasow point out, admittedly somewhat unsystematically, other properties which the categories in both languages share.

Their argument has not gone unchallenged. Pullum (1981) enumerates differences between what Akmajian, Steele, and Wasow call an instantiation of AUX in Luiseño and what they call an instantiation of AUX in English, implying that these differences are at least as important as the definitional and nondefinitional properties under which Akmajian, Steele, and Wasow argue for similarity. In addition, new analyses have been presented for the languages with which Akmajian, Steele, and Wasow were concerned, analyses which argue, in effect, that the categorial label applied in either case is wrong. Pullum (ibid.) and Kaisse (1981) argue that the set of Luiseño clitics presented in Akmajian, Steele, and Wasow as an instance of the category AUX is really just a set of clitics; in Gazdar, Pullum, and Sag (1980), a paper which temporally follows Akmajian, Steele and Wasow, what was analyzed as Aux is covered by the symbol V_n. That is, the response to Akmajian, Steele, and Wasow argues, first, that if their definition allows the identification of elements which have demonstrably different properties in certain respects, it cannot be a good definition. Further, the argument goes, why employ AUX when such familiar notions as Clitic or $V_{(n)}$ are available and, perhaps, more reasonable language-internally?

The objections are not entirely without merit, largely because of the insistence in Akmajian, Steele, and Wasow that the category AUX is also employed language-internally. However, the problem is not one of language-internal labels. Rather, the responses to Akmajian, Steele, and Wasow fail to stipulate cross-linguistically identifiable properties of the categories they employ (e.g. Verb, Clitic, V_n, etc.) and, as a result, their arguments are essentially incomplete. Akmajian, Steele, and Wasow of course did not deny that the Luiseño clitics are, in fact, clitics. While we would not agree with Gazdar, Pullum, and Sag's characterization of the members of their category V_n as verbs, we could accept their language-internal label and still ask whether this category, under some definition and empirical tests of the definition, can be argued to be equivalent to a category labeled, say, Clitic Complex in a language like Luiseño. In fact, it is important to point out that Gazdar, Pullum, and Sag are implicitly assuming a definition of what they label Verb, such that it covers all English verbs, modal auxiliaries, have, and be. Since they do not define the equivalence class they assume--and it cannot depend on identity, because there are clearly differences among the elements explicit even in their analysis--the label V_n is no more explanatory than any other they might have invoked.

1.5 Conclusion

In this chapter we have presented a framework within which categories can be systematically justified across languages. We turn, then, to the specifics of the case: justification of the category AUX. Chapter 2 contains a definition of the category and an extended discussion of the set of categories which this definition identifies in a sample of quite different languages. In chapter 3 we argue for a cluster of nondefinitional properties which accompany the definitional ones and for certain limits on them. The arguments of these two chapters comprise a systematic justification of the category AUX across, at least, the set of languages in chapter 2. Within this framework, the characteristics of the category, as a language-independent object, are clearly specified. Chapter 4, the final chapter, is less a conclusion than a prospectus. Given that we have established an equivalence class labeled AUX, a number of questions arise about its various members, questions that depend on the argument which precedes them but which extend far beyond it.

Following these chapters are two appendices. The languages discussed in chapter 2--with the exception of Luiseño--are not languages upon which the controversy over the category AUX has focused. In the appendices we consider languages which have been in the eye of the storm. Appendix A focuses on

English. Appendix B considers modern German and the history of English.

Notes

1. Examples of the lack of point-by-point identity are fairly easy to cite: the properties of traditionally assigned case labels, subordinate clauses, or even sentences. Since this work is an extended example of this fact, we will not pause here to give details of others.

2. Insofar as other linguists have been concerned with cross-linguistic identification, it seems to us that they have ignored the necessity or providing a priori a definition against which language-particular phenomena may be tested. The arguments presented for the category SUBJECT are a good case in point. Perlmutter and Postal (1977) argue that the notion Subject is needed to allow the statement of the equivalence of certain (intuitively equivalent) language-particular phenomena--specifically, the passive. Actually, they say that something is a passive in language L_1 and something else is a passive in language L_2--although they never state how we are to know a passive when we see one--and that the only way of stating the identification is by referring to such grammatical relations as Subject and Direct Object. However, they do not begin with a definition of SUBJECT that allows us to test whether or not each of the language-particular cases is an instantiation of it. The argument, therefore, is essentially circular.

3. Since categories are commonly presumed for the purpose of illustrating rules which make reference to them, the usual (indirect) arguments for establishing them are primarily syntactic ones.

4. Note further that the specifications + and - do not have a single interpretation throughout, so + can mean either 'takes a' or 'is a'.

5. This example of a definition does not employ semantic criteria, as it is meant simply to be

illustrative. However, there is no reason to think that the use of semantic criteria necessarily protects against a tautological or otherwise uninteresting result.

6. Since the term <u>equivalence</u> could be applied to any relationship which is symmetrical and transitive, the set of categories identified under a definition are equivalent. However, we will label this an <u>identification</u> and reserve the terms <u>equivalence</u> and <u>equivalence class</u> for a linguistically significant identification, i.e. one in which the members of the set of categories share certain nondefinitional properties.

7. Perusing the literature which discusses Universal Grammar (or Core Grammar) immediately reveals that the construct it is intended to identify varies from individual to individual, or even within the writings of a single individual. We do not intend to sort the various specifications out here; rather, we will focus on particular aspects of the discussion which are clearly to be distinguished from the endeavor we are undertaking.

8. Of course, if the only syntactic rule is Move α, the necessity of distinguishing one category from another will be shifted to the morphology or to "logical form".

9. As the preceding discussion suggests, it is critical to distinguish between language-internal categorial labels and the label of an equivalence class which may subsume them. The difference between the two will be consistently represented in this work in the following fashion: a label the initial letter of which is capitalized identifies a language-internal category, e.g. Verb; a label in upper case, e.g. AUX, identifies an equivalence class. That is, Aux identifies the English constituent proposed in certain analyses of English and AUX a set of elements which may include English Aux. Although we will not have established, until chapter 3, that there is indeed an equivalence class

which we will label AUX, this is the point we are attempting to prove. We will therefore use the upper case label to refer to that class, in advance of the proof.

Chapter 2

A DEFINITION AND ITS INSTANTIATIONS

2.1 Introduction
Given a set of language-internal analyses, those constituents which may contain only a specified (i.e. fixed and small) set of elements, crucially containing elements marking tense and/or modality, will be identified as nondistinct.[1] We could use any term to label the definition, that is, to refer to the set of constituents subsumed under the definition, but AUX is the term introduced by Chomsky (1957) for the English analysis discussed in chapter 1. Since his analysis of this aspect of English falls within our definition (as do the analyses which follow it), we will use this term here--in the specific sense, however, of referring to the set of constituents which are nondistinct under the definition.

As we argued to be critical in chapter 1, the elements of the definition comprise a small set: constituent, tense, and modality. They are presumed for the purposes of the cross-linguistic comparison. However, it is reasonable to ask what we take them to include. Elements marking tense are a subset of those elements marking temporal reference. Specifically, temporal reference includes marking for relative time and absolute time; tense refers only to the latter. That is, an element marking tense will indicate time from the point of view of the speech event, rather than time relative to a time indicated in the speech event. Elements expressing modality will mark any of the following: possibility or the related notion of permission, probability or the related notion of obligation, certainty or the related notion of requirement.[2] By specifying in the definition that the set of elements in the constituent with which we are concerned must be fixed and small, we are, in effect, recognizing the grammatical--as opposed to lexical--status of tense; the term is commonly used in such a fashion. The specification is more important for the term <u>modality</u>, since there is no systematic terminological distinction in this realm equivalent to the distinction between the terms <u>tense</u> and <u>temporal reference</u>. Therefore, by requiring that the constituent identified by the definition contain a specified set of elements, we exclude such English words as <u>possible</u> or <u>possibly</u> and their equivalents in other languages. These belong to open classes.

<u>Constituent</u> is much more difficult to delimit adequately, in large part because it is basic to standard syntactic theory. That is, by presuming it we base our definition on something which is generally presumed. Syntactic analysis is generally assumed to involve parsing a sentence into certain smaller units, constituents. Given our proposed definition, there are two questions which must be faced squarely. First, what is the evidence for the parsing? There is a large literature on tests for constituency, dating back beyond <u>Syntactic Structures</u>.[3] However, there is no compelling reason to think that the test(s) for a given parsing will be anything other than language-particular. Thus, the analyses to follow provide evidence for the particular parsing which is proposed, although the tests vary from language to language. At any one point, the tests may not be formalized to the extent some readers might like, but the problem of an adequate theory of parsing procedures is by no means peculiar to our investigation. The second question is at least as tricky: At what level does the parsing apply? Clearly, given an abstract enough analysis, almost any parsing could be proposed; many theories of grammar are powerful enough to admit rules which remove any evidence of the proposed constituent analysis. Furthermore, it is not at all obvious that analyses at different levels of structure, if we admit such a possibility, are comparable. We cannot hope to give a theory of constituent structure which solves the abstractness issue. However, we endeavor to make our analyses as concrete as possible, in an attempt to obviate it. On the other hand, in no case are our analyses

simply a statement of the surface facts; all are
abstracted--regularized--away from them. The tension
created by attempting to meet both of these
requirements allows, then, that our analyses are
reasonably consistent with one another.

In the following sections of this chapter, we
will discuss analyses of four language--Luiseño,
Lummi, Egyptian Arabic, and Japanese--specifically
considering whether or not there is in each case a
constituent which conforms to the definition given
above. In all instances, it will be shown that such
an argument can be made. Thus, since there is no
logical necessity that such a situation hold, our
definition meets the first test of a definition in a
framework of cross-linguistic investigation: it has
instantiation.[4]

2.2   Luiseño[5]

2.2.1 Introduction Following the first element in a
Luiseño sentence may be one or more of a number of
particles. Consider, for example, the following
sentences:[6]

(1)
a. noo   n   hunwuti   patiq
   I   PRT   bear:obj   is:shooting
   'I am shooting the bear.'

b. noo   nu   po   hunwuti   patin
   I   PRT   PRT   bear:obj   will:shoot
   'I will shoot the bear.'

c. noo   xu   n   po   hunwuti   pati
   I   PRT   PRT   PRT   bear:obj   shoot
   'I should shoot the bear.'

(1a) contains only a single particle, one that marks
the number and person of the subject of the
sentence; such particles will be referred to here as
subject marking.[7] In addition to subject marking,
(1b) contains an immediately following particle; and
(1c) contains particles immediately preceding and
following subject marking.

Akmajian, Steele, and Wasow (1979) discuss two properties of this set of particles, with the aim of showing that they form a constituent. First, the set of particles as a whole has certain wordlike properties; most importantly, certain otherwise demonstrably word-internal phonological processes apply to the sequence. Second, the entire sequence of particles must be referred to in the syntax of Luiseño in order to guarantee not only that they are positioned together in sentential second position, but also that nothing interrupts the sequence This discussion does not exhaust, nor was it intended to exhaust, the properties of the particle sequence. Any analysis of Luiseño will have to deal with these phonological and syntactic characteristics, but it will also have to account adequately for another: the sequence of particles is a semantic unit. Section 2.2.2 will provide support for this claim, as further evidence for the constituency of the sequence of second-position particles.

While section 2.2.2 is most critically concerned with the semantic interaction of the members of the particle sequence, one consequence of the discussion is a preliminary specification of its internal structure. Sections 2.2.3 and 2.2.4 complete the argument. With these three sections, we will have argued that the Luiseño particle sequence has characteristics that meet the definition in section 2.1: it is a constituent; it marks tense and modality; and its membership is fixed and small.

2.2.2 The Particle Sequence as a Semantic Unit: Constituency   Here and elsewhere in this discussion, we assume the wordlike property of the sequence of particles and its occurrence in sentential second position. We refer the reader who is unfamiliar with the Luiseño particle sequence to Akmajian, Steele, and Wasow (1979); Steele (1977) discusses the second of these facts in more detail. We are concerned here specifically with the semantic property of the particle sequence which was not discussed in these earlier works. However, the arguments presented for the claim follow from and are further support for the position taken in Akmajian, Steele, and Wasow (1979) that the particle sequence is a constituent, insofar as we take a locus of phonological, syntactic, and semantic properties to define this notion.

A brief excursus on tests for constituency is in order. To our knowledge, no theory of constituency has been advanced which provides definitive tests for proving the constituency of a string of elements. However, we think it indisputable that sufficient evidence for constituency is provided if a string of elements has phonological, syntactic, and semantic properties which associate the members of the string and distinguish them as a unit from other parts of the sentence. The members of the Luiseño particle sequence interact with one another, on all counts, in a way that is totally accidental if they are independent elements of the sentence. On the other hand, if the particle sequence is a constituent, there is no reason not to expect an interdependence of the sort which its members exhibit. Specific to the argument here, while a semantic interdependence of the sort which we will describe is perhaps not always reflected in syntactic constituency, the burden of proof is on those who would propose a syntactic analysis which does not reflect the semantic facts. In this case, then, the burden of proof falls on those who would hold that the members of the particle sequence do not form a single constituent.

In fact, objections to the position that the particle sequence is a constituent are offered in Pullum (1981) and Kaisse (1981). Neither article, however, effectively counters the position taken in Akmajian, Steele, and Wasow (1979).[8] Furthermore--and this is critical--neither accounts satisfactorily for the semantic interdependence which we will detail in this section.

Sentences (1a-c) suggest that there are basically three positions in a Luiseño particle sequence, as represented in (2) (where the middle position contains subject marking).

(2)
Particle: - Particle: - Particle:
 Position:1   Position:2   Position:3

That is, the particle sequences in (1) can be represented respectively as follows:

(3)
a. ∅ - Subject:Marking - ∅
b. ∅ - Subject:Marking - Particle
c. Particle - Subject:Marking - Particle

This discussion will show, first, that there is a global property associated with the configuration of particles on either side of subject marking which argues that these two positions must be considered a semantic unit and, second, that the subject marking which intervenes between them depends on the particle types which surround it. That is, the various members of the particle sequence interact with one another--and only with one another--in a way that might be expected if they form a constituent but which is inexplicable if they are independent elements of a sentence.

In this section we will ignore sentences in which the speaker is giving someone else's assessment of some situation, sentences which we will refer to as quotative speech; however, we will return to them in section 2.2.3. The inventory of particles which can occur in positions 1 and 3 in the particle sequence, then, is given in (4):[9]

(4)
a. Position 1

   ɸu
   xu

b. Position 3

   po
   il
   kwa

If (3) represents all the examples in (1), a fourth configuration of particles surrounding subject marking is logically possible.

(3)
d. Particle - Subject:Marking - ∅

(3d) is also attested, as we will see below. Represented in these four possibilities are three "sentence types".[10] Any sentence with the particle configuration in (3a) or (3b) is a simple assertion; any sentence with the particle configuration in (3c) is a modal assertion, an assertion ascribing some possibility to the situation which it describes; and any sentence with the particle configuration in (3d) is a nonassertion.[11]

We could illustrate the global property associating the first and third positions in the particle sequence with essentially any choice from the set of particles in (4); for ease of exposition, we will discuss cases having the particle ṣu in position 1 and the particles il or po in position 3, alternating in either case with the absence of any particle in either position.

(5)
a. ∅ - Subject:Marking - ∅

b. ∅ - Subject:Marking - $\left\{ \begin{array}{c} il \\ po \end{array} \right\}$

c. ṣu - Subject:Marking - $\left\{ \begin{array}{c} il \\ po \end{array} \right\}$

d. ṣu - Subject:Marking - ∅

A consideration of the semantic differences among (5a) and the two cases in (5b) will at once provide evidence for our claim that the corresponding configurations in (3) are nonmodal assertions and lay the groundwork for considering the claims regarding the configurations in (3c) and (3d). When there is no particle in position 1, il and po cooccur with specific suffixes on what we can term the "verb", as does the absence of any particle in the same position. (6) below is a list of the

Luiseño suffixes which mark tense (and various aspects). The aspectual glosses are given, where appropriate; the suffixes following the slashes are the plural forms. The variation between <u>ax</u> and <u>'ya</u> depends on the form to which it attaches, as does the alternation between <u>wun</u> and <u>an</u>, the plural forms of <u>q</u>.[12]

(6)

	Nonfuture		Future
Distant		Near	
qu$ 'durative'		q/wun or an 'durative'	an
uk 'habitual'			
ax or 'ya 'completed'			

The configuration in (5a) cooccurs with the suffix labeled <u>near nonfuture</u>.

(7)
noo   n   heyi-q
I   ∅-subj:mark-∅   dig-Q
'I am digging.'

The configuration in (5b) with <u>il</u> cooccurs only with the suffixes labeled <u>distant nonfuture</u> (i.e. (distant) past tense); the configuration in (5b) with <u>po</u> cooccurs only with the suffix labeled <u>future</u>.

(8)
a. noo   n-il   heyi-qu$
    I   ∅-subj:mark-IL   dig-QU$
    'I was digging.'

b. noo   n-il   heyi-k
    I   ∅-subj:mark-IL   dig-UK
    'I used to dig.'

c. noo   n-il   hey-ax
    I   ∅-subj:mark-IL   dig-AX
    'I dug.'

(9)
noo   nu-po   heyi-n
I   ∅-subj:mark-PO   dig-AN
'I will dig.'

(10) is a schematic representation of the distribution of (5a) and (5b) just discussed.[13]

(10)
         Nonfuture   Future

Distant   Near

∅-..-il   ∅-..-∅   ∅-..-po

Representative examples of (5c) are given in (11) through (13).

(11)
wunaalum   ǰu-m-po   pomyo'   qalwun
they   ǰU-subj:mark-PO   their:mothers   are
'They must have mothers somewhere.'

(12)
ku'aalum   ǰu-m-il   nowiiwiyk   yuchiwun
flies   ǰU-subj:mark-IL   in:my:wiwish   sank
'I see that flies sank in my wiwish.'

(13)
wunaalum   ǰu-m-il   heyiwun
they   ǰU-subj:mark-IL   are:digging
'They are digging (but I didn't know it until just now).'

The combination of ǰu and po, as in (11), indicates a speaker supposition which lacks any immediate and obvious external verification, a supposition based on some general knowledge. The combination of ǰu and il indicates a supposition of a somewhat different sort. The speaker has some reason to believe that the sentence describes an actual state of affairs, but either has adduced this conclusion from some observation or is in doubt about some particular aspect of the situation. (12) is an example of the former case; (13) of the latter. (14) is a schematic representation of the combinations of ǂu and po or il.

(14)
Supposition with   Supposition from
   External Verification   General Knowledge

     ǂu-...-il   ǂu-...-po

It should be clear from the examples and the discussion that it is reasonable to call sentences in the configuration (3c) modal assertions.

A comparison of the examples illustrating (5b) and (5c) does not, however, clearly prove our claim about the global property associating the positions on either side of subject marking in the particle sequence. Certainly, compared to instances containing ǂu, po and il are different when there is no particle in position 1. We could say that il and po in either case are accidental homophones, a particularly unappealing proposal since there is some intuitive connection between pastness and verifiability on the one hand and futureness or unverifiability on the other. However, the basic problem for our proposal--that the presence or absence of ǂu alone appears central to the interpretation of the "sentence type"--remains.

Once we consider (5d), the problem dissolves; the necessary association of the position preceding subject marking and the position following it is self-evident. The configuration in (5d) marks the sentence in which it occurs as a question; this is a special case of the claim that the configuration in (3d) indicates that the sentence in which it occurs is not an assertion. (15) contains examples of (5d).

(15)
a. wunaalum   ǂu-m   heyiwun
   they   ǂU-subj:mark-∅   are:digging
   'Are they digging?'

b. wunaalum   ǂu-m   heyiquǂ
   they   ǂU-subj:mark-∅   were:digging

'Were they digging?'

c. wunaalum   ǵu-m   heyin
   they   ǴU-subj:mark-Ø   will:dig
   'Will they dig?'

There is no distinction in word order between (yes/no) questions and statements, nor is there any obvious intonational difference. The one critical difference resides in the shape of the particle sequence. Questions contain the particle ǵu and lack any particle in position 3. Thus, in (15b) the verb is inflected with quǵ 'distant past durative' and in (15c) with -an 'future', but neither il nor po, respectively, is possible--if the sentence is a question. Neither the property of containing ǵu nor the property of lacking il or po is alone sufficient to identify a sentence as a question, since there are (modal) statements which contain ǵu--those discussed above in regard to (5c)--and there are statements which lack il and po--those in which the verb is inflected for some near time, as illustrated in (7).[14]

There can be little doubt that the ǵu in (5d) is the same ǵu as the one in (5c), rather than an accidental homophone--aside from the fact that if we took the latter position here and (noting that il and po have potentially different interpretations as well) the same position in regard to them, the accidental homophony in the particle sequence would be startling. Ǵu in questions has the same cooccurrence restrictions with the other position 1 particle xu (an example of which is found in (1c) above) in questions as it does in statements. Ǵu and xu may not cooccur in the particle sequence of a statement, regardless of their relative order.

(16)
a. *wunaalum   ǵu-xu-m-po   toonav
    they   ǴU-XU-subj:mark-prt:3   make:baskets

b. *wunaalum   xu-ǵu-m-po   toonav
    they   XU-ǴU-subj:mark-prt:3   make:baskets

Analogously, the particle sequence in questions may not contain xu. (18) is the question corresponding to the modal assertion in (17).

(17)
wunaalum xu-m-po   toonav
they   XU-subj:mark-prt:3   make:baskets
'They should make baskets.'

(18)
wunaalum ʂu-m   toonav
they   ʂU-subj:mark-Ø   make:baskets
'Should they make baskets?'

(19) with both ʂu and xu is impossible.

(19)
*wunaalum ʂu-xu-m   toonav
 they   ʂU-XU-subj:mark-Ø   make:baskets

If ʂu cannot cooccur with xu in statements, it follows, if ʂu is the same element, that it should not be able to cooccur with xu in questions.¹⁵ If ʂu in (5d) is the same particle as the one in (5c), the presence of ʂu alone does not mark a sentence as a modal assertion. The potential objection that ʂu alone determines "sentence type"--the objection raised in regard to (5a) through (5c)--is, then, laid to rest.

In sum, the claim which we made about the configurations in (3) is substantiated by our consideration of the particular cases in (5). In the face of the semantic interdependence between the positions preceding and following subject marking in the particle sequence, the proposal that the elements which may occur in either position are not part of a single constituent appears singularly untenable--again, insofar as we are willing to accept semantic arguments for constituency. However, advocates of the nonconstituency position would be hard pressed to find a natural explanation for this interaction, to the exclusion of any similar interaction with the other sentence elements. The semantic argument for constituency is obviously not complete, since the first and third positions in the particle sequence are not necessarily contiguous, being separated by another particle. That is, we appear to have argued for a constituent the parts of which are not adjacent to one another. We will turn to completing the argument shortly, but, first, some brief remarks are in order.

The preceding discussion argues that the configuration of particles on either side of subject marking determines the "sentence type". We have also seen from the discussion of the particles ṣu, po, and il that their meaning is a property of the configuration in which they occur. That is, it seems unenlightening to try to give a single meaning for any of these three particles, either a meaning which is modified in a particular context to some (related) meaning or some abstract meaning which receives a particular realization in a given context.[16]

In earlier discussions of the Luiseño particle sequence (cf. Akmajian, Steele, and Wasow (1979)) it was suggested that the first member of the particle sequence marked modality and the third tense. On the other hand, the arguments given above would suggest that modality or tense is marked by some configuration of particles in the first and third positions of the particle sequence. In some sense, both of these positions are right.

Clearly, by saying, for example, that ṣu alone does not determine that a particular sentence is a modal assertion, we are not claiming that some particular modal notion cannot be localized to ṣu, assuming some context. Ṣu and the other particle which occurs in first position in the particle sequence, xu, can be shown to have different modal forces in sentences having the configuration in (3c). While sentences with ṣu (and some particle in the third position) carry some notion of supposition, sentences with xu (and some particle in the third position) do not. Sentences with xu and po, for example, indicate instead logical necessity (20), obligation (21), or speaker desire (22):

(20)
```
wunaalum   xu-m-po              waayax    qay
they       XU-subj:mark-PO      swim      neg

machavichuqanik
wanting:to:drown
```
'They must swim, if they don't want to drown.'

(21)
```
'omom    xu-m-po              pokwaxma         cho'on    temeti
you      XU-subj:mark-PO      run:habitual     every     day
```
'You should run every day.'

(22)
```
noo   xu-n-po              heelax
I     XU-subj:mark-PO      sing
```
'I wish I could sing.'

Similarly, in regard to il and po, we have shown that when there is no particle in the first position in the particle sequence, these particles (and their absence) have a particular cooccurrence pattern with tense suffixes. While the argument for labeling these elements as tense is somewhat weaker, they are to be distinguished in this particular context entirely in terms of tense.

(At this point, we must note a fact which was at least implicit in the discussion of (5b) and (5c). If il and po have a particular cooccurrence pattern with tense suffixes when there is no particle in position 1 in the particle sequence, this pattern is obliterated when there is a particle present in position 1. So, for example, all the sentences in (11) through (13) have some form with the suffix wun 'near nonfuture plural'. Were no particle present in position 1, neither il nor po could cooccur with this suffix.)

In any event, marking both modality and tense is clearly a property of the Luiseño particle sequence, regardless of the validity of assigning these labels to some subpart of it. Therefore, the Luiseño particle sequence meets the requirement of marking tense and modality contained in the

A Definition and Its Instantiations

definition proposed at the beginning of this chapter.

We have argued, then, for the semantic association of the positions on either side of subject marking. The specification of subject marking also depends on the presence or absence of particles preceding and following it. The pattern argues, at least, that the entire particle sequence has an internal consistency, but it can also be interpreted as showing that subject marking is part of the semantic unit which surrounds it.

Four sets of forms are subsumed under subject marking. Three are listed here in (23a), (23b), and (23c); we will refer to these respectively as Set 1, Set 2, and Set 3.[17,18]

(23)

		Singular	Plural
a.	$\frac{1}{2}$	n	cha
	$\frac{2}{3}$		um
			pum
b.	$\frac{1}{\text{non-}1}$	n	cha(m)
			m
c.			m

Set 1 contains forms marking three persons and two numbers. The following sentences illustrate this set.

(24)
a. noo   n   hunwuti   patiq
   I   1ST:SG bear:obj is:shooting
   'I am shooting a bear.'

b. chaam cha   hunwuti   patiwun
   we   1ST:PL bear:obj are:shooting
   'We are shooting a bear.'

c. 'omom   um   hunwuti   patiwun
   you   2ND:PL bear:obj are:shooting
   'You (pl.) are shooting a bear.'

```
d. wunaalum  pum      hunwuti    patiwun
   they      3RD:PL   bear:obj   are:shooting
   'They are shooting a bear.'
```

In Set 2 the person distinctions are reduced to two. A comparison of (25c) and (25d) reveals that subject marking can be the same for a third plural subject as it is for a second person plural subject.

(25)
```
a. noo    n-il              hunwuti    patiquɬ
   I      1ST:SG-prt:3      bear:obj   was:shooting
   'I was shooting a bear.'

b. chaam  cham-il           hunwuti    patiquɬ
   we     1ST:PL-prt:3      bear:obj   was:shooting
   'We were shooting a bear.'

c. 'omom  m-il              hunwuti    patiquɬ
   you    NON:1ST:PL-prt:3  bear:obj   was:shooting
   'You (pl.) were shooting a bear.'

d. wunaalum  m-il              hunwuti
   they      NON:1ST:PL-prt:3  bear:obj

   patiquɬ
   was:shooting

   'They were shooting a bear.'
```

In Set 3 there is only a number distinction. A comparison of (26b), (26c), and (26d) illustrates that the subject marking can be the same for any plural subject; comparing (26a) with (24a) and (25a) shows that a first person singular subject can have the singular form of Set 3--∅.

(26)
```
a. noo  xu-po           heelax
   I    prt:1-prt:3     sing
   'I wish I could sing.'

b. chaam  xu-m-po             heelax
```

we   prt:1-PL-prt:3   sing
   'We wish we could sing.'

c. 'omom   xu-m-po   heelax
   you   prt:1-PL-prt:3   sing
   'You should sing.'

d. wunaalum   xu-m-po   heelax
   they   prt:1-PL-prt:3   sing
   'They should sing.'

Which of these three sets occurs in the particle sequence is determined entirely by the configuration of particles surrounding it. (27) represents the possibilities schematically.

(27)
a. $\emptyset$ - Set:1 - $\emptyset$

b. $\emptyset$ - Set:2 - Particle:3

c. Particle:1 - $\begin{Bmatrix} \text{Set:2} \\ \text{Set:3} \end{Bmatrix}$ - Particle:3

d. Particle:1 - $\begin{Bmatrix} \text{Set:2} \\ \text{Set:3} \end{Bmatrix}$ - $\emptyset$

As (27) suggests, Set 1 subject marking occurs only when subject marking is the only member of the particle sequence present, that is, only in the configuration in (3a). Only the sentences in (24) meet this condition. Replacing Set 1 subject marking in these sentences with some member from another set yields an unacceptable sentence. For example, in (28) pum '3rd plural' is replaced by m 'nonfirst plural' (in Set 2) or 'plural' (in Set 3).[19]

(28)
*wunaalum   um   hunwuti   patiwun
  they   uM   bear:obj   are:shooting

Set 3 subject marking occurs only when subject marking is preceded by some particle, that is, only in the configurations in (3c) or (3d). Only the sentences in (26) meet this condition. Of course, the sentences in (26) also have a particle following subject marking, but (29) will show that it is only the fact that an element precedes subject marking which is important.

(29)
chaam ∅u-m   toonavqu∅
we   ∅U-PL   were:making:baskets
'Were we making baskets?'

(30), with pum '3rd plural' from Set 1 and some particle in position 1, corresponding to (26d), is not a possible sentence.

(30)
*wunaalum   xu-pum-po   heelax
 they   PRT:1-3RD:PL-prt:3   sing

Set 2 subject marking occurs under two conditions. It is obligatory when subject marking is followed by some particle and not preceded by any particle, that is, in the configuration specified in (3b). The sentences in (25) meet this condition and contain Set 2 subject marking. (31), corresponding to (25d) but incorporating pum '3rd plural' from Set 1, is not a possible sentence.

(31)
*wunaalum   pum-il   hunwuti   patiwun
 they   3RD:PL-PRT:3   bear:obj   are:shooting

Set 2 subject marking can also occur in the environment specified for Set 3, that is, when subject marking is preceded by some particle (as in the configurations specified in (3c) or (3d)). The sentences in (32) are the same as those in (26), except that instead of Set 3 subject marking we find Set 2.

(32)
a. noo   xu-n-po   heelax
   I   PRT:1-1ST:SG-prt:3   sing
   'I wish I could sing.'

```
b. chaam    xushpo              heelax
            xu-cha-po
   we       PRT:1-1ST:PL-prt:3  sing
   'I wish we could sing.'

c. 'omom    xu-m-po                 heelax
   you      PRT:1-NON:1ST:PL-prt:3  sing
   'You (pl.) should sing.'

d. wunaalum  xu-m-po                 heelax
   they      PRT:1-NON:1ST:PL-prt:3  sing
   'They should sing.'
```

And (33) is the same as (29), except that Set 3 subject marking is replaced with Set 2.

```
(33)
chaam    ¢u-sh   toonavqu¢
we       ¢U-cha  were:making:baskets
'Were we making baskets?'
```

(27) suggests at least a formal interdependence between subject marking and the elements which surround it. It might be possible to capture the dependence of subject marking on the other members of the particle sequence, were the particle sequence not a constituent, but such an analysis offers no explanation for this dependence or the lack of similar dependence on any other sentence element. Furthermore, given that the particle positions immediately preceding and following subject marking are a semantic unit, the distribution which we have described for subject marking is evidence that this member of the sequence, too, is part of the same unit. Finally, and most importantly, a consideration of (27) suggests immediately that the distribution of the three different sets of subject marking intersects with the determination of "sentence type". Set 1 subject marking occurs only in nonmodal assertions which describe a situation occurring in near time--the sentence type described by the particle configuration in (3a). Set 2 subject marking occurs in any sentence type other than the

one specified for Set 1--those sentence types described by the particle configurations in (3b), (3c), or (3d), that is, any sentence which does not describe a situation in near time. Set 3 subject marking occurs in any sentence which is not a nonmodal assertion--those sentence types described by the particle configurations in (3c) and (3d). In sum, the distinctions in number and person vary directly with the verifiability of the situation described in the sentence.

A final point is in order. We began this discussion with the claim that there were four sets of subject marking; we have presented only three. The fourth set--which we will label Set 4--reduces the distinctions in Set 3 to none. That is, there is a set of subject marking which expresses no number or person distinctions; this type of subject marking can occur wherever Set 3 subject marking is allowed. Since Set 3 subject marking simply indicates a plural/nonplural distinction, the best illustration of Set 4 is a comparison of (26b,d) with (34a,b):

(34)
a. chaam   xu-po   heelax
   we   prt:1-Set:4-prt:3   sing
   'We wish we could sing.'

b. wunaalum xu-po   heelax
   they   prt:1-Set:4-prt:3   sing
   'They should sing.'

In (34) we are analyzing the particles xu and po as being separated by subject marking which has no phonological manifestation.[20]

(35), then, is a revision of (27), based on the discussion of subject marking just given.[21]

(35)
a. ∅ - Set:1 - ∅

b. ∅ - Set:2 - Particle:3

c. Particle:1 - $\left\{\begin{array}{l}\text{Set:2}\\\text{Set:3}\\\text{Set:4}\end{array}\right\}$ - Particle:3

d. Particle:1 $\left\{\begin{array}{l}\text{Set:2}\\\text{Set:3}\\\text{Set:4}\end{array}\right\}$ - ∅

We have argued that the configuration of particles on either side of subject marking determines the "sentence type" and that distinctions among the elements included under subject marking can be drawn on essentially the same grounds. The final argument that the entire particle sequence is a semantic unit pertains to its presence or absence. Quite simply, imperatives and all subordinate constructions have none of these particles. That is, just as the shape of the particle sequence determines the "sentence type", its complete absence serves to distinguish certain constructions.

(36) contains examples of imperatives.

(36)
a. nooli
   read
   'Read!'

b. maamayu   mariyi
   help   Mary:obj
   'Help Mary!'

As (36a,b) suggest, imperatives are characterized in Luiseño as containing a "verb" which lacks any of the tense/aspect suffixes given earlier in (6)--more specifically, it is uninflected for any temporal or aspectual notion--<u>and</u> as lacking any of the members of the particle sequence. Subordinate constructions are much more diverse. On functional grounds, there is reason to distinguish among at least three types: complements, relative clauses, and what we will term <u>adjuncts</u>.[22] Examples of these three types are given in (37), (38), and (39), respectively. As (37) through (39) suggest, subordinate constructions may contain some "verb" form with one of a set of

(37)
a. noo   n   wingeeq   mariya
   I   prt:seq   think   Mary

   po-waaqi-pi-y
   3rd:sg-sweep-temporal:reference-obj

   'I think that Mary will sweep.'

b. noo   nil   tiiwik   moyil   kari'a-qal
   I   prt:seq   saw   moon:obj   rise-aspect
   'I saw the moon rising.'

(38)
a. noo   n   chaqalaqiq   hengeemali
   I   prt:seq   is:tickling   boy:obj

   'o-'ayali-vo-y
   you-know-temporal:reference-obj

   'I am tickling the boy that you know.'

b. noo   n   chaqalaqiq   hengeemali
   I   prt:seq   is:tickling   boy:obj

   'oy   'ayali-mokwish-i
   you:obj   know-temporal:reference-obj

   'I am tickling the boy who knows you.'

(39)
a. xwaan   po-waaqi-qala   noo   nil
   John   he-sweep-aspect   I   prt:seq

   tooyaquʂ
   was:laughing

   'While John was sweeping, I was laughing.'

b. tooya-at   mariya   upil   heelaquʂ
   laugh-aspect   Mary   prt:seq   was:singing
   'While laughing, Mary was singing.'

suffixes marking aspectual or temporal reference, but it is a different set from that found in (6); most importantly, these subordinate constructions must lack any members of the particle sequence.

If the particle sequence were simply a sequence of independent elements, the absence of each particle in imperatives and subordinate constructions would have to be justified separately. While there may be grounds for arguing that some subset of various members of the particle sequence are necessarily absent in either imperatives or subordinate constructions, no reasoned justification can be given for the absence of all. Hence, the entire particle sequence acts as a semantic unit in its absence--it differentiates imperatives and subordinate constructions from the "sentence types" discussed above--just as its configuration differentiates among those sentence types.

2.2.3   Three   More   Particles   The   case   for   the constituency of the sequence of second-position particles thus appears relatively secure. The semantic facts just discussed can be described quite easily if the members of the particle sequence form a constituent; on the other hand, it is not at all obvious that such facts are to be expected, much less described, if the members of the particle sequence are independent elements. Language-internally, we could call this constituent anything we liked, as long as its label distinguished it from whatever other constituents it might be reasonable to hypothesize for Luiseño. Let us call it <u>Particle Complex</u>, a term as descriptive as any.

One consequence of the earlier discussion in section 2.2.2 is that we have given a preliminary specification of the internal structure of the constituent which is the Particle Complex; it was stated, in fact, in (35). In this section and the next, we will expand and elaborate on it. In this section, we are concerned explicitly with enumerating three particles which were not included, for reasons that will become obvious, in the list of particles given in (4);[23] in section 2.2.4 we will consider a number of ways in which the internal

structure could be given in a grammar of Luiseño.
  We mentioned when we introduced the configurations in (3) that these excluded the configurations found in what we called there <u>quotative speech</u>. (40) is an example of a sentence to which we will apply this label.

(40)
noo   kun-un   takwayaq
I   prt:com   is:sick
'I'm sick, I'm told.'

The gloss of (40) is the best English approximation of sentences in "quotative speech"; that is, such sentences are the speaker's report of what someone else has said. In quotative speech the deictic orientation is that of the speaker, but the observation made in the sentence is someone else's. Therefore, <u>quotative speech</u> is not meant to cover direct quotations. Compare, for example, (41) and (42).

(41)
mariya   pil   yaa   noo   n   takwayaq
Mary   prt:com   said   I   prt:com   is:sick
'Mary said, "I'm sick."'

(42)
mariya   pil   yaa   noo   kunun   takwayaq
Mary   prt:com   said   I   prt:com   is:sick
'Mary said that I'm sick.'

(42), but not (41), is an example of quotative speech. <u>Noo</u>, the first person singular pronoun, refers in (41) to Mary, but in (42) to the speaker.[24]
  Sentences in quotative speech are also to be distinguished from sentences containing any of the particle configurations in (37), in that, although these are to be distinguished from one another on various grounds, they all are found in sentences which report the speaker's assessment of some situation--not the speaker's report of someone else's assessment. Sentences in quotative speech are identified by the presence in the Particle Complex

of the particle kun. A comparison of (40) to (43) makes the point quite clearly.

(43)
noo   n   takwayaq
I   prt:com   is:sick
'I'm sick.'

The only difference between (40) and (43) is the presence in the former sentence--and the absence in the latter--of the particle kun; in (40), kun is followed by a form of the first person singular subject marking.
  The examples of sentences in quotative speech have a particle sequence which, it might appear, should be subsumed under (3d); that is, each contains kun, followed by subject marking and only subject marking. Furthermore, the subject marking possibilities are precisely those we would expect, given the expansion of (3d) in (35d): Set 2, Set 3, or Set 4. Thus, it might seem reasonable to analyze the particle sequence in (40) and (42) as shown in (44), an instance of (3d).

(44)
$$\text{kun} - \begin{Bmatrix} \text{Set:2} \\ \text{Set:3} \\ \text{Set:4} \end{Bmatrix} - \emptyset$$

Insofar as sentences in quotative speech are also not assertions, they appear consistent with our claims about the configuration in (3d). However, our characterization of quotative speech suggests that we consider such sentences to be of a different type altogether. Furthermore, a closer examination of the particle sequence of such sentences argues that, in fact, it is not possible to subsume it under our analysis of the Particle Complex.
  We begin by arguing explicitly against subsuming this particle sequence under the configurations specified in (3d). Quite simply, (3d) does not cover all the particle sequence possibilities found in quotative speech. Kun and the particles specified in (4) as occurring in the third position in the

A Definition and Its Instantiations   46

Particle Complex--<u>po</u>, <u>il</u>, and <u>kwa</u>--never occur in a single particle sequence. However, there is a particle--<u>a'</u>--which acts like <u>po</u>, <u>il</u>, and <u>kwa</u> in the instantiations of (3b) in that it marks tense; this particle is peculiar to sequences with <u>kun</u>. (45) and (46) give examples of particle sequences with <u>a'</u>. In (45), we find the suffix -<u>uk</u> 'past habitual' and, in (46), the suffix -<u>quṣ</u> 'past continuous'. Both suffixes are included in the nonfuture distant (i.e. past tense) column in (6).

(45)
```
wunaalum    kun-a'    'oy        'ayali-k
they        kun-A'    you:obj    know-UK
```
'They used to know you, I'm told.'

(46)
```
yamayk              kun-a'    cho'on    'ivi'    'exla
a:long:time:ago     kun-A'    all       this     earth

'ataaxum    pommiix              miy-quṣ
people      their:possession     be-QUṢ
```

'A long time ago, all this land was the Indian's.'

However, a sentence like (47a) with the suffix -<u>an</u> 'future' from (6) does not allow <u>a'</u>, as (47b) shows.

(47)
```
a. wunaal    kun    'oy        'onani-n
   he        kun    you:obj    meet-AN
```
   'He will meet you, he says.'

```
b. *wunaal   kun-a'    'oy        'onani-n
    he       kun-A'    you:obj    meet-AN
```

In any sentence whose particle sequence contains <u>a'</u> (and <u>kun</u>), there is some suffix which marks distant nonfuture. This situation is reminiscent of the discussion of <u>il</u>, when it occurs in a particle sequence lacking a particle preceding subject marking, i.e. (3b). It is parallel in a broader sense to <u>po</u> as well in the same configuration in that it cooccurs only with a subset of the possible suffixes in (6). That is, it is not the case that a particle sequence with kun does not allow some particle which can mark tense; however, (3d) does not include this possibility.

It is clearly not helpful to divide the particle sequences in quotative speech among the configurations specified in (3c) and (3d), on the basis of the facts we have just discussed in regard to a'. Aside from the fact that this would support our original claim that (3d) does not include all the particle sequence possibilities in quotative speech, the distinction between a particle sequence which contains a' and one which does not is not the distinction which we have argued to hold between (3c) and (3d). It is a simple tense distinction, not the difference between a modal assertion and a nonassertion. That is, the distinction between the presence of a' and the absence of a' is reminiscent of the contrast between (35a) and (35b), although both of those lack any particle in the first position in the Particle Complex.

We will take the position, therefore, that the particle sequence in quotative speech is not to be subsumed under (35); we will thus be concerned with stating its internal structure. The structure which we will propose is further support for distinguishing it from the sequences given in (35).

We stated above that kun can be followed by any of Set 2, Set 3, or Set 4 subject marking. (48) contains examples of each.

(48).
a. chaam   kun-ush   takwayaan
   we   kun-cha:1ST:PL:SET:2 are:sick
   'We are sick, so I'm told.'

b. chaam   kun-um   takwayaan
   we   kun-PL:SET:3   are:sick
   'We are sick, so I'm told.'

c. chaam   kun   takwayaan
   we   kun-SET:4   are:sick
   'We are sick, so I'm told.'

However, the particle a' is mutually exclusive with all but Set 4. Therefore, (45) has a particle sequence which we will analyze as <u>kun - Set:4:Subject:Marking - a'</u>. It is impossible to replace Set 4 subject marking with either Set 2 or Set 3, as (49) illustrates. (With a third person plural subject, there is no distinction between the two sets.)

(49)
*wunaalum   kun-um-a'   'oy   'ayalik
 they   kun-SET:2/3-a'   you:obj   used:to:know

Thus, we can specify two particle sequences for quotative speech, as given in (50a,b), where the second is specific to sentences in which there is some element inflected for the distant nonfuture.[25]

(50)

a. kun - $\begin{Bmatrix} \text{Set:2} \\ \text{Set:3} \\ \text{Set:4} \end{Bmatrix}$ - ∅

b. kun - Set:4 - a'

(50) does not exhaust the particle sequences in quotative speech. While it is impossible for a sequence of particles to precede subject marking in the instantiations for the analysis given in (3) or (35) (but see footnote 23), this may happen in quotative speech. Consider the following example.

(51)
'aw'quɸ   ɸu-kun-a'   ya'ash   potuung   xwaan
was   ɸu-kun-Set:4-a'   man   his:name   John
'Was there such a man named John?'

(51) contains an instance of the sequence in (50b), preceded by ɸu--undoubtedly the same particle ɸu which has already been discussed in some detail in nonquotative speech. Since ɸu can also precede the sequence in (50a), the possibilities given in (52) exist in addition to those in (50).

A Definition and Its Instantiations 49

(52)

a. ṣu - kun - $\begin{Bmatrix} \text{Set:2} \\ \text{Set:3} \\ \text{Set:4} \end{Bmatrix}$ - ∅

b. ṣu - kun - Set:4 - a'

All the sentences with the particle sequences in (50) are statements; the sentences with the particle sequences in (52) admit of no such simple characterization. (51) is glossed as a question; however, an English gloss like the following might be a better approximation of the force of this sentence: 'I've been told there was such a man named John; can you verify this report?' That is, kun marks 'aw'quṣ ya'ash potuung xwaan as the speaker's report of someone else's assertion, and xu indicates that the speaker is asking for confirmation of this assertion. A question about a (reported) statement is only one of the possible interpretations of the particle sequences in (52). They may also indicate a report of someone else's question. For example, if someone asked (53),

(53)
hax   ṣu   'iva'   'aw'q
someone prt:com   here   is
'Who is here?'

the speaker could report this question as shown in (54).

(54)
hax   ṣu-kun   'iva'   'aw'q
someone ṣu-kun-subj:mark-∅   here   is
'(He asked) who's here.'

That is, ṣu here marks the fact that hax 'iva' 'aw'q is a question and kun indicates that the question hax ṣu 'iva' 'aw'q is to be attributed to someone other than the speaker. Finally, the sequences in (52) occur in the Luiseño equivalent of what are commonly termed echo questions. (55) can be interpreted either as a question about whether the statement 'awaal wa'iq 'The dog is barking' is what someone has said or as a question about whether the question 'awaal ʃu wa'iq 'Is the dog barking?' is what someone has said.²⁶

(55)
'awaal   ʃu-kun   wa'iq
dog   ʃu-kun-subj:mark-∅   is:barking
a. 'The dog is barking, is that what you said?'
   or
b. 'Is the dog barking, is that what you said?'

Regardless of how we characterize the particle sequences in (52), the force of the sentences in which they occur is to be distinguished from the force of those containing the sequences in (50), entirely again by the Particle Complex. Since, furthermore, the specifications in (50) and (52) are not to be collapsed with those for nonquotative speech, (50) and (52) can be added to (35) to more completely characterize the possible forms of the Particle Complex.

This discussion adds two particles to the list given earlier in (4): kun and a'. There is another particle which was mentioned briefly in footnote 18, the particle up, which is not included in any of the specifications of the Particle Complex. Once we have considered it, we will have exhausted the list of particles which can occur in the Particle Complex.

First, let us examine the following sentences.

(56)
a. 'om   up   hunwuti   patiq
   you   UP   bear:obj   is:shooting
   'You are shooting a bear.'

b. wunaal   up   hunwuti   patiq
   he   UP   bear:obj   is:shooting
   'He is shooting a bear.'

(57)
a. 'om   up-il   hunwuti   patiquʃ

```
    you    UP-prt:3   bear:obj   was:shooting
    'You were shooting a bear.'

b.  wunaal  up-il      hunwuti    patiquş
    he      UP-prt:3   bear:obj   was:shooting
    'He was shooting a bear.'
```

(58)
```
a.  'om    up-po     hunwuti    patin
    you    UP-prt:3  bear:obj   will:shoot
    'You will shoot a bear.'

b.  wunaal  up-po     hunwuti    patin
    he      UP-prt:3  bear:obj   will:shoot
    'He will shoot a bear.'
```

These sentences suggest that <u>up</u> be treated as one of the elements which we have labeled <u>subject marking</u>. They are all examples of nonquotative speech; therefore, these particle sequences should be included in the schemas in (3) or its revision (35). (56a,b) appear to be like the (a) case of (3) or (35), that is, the case which contains a particle in position 2 only; (57a,b) and (58a,b) appear to be like the (b) case, that is, the case having particles in positions 2 and 3 only.

However, there is good reason not to treat <u>up</u> as subject marking, although it occurs in the same position as those elements. We identified those elements to which we gave the label <u>subject marking</u> as marking the number and possibly the person of the subject of the sentence. Therefore, for example, <u>n</u> occurs only with a first person singular subject. However, there are different restrictions on the occurrence of <u>up</u>. In brief, certain sentences occur in Luiseño which obligatorily contain an element with a possessive prefix, and <u>up</u> regularly appears in the particle sequence of such sentences. One type we can label <u>sentences of possession</u>, examples of which are given below.[27]

(59)
```
a.  noo    p    no-toonav              qala
```

```
    I    UP   POSSESSIVE-basket    is
    'I have a basket.'

b.  noo   p-il        no-puush            konoknish
    I     UP-prt:3    POSSESSIVE-eye      green

    miyxuk
    used:to:be

    'I used to have green eyes.'

c.  noo   p     no-te                 tiiwuq
    I     UP    POSSESSIVE-stomach    aches
    'I have a stomach ache.'

d.  noo   p     po-toonavi              yawq
    I     UP    POSSESSIVE-basket:obj   "have"
    'I have his basket.'
```

Regardless of the number and person of the subject of such sentences, up is possible.[28]

Up is also different from the elements in (23) by virtue of its distribution in what we have been calling "sentence type". The sentences in (56) through (58) suggest that up should be part of both Set 1 and Set 2 subject marking. As we have stated, Set 1 subject marking is restricted to the (a) cases in (35); Set 2 subject marking is possible in any of the other three cases in (35), as well as in (58a) and (59a). Up, however, is restricted to particle sequences like those in (56) through (58), i.e. to only the (a) and (b) cases in (35). That is, unlike the members of Set 2 subject marking, up cannot occur in any particle sequence preceded by another particle (thus, not in (35c), (35d), (50a), or (52)); or in other words, up is restricted entirely to nonmodal assertions in nonquotative speech.

For the moment, we can treat up as alternating with subject marking--in the particle sequences given in (35a) and (35b)--under specifiable conditions. It is necessarily present in either when there is no phonologically specified subject marker, that is, in sentences with second and third person singular subjects (as in (56) through (58)

A Definition and Its Instantiations 53

above). It will be optionally present (cf. footnote 28) in either sequence when the sentence in which it occurs necessarily contains an element with a possessive prefix, that is, in sentences like those in (59). (60), then, is a revision of (35) which includes this last particle.

(60)

a. $\emptyset - \left\{\begin{matrix}\text{Set:1}\\ \text{up}\end{matrix}\right\} - \emptyset$

b. $\emptyset - \left\{\begin{matrix}\text{Set:2}\\ \text{up}\end{matrix}\right\} - \text{Particle:3}$

c. $\text{Particle:1} - \left\{\begin{matrix}\text{Set:2}\\ \text{Set:3}\\ \text{Set:4}\end{matrix}\right\} - \text{Particle:3}$

d. $\text{Particle:1} - \left\{\begin{matrix}\text{Set:2}\\ \text{Set:3}\\ \text{Set:4}\end{matrix}\right\} - \emptyset$

While one result of this discussion is a revision of (35) and the addition of another set of statements--those in (50) and (52)--to the schemas represented there, the discussion has been aimed primarily at completing the list of elements which can be found in the Particle Complex. If we intend this list to be exhaustive, we must return to the question raised in footnote 10: whether or not the inventory of particles in positions 1 and 3 in (60) should be expanded to include $\emptyset$. A similar question could be raised about the sequences in (50) and (52), but since we will argue against the proposal, we will focus on (60) only.

If we took the view that $\emptyset$ is one of the particles which can occur in position 1 and one of the particles which can occur in position 3 in (60), there would be a single statement of the Particle Complex, as given in (2) (repeated here):

(2)
Particle:1 - Particle:2 - Particle:3

The statements regarding the list of possibilities in (60)--which are subsumed in (2)--would require substantial revision from those given at the beginning of section 2.2.2. If the particle ∅ is present in position 1, the sentence in which the Particle Complex occurs is a nonmodal assertion--(60a) and (60b); if any other particle is present in position 1, the sentence in which the Particle Complex occurs is either a modal assertion or a nonassertion. The first is the case only if the particle in position 3 is something other than ∅--(60c); the second, only if the particle in position 3 is ∅--(60d).

One consequence, then, of including ∅ in the inventory of particles in positions 1 and 3 is that ∅ is peculiar among the particles in the statements of "sentence type". That is, ∅ alone among the particles must be specifically referred to in making generalizations about the relationship between "sentence type" and Particle Complex. When we attempt to state the distribution of the various sets of subject marking, the same problem arises. That is, if two ∅'s were included in the inventory of particles, the statement of the distribution of the sets of subject markers would be sensitive to these ∅'s and <u>only</u> these particles among the set of particles. Set 1 subject marking would occur between ∅ in position 1 and ∅ in position 3; Set 2 subject marking would occur between ∅ in position 1 and any other particle except ∅ in position 3 or between any particle but ∅ in position 1 and any particle in position 3; Set 3 and Set 4 subject marking would occur between any particle but ∅ in position 1 and any particle in position 3. In sum, ∅ would have a special status with respect to the other particles, a fact which argues against including it in the particle inventory.

2.2.4 <u>Questions of Analysis</u> We have given a set of schemas--(50), (52), and (60)--which correctly and exhaustively specify all the particle sequences found in Luiseño, to the best of our knowledge. The status of the schemas in the grammar of Luiseño remains an open question; that is, whether these schemas, and their relationship to "sentence type", are directly represented in the grammar of Luiseño depends entirely on the analysis which is proposed. This section will consider essentially two possible analyses, both of which raise questions which we cannot adequately deal with here.

A number of analyses come to mind for the Particle Complex in a grammar of Luiseño. These possibilities can be reasonably classified as either syntactic or lexical. In the first type, the syntax of Luiseño will, in some fashion, specify the linear string which is the Particle Complex. In the second, the strings of particles are syntactically unanalizable; any possible string of particles is treated lexically as a word.

A grammar which attempts a syntactic analysis of the Particle Complex could (a) specify a set of phrase structure rules, precisely like the schemas given in (50), (52), and (60); (b) collapse the schemas in (50) and (52) and those in (60) (see, for example, (61) and (62) respectively); or (c) adopt various intermediate possibilities.

(61)
(ʃu) - kun - Subject:Marking - (a')

(62)
(Particle:1) - Particle:2 - (Particle:3)

Obviously, only the first possibility would directly represent in the syntax the schemas which we have discussed--and would then directly represent the "sentence types" associated with those sequences only if the various rules which specify the sequences were so labeled. For example:

(63)
Particle Complex$_{\text{Modal Assertion}}$ ──────>

     Particle:1 - Particle:2 - Particle:3

Any syntactic analysis of the Particle Complex, any analysis which attempts to specify the linear string in the syntax, faces one obvious problem.

Under this hypothesis, each particle which is analyzed as being part of the particle sequence(s) would be treated as a different lexical item; that is, each would receive a separate lexical entry. However, not only would the lexical entry for, at least, the particles ǵu, kun, xu, po, il, and kwa have to repeat some subpart of the syntactic specification for the Particle Complex, but also it would be impossible to give any semantic specification for the particular lexical item outside of the set of particle configurations in which it occurs. For example, ǵu might receive the following lexical entry.

(64)
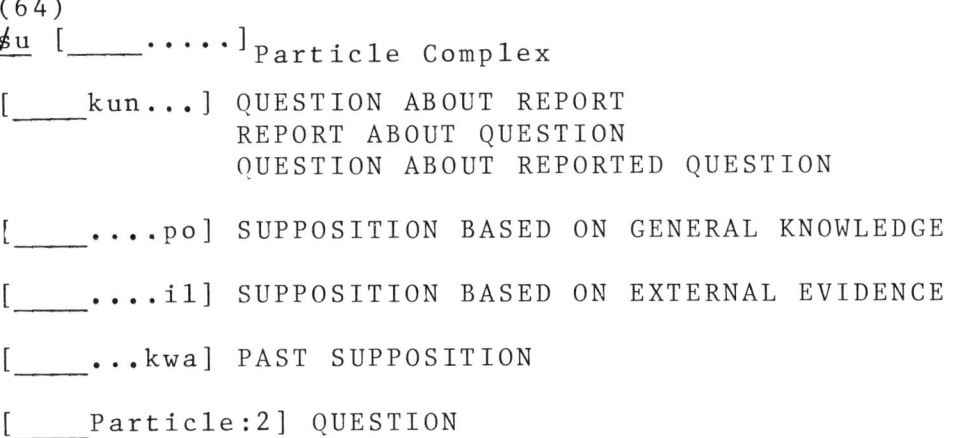

That is, the syntactic specification of the linear string provides information which must be given elsewhere, as well. Furthermore, although ǵu and the rest of the particles in the list above are necessarily the lexical entries, they can be given no semantic identification outside of the particular configurations in which they appear. Finally, aside from the possibility of labeling a set of rules with some general "sentence type" identification, the rules which are given for the linear string of particles say nothing about the semantics of the Particle Complex.

If we adopt a lexical analysis of the Particle Complex, these problems are obviated--although another is raised. Under a lexical analysis of the

A Definition and Its Instantiations 57

Particle Complex, all the possible combinations of particles would be listed independently in the lexicon. That is, the lexicon of Luiseño would include, for example, the following items:

(65)
nil   Particle Complex   first person singular past

chamil   Particle Complex   first person plural past

mil   Particle Complex   nonfirst person plural past

ŝunpo   Particle Complex   first person singular, supposition based on general knowledge

ŝushpo   Particle Complex   first person plural, supposition based on general knowledge

ŝumpo   Particle Complex   nonfirst person plural, supposition based on general knowledge

ŝun   Particle Complex   first person singular, question

ŝush   Particle Complex   first person plural, question

ŝum   Particle Complex   nonfirst person plural, question

etc.

The problem with this approach is obvious. Clearly, there are generalizations which can be made about the composition of the various words in (65): for example, the piece ŝu is always initial to the sequence; the piece m has a consistent specification. That is, the regularities which allowed us to state the schemas in (50), (52), and (60) are not directly represented in the lexical analysis and, assuming that we want to include them in the grammar of Luiseño, we would have to add somewhere--perhaps in some morphological component--the information which can be generalized from the various words identified as Particle Complex listed in the lexicon.

On the basis of the evidence we have given regarding the Luiseño Particle Complex, it is not obvious that we can choose between a lexical analysis and a syntactic analysis. It is possible, of course, that the issue could be decided on grounds outside the specifics of the particle sequence. A study of change as it affects the particle sequence could provide evidence for one or the other analysis; were change to affect only the words which are listed in (65), it would argue for the lexical analysis. Or an analysis of other aspects of Luiseño could decide the question. That is, if Luiseño can be reasonably analyzed as a nonconfigurational language--or what Hale (1980) has called a W* language--the lexical analysis of the Particle Complex would obviously follow. Since the syntax of a nonconfigurational language specifies only that an expression is composed of a sequence of words--there are no syntactically specified constituents larger than words--a word which is a particle sequence would be one of the possible lexical choices, constrained, unlike other lexical choices, to occur in sentential second position. The evidence isn't in on this larger question about Luiseño syntax (however, see Steele (1981)).

Apparently, then, there is no reason to assume that the grammar of Luiseño will necessarily directly represent the generalizations which we have made about the Particle Complex. This does not change the fact that a sequence of those second position particles which we have exhaustively listed must be considered a constituent. However, the choice of an analysis does affect what we take to be the list of elements subsumed under the label which identifies that constituent. On the syntactic analysis, the set of elements includes those given in (4) and (23) and those added in section 2.2.3. On the lexical analysis, the set of elements is the list of possible combinations of these elements, a subset of which is given in (65). In either case, of course, the members of the set can be easily listed.

2.2.5 Conclusion

We have argued that the set of second position particles in Luiseño forms a constituent, that this constituent contains elements marking tense and modality, and that the members of the constituent--regardless of the analysis which we propose--comprise a specifiable set. That is, we have argued that the definition given in section 2.1 is instantiated in Luiseño, specifically by what we have called the Particle Complex.

2.3 Lummi [29]

2.3.1 Introduction

A typical Lummi sentence consists of a predicate head to which various clitic elements may be attached. Any additional nouns follow the initial predicate; in the case of transitive sentences with two full nouns (not pronouns), the unmarked sentence order is V(erb) - S(ubject) - O(bject). Sentences (66a-c) are representative.

(66)
a. xčit-sən   cə   swəy?qə?
   know-I   the   man
   'I know the man.'

b. xčit-sx^w cə   swəy?qə?
   know-you   the   man
   'You know the man.'

c. xčit-ł   cə   swəy?qə?
   know-we   the   man
   'You know the man.'

d. xčit-s   cə   swəy?qə?
   know-3rd the   man
   'Someone knows the man.'

e. xčit-s   cə   swəy?qə?   cə   swi?qo?əł
   know-3rd the   man   the   boy
   'The man knows the boy.'

A straightforward analysis of these sentences isolates the following morphemes: an initial

A Definition and Its Instantiations 60

predicate (verb) x̌ċit 'know'; a set of pronominal enclitics indicating subject, -sən 'I', -sxʷ 'you', -ɬ 'we', -s '3rd person subject';[30] an article cə 'a/the'; nouns swəy?qə? 'man' and swi?qo?əɫ 'boy'.

All the sentences in (66) exhibit bound pronominal subject markers; however, they do not exhaust the clitic types which attach to the predicate head. The following sentences illustrate clitics marking other notional categories which occur in the same position.

(67)
a. x̌ċit-lə-sən   cə   swəy?qə?
   know-PAST-I the   man
   'I knew the man.'

b. x̌ċit-sən-sə   cə   swəy?qə?
   know-I-FUTURE the   man
   'I will know the man.'

c. x̌ċit-ə-lə-sxʷ
   know-QUESTION-PAST-you
   'Did you know it?'

d. x̌ċit-q-sən   cə   swəy?qə?
   know-POSSIBILITY-I   the   man
   'I might know the man!'

e. x̌ċit-ə-q-lə-sxʷ
   know-QUESTION-POSSIBILITY-PAST-you
   'Could you have known it?'

f. x̌ċit-yəq-lə-sən
   know-OPTATIVE-PAST-I
   'I wish I would have known it.'

g. x̌ċit-cə-sən
   know-QUALIFIED:KNOWLEDGE-I
   'Maybe I know it.'

h. x̌ċit-yəxʷ-sən   cə   swəy?qə?
   know-PROBABILITY-I   the   man
   'I'm quite certain that I know the man.'

A Definition and Its Instantiations

The sentences in (67) exhibit a representative cross section of the enclitic particles in Lummi. That is, as an examination of (66) and (67) will suggest, the Lummi enclitic particles mark yes/no questions, modality (possibility, optative, qualified knowledge, and strong probability), tense (past and future), and a range of person subjects. There are other modalities, but examples of them are scarce in the Lummi data and they will not be discussed here. The most common occurrences of the Lummi clitic particles, which have been given in (66) and (67), are displayed in table 2.1 for ease of reference.

Table 2.1

Question	Modality	Tense	Person Subject
ə	q	sə	sən
	(possibility)	(future)	(1st pers. sg.)
	yəq	lə	sx^w
	(optative)	(past)	(2nd pers.)
	čə		ł
	(qualified knowledge)		(1st pers. pl.)
	yəx^w		s
	(strong probability)		(3rd pers.)

Since this set of clitic particles contains elements marking tense and modality, and since its membership can be specified, two of the criteria in the definition given at the beginning of this chapter are met. The following discussion argues for the constituency of the set of clitic particles given in table 2.1.

2.3.2 Arguments against What the Phonology Suggests

The Lummi case regarding the question of the constituency of the set of clitic particles is significant because it poses the more general question of whether a sequence of obligatorily bound particles can be analyzed as an autonomous syntactic constituent. That is, as the sentences in (66) and (67) imply, a clitic element is never a phonological word, but is always bound to the element to its immediate left. Thus, for the sentence in (67c), for example, the following analysis might seem plausible.

(68)

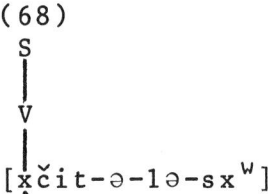

(68) represents an analysis in which the clitic elements which are attached to the verb are affixes, and thus form a unit with the verb. In this section we will argue against this analysis.

The following syntactic facts are crucial to the argument: (a) <u>The Second Position Condition</u>. The clitic sequence satisfies a distributional condition in that it appears attached to the first major constituent of a Lummi sentence. (b) <u>The Sentence Level Interpretation Condition</u>. Although the sequence of clitics is attached to the first element of the sentence, they are not interpreted compositionally with that element; rather, they are interpreted over the sentence. (c) <u>The Minimal Interaction Criterion</u>. Although the sequence of clitics forms a phonological unit with the word to which it is attached, its presence does not interfere in a primary way with the other phonological properties of the word to which it is attached. Moreover, the phonological shape of the clitic sequence remains constant, regardless of the word to which it is attached.

2.3.2.1 The Second Position Condition Among the most prominent conditions involving the string of clitics in Lummi is the fact that they will normally appear attached to the sentence-initial constituent. (69a-e), which are similar to (67a-e), exhibit this "Second Position" property.

(69)
a. λ'el-lə-sən   ʔuʔ   xčit   cə   swəyʔqəʔ
   also-PAST-I   connective: know   the   man
                      particle
   'I knew the man too.'

b. λ'el-ə-sə-sən   ʔuʔ   xčit   cə
   also-QUESTION-FUTURE-I   connective: know   the
                                 particle

   swəyʔqəʔ
   man

   'Will I know the man too?'

c. λ'el-ə-lə-sxʷ   ʔuʔ   xčit
   also-QUESTION-PAST-YOU   connective: know
                                 particle
   'Did you know it?'

d. λ'el-q-sən   ʔuʔ   xčit   cə
   also-POSSIBILITY-I   connective: know   the
                                 particle

   swəyʔqəʔ
   man

   'I might know the man too.'

e. λ'el-ə-q-lə-sxʷ   ʔuʔ
   also-QUESTION-POSSIBILITY-PAST-YOU   connective:
                                                       particle

   xčit
   know

   'Could you possibly have known it too?'

The particles attached to x̣čit in (67a-h) are now attached to λ'el. These sentences exhibit a property which furnishes important evidence against the analysis in (68): the sequence of clitic particles must appear attached to the initial element of the sentence, and regardless of the categorial status of that element. For the argument to be valid, it must be shown that x̣čit and λ'el can reasonably be assigned to different categories. That is, it must be shown that λ'el is not a predicate. Precisely how--and whether--categories may be distinguished is a notoriously complex issue in the languages of the Northwest.[31] There are two properties, however, that are typical of elements such as x̣čit, which we will identify as properties of Lummi predicates. λ'el exhibits neither property. First, elements such as x̣čit require that phrases containing additional predicates be subordinated. Consider, for example, the following sentence:

(70)
x̣čit-s   k^w   nə-s-x̣čit
know-3rd   complementizer   my-nominalizer-know

cə   swəy?qə?
the   man

'He knows that I know the man.'

(70) has three features which show that subordination is involved. First, k^w is a subordinating particle (complementizer); second, the possessive pronoun form nə- of the first person pronoun is used; and third, x̣čit has the prefix s (labeled in (70) as a nominalizer).[32] None of these features of subordination is found in any of the sentences of (69). It would appear, then, that λ'el is simply an additional sentence-level element which can occur in Lummi sentences, an element which does not alter the basic sentence structure, other than bearing the sequence of clitics.

The second property that distinguished λ'el from elements such as x̣čit concerns word order. Elements such as x̣čit--true predicates--must precede any arguments in their sentence. A typical Lummi sentence containing two predicates has already been given in (70). In this sentence, each occurrence of x̣čit appears at the beginning of its respective clause. In contrast, the λ'el that appears in sentence-initial position in (69a-e) may also appear in sentence-final position. Some contrasting Lummi sentence types which are variants of (69a) are given in (71).[33]

(71)
a. λ'el-lə-sən   ʔuʔ   x̣čit   cə   swəyʔqəʔ
    ALSO-past-I   connective: KNOW   the   man
                   particle
    'I knew the man too.'

b. x̣čit-lə-sən   cə   swəyʔqəʔ   λ'el
    KNOW-past-I   the   man   ALSO
    'I knew the man too.'

c. *λ'el-lə-sən   ʔuʔ   cə
    ALSO-past-I   connective: the
                   particle

    swəyʔqəʔ   x̣čit
    man   KNOW

Sentence (71b) is a grammatical variant of (71a) in which only a change of focus is involved.[34] In contrast, sentence (71c) is ill-formed because the expression cə swəyʔqəʔ precedes x̣čit in the sentence. λ'el, then, is one of a number of items that can appear both sentence-initially and sentence-finally, without changing the grammatical relations of the sentence. Words of the x̣čit class (verbs) do not have this distributional property.

Another class of sentences further strengthens the case against the affix analysis in (68). These are copular sentences in Lummi.

(72)
a. šx̌ʷnem-ə-lə-sx̌ʷ
    doctor-question-past-you
    'Were you a doctor?'

b. ʔəyʔ-ə-lə-sxʷ
   good-question-past-you
   'Were you good?'

Sentences such as (72a,b) are typical of Salish languages generally and have led many linguists to propose that there are no categorial distinctions in these languages. That is, because the enclitics attach to whatever is initial, every lexical item in these languages belongs to the same category--they are all "Predicates" (cf. Kuipers (1968)). However, it can be shown that there are in fact reasons to distinguish a number of different categories. Nouns, for example, are the class of words that can take possessive pronoun affixes when serving as arguments in independent clauses.[35] Verbs, on the other hand, are the class of words that can be used in the imperative. Sentences such as ʔəyʔ mean 'Something is good', not 'Be good!' A semantic reason for distinguishing nouns from verbs is the unpredictability of meaning relationships between morphologically related verbs and nouns. Instrumental nouns can be formed from verbs by adding the suffix -tən. For example, the verb root təqə(s) means 'to shut off' or 'to close'. When this verb root is combined with -tən, the word təqəstən is created. The meaning of this word is quite narrow, however, and refers to a net on poles used for trapping ducks. Thus, two lexical entries are required, one for the noun and one for the verb.

The reason that nouns and adjectives appear to be verblike, then, is that (a) Lummi does not have a copular verb, and (b) the Lummi clitics must be attached to the first element of a Lummi sentence, and thus be in second position. Below is a preliminary formulation of the second-position condition in Lummi.

(73)
Lummi Sentence Well-Formedness Condition

[C+Enclitics-Y]$_S$

Lummi sentences (in the unmarked case) conform to

condition (73), which may be viewed as a surface filter in the sense of Chomsky and Lasnik (1977).[36] In the formula, C is any major lexical category and Y is a syntactic variable. This second-position property of the Lummi clitic sequence, as specified by (73), yields a superficial similarity among all major lexical categories; it does not argue, however, for their identification.

The clitics which are attached to xcit in (68), then, are not there because of a morphological rule of Lummi; rather, they are there as the result of a sentence-level condition of Lummi syntax. Additional evidence for their sentence-level analysis is found in the next section.

2.3.2.2 The Sentence-Level Interpretation Condition

This condition requires that the set of clitics in Lummi be analyzed at the sentence level, even though they may be bound to a particular word and thus appear to be part of the morphological structure of that word. That the clitics are not always interpreted as part of the word to which they are attached is shown clearly by the following case. The sequence ʔəneʔ-sən 'come-I' is translated as 'I came/come' in English. The sequence leŋ-t-ŋ is a type of passive and means 'Something was seen'. Now consider (74), apparently formed by combining the two previous sentences.

(74)
ʔəneʔ-sən   leŋ-t-ŋ

Based on the previous discussion, one would predict that (74) should be interpreted as either 'I came (in order) to be seen' or perhaps 'I came (in order that) it was seen'. However, (74) has the somewhat surprising interpretation 'Someone came to see me'. That is, -sən, which is present on ʔəneʔ, is not interpreted as the subject of that verb, but rather is interpreted as the subject of leŋ-t-ŋ (the sentence leŋ-t-ŋ-sən means 'I am/was seen'). The sequence ʔəneʔ leŋ-t-ŋ is an idiosyncratic purposive construction with the meaning 'Someone came in order that someone was to be seen'. Apparently, condition (73) is being satisfied in sentence (74), and the

-sən which "normally" would appear on leŋ-t-ŋ occurs instead on the sentence-initial element ʔəneʔ. Thus, the existence of sentences such as (74) supports what was implicit in (73), that the Lummi clitics are members of S and are not necessarily interpreted as a part of that to which they are encliticized.

Condition (73) even allows the splitting of compound words. For example, mək̓ʷ by itself means 'every, all', and wet is an interrogative word corresponding to 'who'. The combination mək̓ʷ-wet means 'everybody'. Note, however, the position of the clitic sequence in the following sentence.

(75)
mək̓ʷ-ə-q-lə-wet   ʔuʔ   yeʔ
all-QUESTION-POSSIBILITY-PAST-who   connective: go
                                    particle
'Could everyone have gone?'

Based on sentences such as (74) and (75) (and earlier (69)), we conclude that the domain of interpretation for the members of the clitic sequence is distinct from the item to which they are attached (satisfying condition (73)). The domain of interpretation is the sentence (or perhaps, phrase) in which they are found.

2.3.2.3 The Minimal Interaction Condition

Although the Lummi clitics are encliticized onto sentence-initial words, they interact with that word only minimally. This lack of interaction is in marked contrast to other sets of morphemes which are attached to particular lexical categories. For example, there is a rich set of affixes which are found on verbs. Consider the different forms of the verb root čəs 'hit' (actual aspect; cf. Thompson and Thompson (1971)) in the following paradigm.

(76)

   a. čəs-sən   'I got hit.'

   b. čəs-t-sən   'I hit it (on purpose).'

   c. čəs-nəxʷ-sən   'I hit it (accidentally).'

A Definition and Its Instantiations   69

d. čəs-t-ŋ-sən   'I got hit (on purpose).'

e. čəs-n-ŋ-sən   'I got hit (accidentally).'

f. čəs-t-óŋəs-sən   'I hit you (on purpose).'

In sentences (76b), (76d), and (76f), the transitivizing suffix t occurs. This suffix indicates that the subject has some degree of willful control over the action expressed by the verb. In sentences (76c) and (76e), in contrast, the suffix nəx^w (or its morphologically conditioned variant n) indicates restricted control over the action expressed by the verb. Sentences (76d) and (76e) exhibit the detransitivizing suffix n, which is best translated with the English passive. Finally, sentence (76f) introduces the second person object suffix, oŋəs. The important differences between the affixes in (76) and the enclitic particles previously discussed are (a) the affixes are always bound to the verb, and (b) the affixes interact phonologically with the verb, frequently determining some of its phonological properties.

The rigidity of the suffixes' attachment is shown by the ungrammaticality of (77b) and (77c).

(77)
a. λ'el-lə'sən   ʔuʔ
   also-past-I   connective:
                 particle

   čəs-t-óŋəs
   hit-TRANSITIVIZER-YOU:OBJ

   'I hit you too.'

b. λ'el-t-oŋəs-lə-sən   ʔuʔ
   also-TRANSITIVIZER-YOU:OBJ-past-I connective:
                                     particle

   čəs
   hit

   *λ'el-oŋəs-lə-sən   ʔuʔ

```
        also-YOU:OBJ-past-I  connective:
                             particle

    ʔčəs-t
    hit-TRANSITIVIZER
```

The affixes exhibited in (76), then, differ from the enclitic particles in that the latter are not rigidly bound to the verb and may be attached to whatever occurs sentence-initially.

That the verbal affixes interact phonologically with the verb is similarly easy to illustrate. These affixes may influence phonological properties of the verb to which they attach. For example, the suffix <u>onəs</u> always bears the primary stress in constructions in which it occurs (as indicated by (76f)). Otherwise (unless certain other suffixes are present) the verb root will bear the primary stress. In contrast, although they too may directly follow the verb root, the enclitic particles do not "attract" the stress from the root. The affixes exhibited in (76), then, differ from the enclitic particles in terms of the phonological independence of the word (or stem) to which they attach. A somewhat stronger observation is in order. Not only does the word to which the enclitics are attached have a degree of phonological independence, but also the phonological shape of the clitic sequence remains unaffected by the word which precedes it--and to which it is attached. That is, although the enclitics attach to some word which immediately precedes them, there is <u>no</u> phonological interaction between the two.

<u>2.3.2.4   Summary</u>   We have presented evidence internal to Lummi that the phonological unit consisting of a word plus a sequence of enclitic particles is not a morphological unit; that is, (68) does not correctly describe the syntactic facts of Lummi. In support of this position, we appeal to the more general fact that languages frequently group portions of sentences into units of phonological organization that do not correspond to labeled syntactic structures. For instance, the English sentence [<u>This is</u> [<u>the cat that caught</u> [<u>the</u>

rat that stole the cheese]]] is frequently cited as an example in which intonation breaks (between cat and that, and rat and that) do not correspond to the major constituent breaks (indicated with square brackets). A more extreme case from English is the casual speech pronunciation of the sentence What do you want? (wʌDəyə wan?). The initial phonological sequence wʌDəyə is wordlike in that it obeys the intonation and stress contours of English as well as the low-level phonetic rules of words. It appears, then, that languages may have phonological sequences which need not correspond to syntactic constituents. The fact that Lummi clitics are obligatorily bound to sentence-initial words (as represented in (68)) is, therefore, not evidence that these clitics are morphologically part of that initial word; rather, the evidence presented in this section shows that (68) does not represent the syntactic facts of Lummi.[37]

2.3.3 Constituency If we have argued against the analysis in (68), it remains to argue in favor of some other analysis of the sequence of Lummi enclitic particles. Two possibilities, both of which are consistent with previous discussion of the enclitic sequences, are given in (78):

(78)

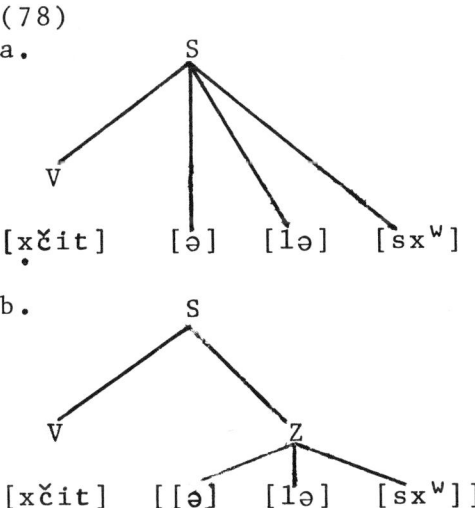

Tree (78a) represents an analysis in which the elements which are attached to the verb are essentially independent and have no structural relationship to each other. Tree (78b) represents an analysis in which the sequence of clitics is a constituent. In this section, we will argue for the analysis represented in (78b); with this argument, we will have shown that the set of Lummi enclitics can be identified as an instantiation of the definition given in section 2.1.

First, the set of enclitics has an internal structural integrity which can be represented by the formula in (79).

(79)
$\{(Q) \longleftarrow (Modality)\} \quad \left\{ Tense \longleftarrow \begin{array}{l} Person \\ Subject \end{array} \right\}$

That is, the order of the Lummi enclitics is Q (question marker), Modality, Tense, and Subject Person marking. The braces around the first and second pairs of elements reflect the fact that the order of the elements within them occasionally varies (under conditions not understood at present). However, the order of the two sets of braces themselves is strict. Another difference is also found between the two sets of braced elements. Whereas Question and Modality are optional categories, Tense and Person are obligatory. The standard parenthesis notation for optionality represents this fact.

Of course, either analysis in (78) can describe the statement in (79). However, if the set of enclitics is a constituent, we might expect it to have an internal coherence. The analysis in tree (78a) makes no such prediction.

Second, and perhaps more strongly, there is a phonological regularity unique to the enclitic sequence. For example, the sentence ye?-sə-ɫ 'We will go' is actually pronounced as ye?ɫəɫ. The future marker sə becomes ɫə by regressive assimilation to the following first person marker ɫ. This regressive assimilation does not extend beyond the sequence of enclitics. That is, an s in a word to which the first person marker attaches will not assimilate to ł. In fact, this regular regressive assimilation is limited to the sequence of enclitics. Consider, for example, the word for 'bored out', which is ʔəsəłqʷ, not *ʔəłəłqʷ. We can handle these facts quite nicely by stating that the assimilation cannot extend beyond a category boundary and that it is limited to a particular category. However, the first generalization requires that (78b), and not (78a), be the correct representation of the relationship among the enclitics, and the second requires that the category which is the clitic sequence be distinct from whatever other categories we might propose for Lummi.

Finally, the Lummi Sentence Well-Formedness Condition (73) can be stated most simply if the sequence of enclitics is a constituent. If the analysis in tree (78a) were correct, it would be necessary to include the list of all Lummi enclitics in the formula in (73)--given there simply as enclitics. However, if a single constituent subsumes them all, it is necessary only to include the label of this constituent in (73)--and some statement such as (79)--in Lummi grammar to give an account of the positional restriction(s) on Lummi enclitics.

2.3.4 Conclusion   We have argued, then, that the best analysis of Lummi includes a constituent subsuming the elements in table 2.1, in the order given in (79), a constituent which contains elements marking both tense and modality, among other notional categories. In short, Lummi has been shown to offer an instantiation of the definition given in section 2.1. In the analysis in tree (78b), we labeled this constituent Z. This is a perfectly adequate language-internal label; however, in the rest of this work, we will refer to it with the somewhat more descriptively adequate label Enclitic Sequence.

2.4 Colloquial Egyptian Arabic[38]

A Definition and Its Instantiations 74

<u>2.4.1 Introduction</u> Consider the following typical sentences in Colloquial Egyptian Arabic:

(80)
a. biyiktib   ig-gawaab
   writing   the-letter
   'He is writing the letter.'

b. kaan   biyiktib   ig-gawaab
   was   writing   the-letter
   'He was writing the letter.'

c. Haykuun   biyiktib   ig-gawaab
   will:be   writing   the-letter
   'He will be writing the letter.'

(81)
a. katab   ig-gawaab
   written   the-letter
   'He wrote (has written) the letter.'

b. kaan   katab   ig-gawaab
   was   written   the-letter
   'He had written the letter.'

c. Haykuun   katab   ig-gawaab
   will:be   written   the-letter
   'He will have written the letter.'

(82)
a. Hayiktib   ig-gawaab
   gonna:write   the-letter
   'He is gonna write the letter.'

b. kaan   Hayiktib   ig-gawaab
   was   gonna:write   the-letter
   'He was gonna write the letter.'

These three sets of sentences differ in the form of the Arabic equivalent of 'write'. In (80a-c), 'write' is inflected in what is traditionally called the <u>bi-imperfect</u>, a form which marks imperfective aspect; in (81a-c), it is inflected in what is traditionally called the <u>perfect</u>, a form which marks

A Definition and Its Instantiations

(83)
a. bitiktib   ig-gawaab
   writing   the-letter
   bi:imperf:3:f:sg
   'She is writing the letter.'

b. kaanit   bitiktib   ig-gawaab
   was   writing   the-letter
   perf:3:f:sg bi:imperf:3:f:sg
   'She was writing the letter.'

c. Hatkuun   bitiktib   ig-gawaab
   will:be   writing   the-letter
   Ha:imperf:3:f:sg bi:imperf:3:f:sg
   'She will be writing the letter.'

(84)
a. katabna   ig-gawaab
   wrote   the-letter
   perf:1:pl
   'We wrote (have written) the letter.'

b. kunna   katbna   ig-gawaab
   were   wrote   the-letter
   perf:1:pl perf:1:pl
   'We had written the letter.'

c. Hankuun   katabna   ig-gawaab
   will:be   wrote   the-letter
   Ha:imperf:1:pl perf:1:pl
   'We will have written the letter.'

(85)
a. Hayiktibu   ig-gawaab
   gonna:write   the-letter
   Ha:imperf:3:pl
   'They are gonna write the letter.'

b. kaanu   Hayiktibu   ig-gawaab
   were   gonna:write the-letter
   perf:3:pl Ha:imperf:3:pl
   'They were gonna write the letter.'

perfective aspect; and in (82a-c), it is inflected in what is traditionally called the Ha-imperfect, a form which marks prospective aspect. The (b) and (c) sentences also contain a form of the copular verb kaan. It is this verb that will be the focus of our argument that Colloquial Egyptian Arabic has a constituent which instantiates the definition of AUX given in section 2.1.

2.4.2 The Peculiarities of kaan Kaan appears to be a regular member of the morphological class verb; that is, kaan, like katab 'write' in (80) through (82), is inflected for person, number, and gender (in the second and third person singular). In (81) kaan is inflected in the perfect verb paradigm, and in (82) in the Ha-imperfect paradigm.[39] Compare the sentences in (83) through (85) to (80) through (82).

Though kaan is a regular member of the morphological class verb, it is syntactically and semantically distinct from all other verbs in the language. The pattern of kaan relative to the aspectually inflected verb forms shown in the preceding examples is not peculiar to them. Kaan--and kaan alone of all the members of its morphological class--occurs with all predicates in the language. By predicate is meant here those verbs, participles, predicate nouns, predicate adjectives, prepositional phrases, etc., that serve to mark the predicational function of the sentence. Some nonverbal predicates appear in examples (86) through (92) below.

The verb paradigms shown in (80) through (85) are morphologically distinct from other forms traditionally labeled the active and passive participles in Arabic. These participles mark number and gender, but not person. They mark aspect, but they also mark voice.

(86)
huwwa   kaatib   ig-gawabaat
he   written   the-letters
         act:part:m:sg
'He has written the letters.'

(87)
ig-gawabaat maktubiin
the-letters written
             pass:part:pl
'The letters are (have been) written.'

Sentences (86) and (87) with participles exactly parallel those in (80) through (85) with respect to the occurrence and form of kaan, as (88) and (89) illustrate. And the sentences in (90) through (92) exhibit the same pattern of kaan plus other classes of predicates.

(88)
a. huwwa   kaatib   ig-gawabaat
   he   written   the-letters
           act:part:m:sg
   'He has written the letters.'

b. huwwa   kaan   kaatib   ig-gawabaat
   he   KAAN   written   the-letters
                  act:part:m:sg
   'He had written the letters.'

c. huwwa   Haykuun kaatib   ig-gawabaat
   he   HAYKUUN written   the-letters
                    act:part:m:sg
   'He will have written the letters.'

(89)
a. ig-gawabaat   maktubiin
   the-letters   written
                 pass:part:pl
   'The letters have been written.'

b. ig-gawabaat   kaanu   maktubiin
   the-letters   KAANU   written
                          pass:part:pl
   'The letters had been written.'

c. ig-gawabaat   Haykuunu   maktubiin
   the-letters   HAYKUUNU   written
                            pass:part:pl
   'The letters will have been written.'

A Definition and Its Instantiations 78

(90)
a. huwwa   za9laan
   he   angry
            adj:m:sg
   'He is angry.'

b. huwwa   kaan   za9laan
   he   KAAN   angry
                    adj:m:sg
   'He was angry.'

c. huwwa   Haykuun   za9laan
   he   HAYKUUN   angry
                       adj:m:sg
   'He will be angry.'

(91)
a. huwwa   ṭabiib
   he   doctor
            noun:m:sg
   'He is a doctor.'

b. huwwa   kaan   ṭabiib
   he   KAAN   doctor
                    noun:m:sg
   'He was a doctor.'

c. huwwa   Haykuun   ṭabiib
   he   HAYKUUN   doctor
                       noun:m:sg
   'He will be a doctor.'

(92)
a. fii-h   kitaab   9al-maktab
   preposition-pronoun   book   on:the-desk
   'There is a book on the desk.'

b. kaan   fii-h   kitaab   9al-maktab
   KAAN   preposition-pronoun   book   on:the-desk
   'There was a book on the desk.'

c. Haykuun   fii-h   kitaab   9al-maktab
   HAYKUUN   preposition-pronoun   book   on:the-desk
   'There will be a book on the desk.'

A Definition and Its Instantiations 79

The sentences in (80) through (92) do not exhaust the predicate possibilities in Egyptian Arabic, but they amply illustrate the point about the syntax of kaan.

Although kaan shares the inflectional paradigms of other verbs, in a sentence it--and it alone of all members of the morphological class verb--marks tense. The contrasts among the (a), (b), and (c) sentences above suggest this fact. However, there is evidence beyond that offered by the closest English translation. Many languages that mark tense have some sentence or clause types that do not--that are, therefore, nonfinite. Typically, imperatives, some embedded clause types, and (in many languages) subjunctive/jussive clause types exhibit this property. We might expect, then, that if kaan marks tense, the pattern we have illustrated above would be excluded from such clause types. This is, in fact, precisely what occurs.

An imperative in Egyptian Arabic is indicated by a special "imperative" inflection of the verb root; person, number, and gender are marked, but aspect is not. Compare (93a-c) to the sentences in (80) through (82) to illustrate the second point; compare them to one another to illustrate the first.

(93)
a. iktib   'Write!' (m:sg)

b. iktibi   'Write!' (f:sg)

c. iktibu   'Write!' (pl)

However, no finite inflections of kaan occur in imperative sentences.[40]

Some embedded clauses show the pattern of tense marking with kaan illustrated above and some do not. The complements of verbs such as 9irif 'know' allow the pattern of (80) through (92).

(94)
a. ana   9aarif   innu   naayim
   I   knowing   that:he   sleeping
   'I know that he is sleeping.'

```
b. ana    9aarif     innu        kaan     naayim
   I      knowing    that:he     KAAN     sleeping
   'I know that he was sleeping.'

c. ana    9aarif     innu        Haykuun   naayim
   I      knowing    that:he     HAYKUUN   sleeping
   'I know that he will be sleeping.'
```

However, the complements of other predicates, such as 9aawiz 'want', do not allow this pattern.

```
(95)
ana    9aawiz     innu        yiruuH
I      wanting    that:he     go
                              subjunctive:3:m:sg
'I want him to go.'
```

In (25) the verb raaH 'go' is inflected in what is often called the "subjunctive" of Egyptian Arabic (cf. Abdel-Massih, Abdel-Malek, and Badawi (1979, 175)). The important feature of this embedded clause, however, is that it allows none of the inflections of kaan seen in (80) through (82).

```
(96)
a. *ana    9aawiz     innu        kaan      yiruuH
    I      wanting    that:he     KAAN      go

b. *ana    9aawiz     innu        Haykuun   yiruuH
    I      wanting    that:he     HAYKUUN   go
```

Thus, in both imperatives and certain types of embedded clauses, the latter dependent upon the verb or other predicate of the main clause, the paradigm of (80) through (82) is impossible. This fact is consistent with the hypothesis that kaan marks tense, and that such clause types may be untensed. Egyptian Arabic also has independent subjunctive clauses where the paradigm with kaan does not occur; these sentences employ the same subjunctive verb inflection that appears in the nonfinite embedded clause type illustrated in (95) and (96).

(97)
a. yiruuH   fi   daHya
   he:go   in   hell
   'Let him go to hell!'

b. ir-raagil   yikuun   9aa'il
   the-man   be   prudent
   'A man should be prudent.'

c. matiktibš   ig-gawaab
   neg:you:write   the-letter
   'Don't write the letter!'

The fact that these nonfinite sentence types also lack the paradigm with <u>kaan</u> is consistent as well with the hypothesis than <u>kaan</u> marks tense.

In sum, we have argued that <u>kaan</u> alone occurs with all predicates in the language to mark tense contrasts. That is, while <u>kaan</u> is morphologically a verb, it clearly exhibits distinctive syntactic and semantic properties.

<u>2.4.3   Questions   of   Analysis</u>   The preceding discussion assumes an analysis of Egyptian Arabic which requires that every sentence contain a predicate. The sentences in (80) through (92) suggest that the predicate may be preceded by either some inflection of <u>kaan</u> or some subject or both or neither. That is, the sentences in (80) through (92) appear to be of four types, listed in (98):

(98)
a. Predicate (= e.g. (80a))

b. <u>kaan</u> Predicate (= e.g. (80b))

c. Subject Predicate (= e.g. (88a))

d. Subject <u>kaan</u> Predicate (= e.g. (88b))

The schemas in (98) adequately represent all the main clauses in (80) through (92); in fact, with one addition, (98) is an exhaustive list of the superficial structure of all main clauses in

Egyptian Arabic. In all the sentences represented in (98), the predicate is necessarily final; the inflection of kaan is either initial or second; and the subject is initial. It is this last point which is not fully accurate. Consider the following sentences:

(99)
a. kaanu   il-awlaad   naymiin
   kaan:perf:3:pl   the-children   sleeping
                                       act:part:pl
   'The children were sleeping.'

b. Haykuun   ir-raagil   biyištaɣal
   kaan:Ha:imperf:3:m:sg the-man   working
                                        bi:imperf:3:m:sg
   'The man will be working.'

In (99) an inflection of kaan precedes the subject; thus, we may add the schema in (100) to those specified in (98).

(100)
kaan Subject Predicate

Note that the existence of sentences of the form shown in (100) supports what was simply assumed in the list in (98): that there are potentially three major parts to an Egyptian Arabic sentence--Subject, kaan, and Predicate.

The question of critical interest from the point of view of this discussion is how to treat sentences of the forms given in (98a) and (98c), i.e. those that have no inflection of kaan. That is, do we want to analyze sentences, even those which lack kaan, as containing some space--some node, if you will--which happens in some cases to be empty? An examination of the sentences which exemplify (98a) and (98c) will readily reveal that sentences in the present tense are such cases. At least three positions seem possible on this question:

(101)
a. Present tense sentences in Egyptian Arabic have

at most two primary nodes: Subject and Predicate.
b. All finite Egyptian Arabic sentences have a node where tense is marked; in the present tense, this tense marking is phonologically null, a zero inflection of kaan.
c. All finite Egyptian Arabic sentences have a node where tense is marked; in present tense sentences, this node is empty.

The difference between (101b) and (101c) in particular is a subtle one; distinctions of this kind have received little overt discussion in linguistic literature.

We begin, then, with arguments against the first position, (101a). There are sentences which lack some inflection of kaan, as in the sentence types represented in (98a) and (98c), but in which certain other elements appear in just the position where we find some inflection of kaan in (98b) and (98d). These elements are the particles marking sentential negation and subject-marking pronouns. Since these elements are sensitive to a position where an inflection of kaan may occur in past and future tense sentences, their appearing there is evidence against (101a) and in support of a node in present tense sentences analogous to that occupied by kaan in the past and future tense sentences represented by (98b) and (98d).

The argument depends, however, on recognizing an important difference among predicate types that is obscured in (98). There are two types of predicates in Egyptian Arabic: those which mark person subject and those which do not. Specifically, the bi-imperfect, the perfect, and the Ha-imperfect illustrated in (80) through (82) are inflected for person subject. There are also certain nouns and prepositions that function as transitive predicates and mark person subject by means of a different set of bound affixes.[41]

(102)
a. biddaha tifaaHa
   wish:her apple
   'She wants an apple.'

b. biddi   tifaaHa
   wish:my apple
   'I want an apple.'

(103)
a. 9andaha   tifaaHa
   with:her   apple
   'She has an apple.'

b. 9andi   tifaaHa
   with:me   apple
   'I have an apple.'

The class of predicates that do not mark person subject includes participles, nouns, and adjectives. The claim in regard to participles is clear from the literal glosses of (86) through (89); no person indication is specified. The claim in regard to nouns and adjectives can be shown by comparing (90) and (91) to (104) and (105), respectively.

(104)
ana za9laan
I   angry:m:sg
'I am angry.'

(105)
ana ṭibiib
I   doctor:m:sg
'I am a doctor.'

(98b), (98c), and (98d) subsume both predicate types; (98a) allows only predicates which are marked for person subject, for reasons that we will return to presently. That is, (98) might be stated more specifically as shown in (106):

(106)
a.   Predicate
        +person subject

b-1. <u>kaan</u> Predicate
           +person subject

b-2. _kaan_ Predicate
           -person subject

c-1. Subject Predicate
           +person subject

c-2. Subject Predicate
           -person subject

d-1. Subject _kaan_ Predicate
           +person subject

d-2. Subject _kaan_ Predicate
           -person subject

Examples which illustrate these various types are given below, where (107) exemplifies (106a), (108) exemplifies (106b-1), and so forth.

(107)
biyiktib
writing
bi:imperf:3:m:sg
'He is writing.'

(108)
a. kaan   biyiktib
   KAAN   writing
          bi:imperf:3:m:sg
   'He was writing.'

b. Haykuun   biyiktib
   KAAN   writing
             bi:imperf:3:m:sg
   'He will be writing.'

(109)
a. kaan   naayim
   KAAN   sleeping
          act:part:m:sg
   'He was sleeping.'

b. Haykuun   naayim
   KAAN   sleeping
             act:part:m:sg

'He will be sleeping.'

(110)
huwwa biyiktib
he   writing
       bi:imperf:3:m:sg
'He is writing.'

(111)
huwwa naayim
he   sleeping
       act:part:m:sg
'He is sleeping.'

(112)
a. huwwa kaan biyiktib
   he   KAAN writing
                bi:imperf:3:m:sg
   'He was writing.'

b. huwwa Haykuun biyiktib
   he   KAAN   writing
                   bi:imperf:3:m:sg
   'He will be writing.'

(113)
a. huwwa kaan naayim
   he   KAAN sleeping
                act:part:m:sg
   'He was sleeping.'

b. huwwa Haykuun naayim
   he   KAAN   sleeping
                   act:part:m:sg
   'He will be sleeping.'

Given this refinement of (98), which substantially increases the number of statements about the form of sentences in Egyptian Arabic, we can show that (101a) cannot be correct--and at the same time give a somewhat more unified, although not complete, statement of the form of sentences than the one given in (106). (106a) and (106b-1), (106c-1) and (106d-1), (106c-2) and (106d-2) differ only in the presence or absence, respectively, of some inflection of kaan; that is, (106a), (106c-1), and (106c-2) represent present tense sentences, while (106b-1), (106d-1), and (106d-2) represent past and future tense sentences of the same predicate type. However, the negative in sentences of the form represented in (106a), (106c-1), and (106c-2) is sensitive to the position which kaan occupies in their respective counterparts (106b-1), (106d-1), and (106d-2). Consider first the following negative form of the past and future tense sentences given in (108) (an example of (106b-1)), (112) (an example of (106d-1)), and (113) (an example of (106d-2)).

(114)
a. ma-kan-š   biyiktib
   NEG-kaan-NEG   writing
                   bi:imperf:3:m:sg
   'He wasn't writing.'

b. ma-Haykun-š   biyiktib
   NEG-kaan-NEG   writing
                   bi:imperf:3:m:sg
   'He won't be writing.'

(115)
a. huwwa ma-kan-š   biyiktib
   he   NEG-kaan-NEG   writing
                          bi:imperf:3:m:sg
   'He wasn't writing.'

b. huwwa ma-Haykun-š   biyiktib
   he   NEG-kaan-NEG   writing
                          bi:imperf:3:m:sg
   'He won't be writing.'

(116)
a. huwwa ma-kan-š   naayim
   he   NEG-kaan-NEG   sleeping
                          act:part:m:sg
   'He wasn't sleeping.'

b. huwwa ma-Haykun-š   naayim

```
he      NEG-kaan-NEG   sleeping
                       act:part:m:sg
'He won't be sleeping.'
```

(Some Egyptians say **maHaykunš**; most educated Cairenes prefer the variant **miš Haykuun**, where the unattached negative particle **miš** precedes the future tense inflection of **kaan**:

(117)
```
a. miš  Haykuun   biyiktib
   NEG  KAAN      writing
                  bi:imperf:3:m:sg
   'He won't be writing.'

b. huwwa  miš   Haykuun   biyiktib
   he    NEG   KAAN      writing
                          bi:imperf:3:m:sg
   'He won't be writing.'
```

The point here is the tendency of the negative particle to become attached to any inflection of **kaan**.)

In the negative form of the present tense examples given in (107), (110), and (111), the negative **miš** (or **muš**) appears in precisely the position occupied by **kaan** in (114), (115), and (116).

(118)
```
miš  biyiktib
NEG  writing
     bi:imperf:3:m:sg
'He isn't writing.'
```

(119)
```
huwwa  miš  biyiktib
he     NEG  writing
            bi:imperf:3:m:sg
'He isn't writing.'
```

(120)
```
huwwa   miš   naayim
```

```
he       NEG  sleeping
              act:part:m:sg
'He isn't sleeping.'
```

That is, although sentences with the form in (106a), (106c-1), and (106c-2) lack any morphological material marking tense, the negative appears in precisely the position occupied by <u>kaan</u> in (106b-1), (106d-1), and (106d-2).

Although the item under consideration is different, a similar argument further supporting the relationship between (106c-2) and (106d-2) is possible. (106d-2) includes copular sentences.

(121)
```
a. axuuya        kaan    iṭ-ṭabiib
   my:brother    KAAN    the-doctor
   'My brother was the doctor.'

b. axuuya        Haykuun  iṭ-ṭabiib
   my:brother    KAAN     the-doctor
   'My brother will be the doctor.'
```

Where the predicate noun is definite, as in (121), what is traditionally called the "pronoun of separation" appears in present tense sentences, i.e. in sentences of the form (106c-2), in precisely the position occupied by <u>kaan</u> in the non-present tense equivalent of these sentences.

(122)
```
axuuya        huwwa   iṭ-ṭabiib
my:brother    HE      the-doctor
'My brother is the doctor.'
```

These pronouns may appear with attached negative particles, and are then commonly referred to as "<u>negative pronouns</u>".

(123)
```
axuuya        ma-huwwaa-š  iṭ-ṭabiib
my:brother    NEG-HE-NEG   the-doctor
'My brother isn't the doctor.'
```

These "negative pronouns" may follow a pronoun subject.

(124)
huwwa   ma-huwwaa-š   iṭ-ṭabiib
he   NEG-HE-NEG   the-doctor
'He isn't the doctor.'

Compare, for example, the following past and future tense sentences:

(125)
a.   huwwa   ma-kan-š   iṭ-ṭabiib
     he   NEG-KAAN-NEG the-doctor
     'He wasn't the doctor.'

b.   huwwa   ma-Haykun-š   iṭ-ṭabiib
     he   NEG-KAAN-NEG the-doctor

(or: huwwa miš Haykuun iṭ-ṭabiib)

     'He won't be the doctor.'

The constructions in (123) and (124), in which the negative particle is attached to the pronoun, parallel the constructions in (125) having both the negative particle and <u>kaan</u> and, thus, offer evidence that present tense sentences, like non-present tense sentences, have a node where tense is marked. In the present tense form in (106c-2), there happens to be no morphological material marking tense; however, the node remains as a place where the "pronoun of separation" and "negative pronouns" may appear. (The "negative pronouns" are limited to and optional in all present tense sentences where person subject is not marked in the predicate. This peculiarity in the distribution of the "negative pronouns" has previously been ignored in the literature on Egyptian Arabic. (See Jelinek (1980).))
   We have argued, then, that (106a) can be collapsed with (106b-1), (106c-1) with (106d-1), and (106c-2) with (106d-2). We can represent these facts as shown in (126), where the underlined space

indicates that part of a sentence where tense is marked--as well as sentential negation, the "pronoun of separation", and the "negative pronouns", although neither of the latter two are general to all the possibilities given.

(126)
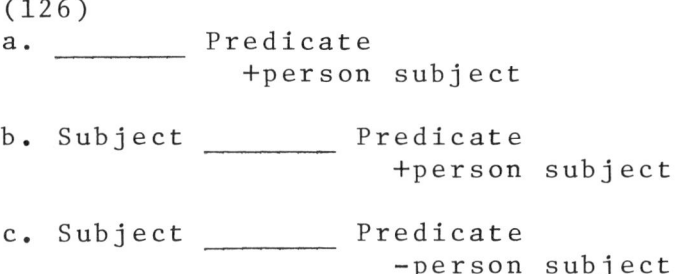
a. _____ Predicate
           +person subject

b. Subject _____ Predicate
                   +person subject

c. Subject _____ Predicate
                   -person subject

Schema (106b-2) is not obviously included in (126); we will defer discussion of this sentence type until after we take up the arguments against (101b).

A final argument against viewing present tense sentences as having at most a subject and a predicate involves the structure of imperative sentences. In (93) we gave examples of imperatives which lacked a subject; but an overt subject is also possible.

(127)
inta   iktib   ig-gawaab
you   write:imperative:m:sg   the-letter
'You write the letter!'

That is, imperative sentences look precisely like (98a) and (98c), if the latter lack some node which marks tense. Thus, if we choose to ignore the evidence presented by the negative particle, the "pronoun of separation", and the "negative pronouns" in present tense sentences, and to treat these sentences as containing at most a subject and a predicate, we would fail to capture an important generalization about finite sentences as opposed to imperative sentences in Egyptian Arabic. It is worth noting, in this regard, that the negative particle is excluded in sentences with an imperative inflection, just as the finite inflections of <u>kaan</u>

are excluded in imperative sentences.

We turn, then, to a consideration of the choice offered by (101b) or (101c). There is good reason to choose (101c) and to argue against (101b), that is, against zero as part of the inflectional system of the verb kaan. However, the first argument is intimately bound up with the conditions on the appearance of subjects in Egyptian Arabic. Thus, we must take up that aspect of the language first.

We have already discussed the distinction among predicate types in Egyptian Arabic in terms of whether or not they are marked for person subject. The class of elements that mark person subject is not limited to predicates; kaan also marks person subject, as noted in section 2.4.2. Given this distinction and the distribution of elements relative to it, we can easily state the conditions for the appearance of an independent subject: an independent subject is obligatory in any sentence where person subject is not marked by some bound pronominal affix. Thus, the (a) sentences in (88) through (91) all contain a subject and obligatorily so, because their predicate does not mark person subject and they also lack kaan. The (b) and (c) sentences in (88) through (91) all have a subject--but not obligatorily, because while they contain a predicate which has no person subject marking, they also contain some inflection of kaan. In short, the sentence type represented in (126a) is a variant of the one represented in (126b), since (126b) obligatorily contains some predicate marked for person subject.[42]

(128)
(Subject) _____ Predicate
                   +person subject

However, the sentence type represented in (126c) will necessarily contain a subject, unless some inflection of kaan or a "negative pronoun", both of which mark person subject, occupies the underlined space. Thus, sentences having the forms (129a,b) and (130a) are perfectly acceptable (see, for example, (113a), (109), and (120), respectively);

however, sentences of the form (130b) are not.

(129)
a. Subject $\left\{\begin{array}{c}\underline{kaan}\\ \text{Negative Pronoun}\end{array}\right\}$ Predicate
$\phantom{\text{Subject kaan Negative Pronoun Predic}}$ -person subject

b. $\left\{\begin{array}{c}\underline{kaan}\\ \text{Negative Pronoun}\end{array}\right\}$ Predicate
$\phantom{\text{kaan Negative Pronoun Predic}}$ -person subject

(130)
a. $\left\{\begin{array}{c}\text{Subject Negative}\\ \emptyset\end{array}\right\}$ Predicate
$\phantom{\text{Subject Negative Predic}}$ -person subject

b. *$\left\{\begin{array}{c}\text{Negative}\\ \emptyset\end{array}\right\}$ Predicate
$\phantom{\text{Negative Predic}}$ -person subject

This distribution of subjects provides the first argument against a phonologically null inflection of kaan in present tense sentences. We cannot collapse the sentence types in (129) and (130) as shown in (131), parallel to (128).

(131)
(Subject) _____ Predicate
$\phantom{\text{(Subject)   Pred}}$ -person subject

This is because statement (131) is true only when person subject is overtly marked in the underlined space. Otherwise, the subject is obligatory. Therefore, unlike any other inflection of kaan, the purported zero inflection would not be marked for person subject. Were it so marked, the sentences which had such a zero inflection would (given our generalizations) also allow a subject to be optional; but it is precisely where kaan is absent that we must depend upon the predicate (or "negative pronoun") to condition whether or not the subject is obligatorily present. That is, a zero inflection of kaan would be absolutely idiosyncratic in comparison with all of its other inflected forms.

The second argument against a phonologically null inflection of kaan (that is, against (101b)) involves sentences like those represented in (100) above. When kaan is overtly present, the subject may either precede it--as represented in (98)--or follow it--as in (100). If there were a phonologically null inflection of kaan in all present tense sentences, one might expect the negative particles (which occupy the same position, as argued above) to exhibit the same two distributional possibilities. But this is not the case. These elements do not have the same privileges of occurrence that an overt inflection of kaan does. That is, in negative present tense sentences with a subject, the negative miš must follow the subject. (132b) is not a variant of (132a).

(132)
  a. huwwa miš za9laan
     he   NEG angry
     'He's not angry.'

≠ b. miš huwwa za9laan (bass)....
    NEG he   angry
    'It's not just that he is angry....'

Having argued against (101a) and (101b), we come to the position that finite sentences lacking an inflection of kaan (i.e. present tense sentences) have a node which may be empty. Thus, if the three statements in (101) exhaust the possibilities, there is negative evidence in support of (101c). However, there is positive evidence as well. In some sentences lacking kaan, but having a predicate that marks person subject, the particle marking sentential negation may attach directly to the predicate.

(133)
a. ma-biyiktib-š   ig-gawaab
   NEG-writing-NEG the-letter
   'He isn't writing the letter.'

b. ma-katab-š   ig-gawaab
   NEG-wrote-NEG   the-letter

'He didn't write (hasn't written) the letter.'

The attachment of the negative particle to the predicate in these examples is consistent with the view that there is an empty node in these sentences, rather than a zero inflection of kaan to which the negative particle would be drawn.

As we have seen, finite sentences without kaan is some ways resemble sentences with a finite inflection of kaan; that is, they lack a verb in either the imperative or the subjunctive inflection. And some sentences without kaan differ from sentences with kaan in the position of the negative particle; this particle must always follow any independent subject if no inflection of kaan appears, at least on the interpretation under consideration. Sentences with finite kaan and sentences with the "negative pronouns" fall together on the optionality of an independent subject, but neither on the position of this subject nor on predicate type. This partial similarity between present and non-present tense sentences seems consistent with the view that present tense sentences have a node, a particular space, where tense is marked and where sentential negation and person subject may be marked. Still, this space does not constitute a phonologically null inflection of kaan, since it does not correspond to all the positions in non-present tense sentences where the various inflections of kaan occur; nor does it always mark person subject. And in some negative present tense sentences as shown in (133), this node may also be empty.

We have argued for the position stated in (101c), namely, that sentences without an overt inflection of kaan contain a node where tense is marked, albeit a potentially empty node in present tense sentences. The arguments presented against (101a) also specify the possible membership of this constituent; in addition to kaan, we may find there the negative element, the "pronoun of separation", and the "negative pronouns". The first argument presented against (101b) offers a revision of statement (126), since the subject is obligatorily present only in sentences where person subject is not marked by some bound pronominal affix. (134), then, schematically represents all these generalizations about Egyptian Arabic sentences.

(134)

a. (Subject) $\left\{\begin{array}{c} \emptyset \\ \underline{kaan} \\ \text{Negative} + \underline{kaan} \\ \text{Negative} \end{array}\right\}$ Predicate
+person subject

b. (Subject) $\left\{\begin{array}{c} \underline{kaan} \\ \text{Negative} + \underline{kaan} \\ \text{Negative Pronoun} \end{array}\right\}$ Predicate
−person subject

c. Subject $\left\{\begin{array}{c} \emptyset \\ \text{Negative} \\ \text{Pronoun of Separation} \end{array}\right\}$ Predicate
−person subject

We must note at this point that (134b) includes the form given in (106b-2), the sentence type the discussion of which was previously deferred.

(106)
b-2. <u>kaan</u> Predicate
        −person subject

Thus, given the conditions on the appearance of a subject in Egyptian Arabic, the specification of which allows a better statement of sentence structure in this language, there is an automatic generalization to a form which had to be ignored when the focus was entirely on the distinction between the two types of predicates.
One final comment is in order. Subject is specified as initial in (134). We noted earlier that the subject may follow the constituent under primary consideration here, and the second argument presented above against (101b) gives the conditions under which that is possible, specifically when <u>kaan</u> is present. Therefore, a subset of the sentences subsumed under (134a) and (134b) may appear in another order.

2.4.4 Conclusion

We have argued in this section that finite sentences in Egyptian Arabic have a constituent, independent of the predicate, where tense is marked--either by kaan or its absence--as well as negation and person subject (the latter marked both in kaan and in the "pronoun of separation"). We will not take a position here on whether the membership of this constituent is best given in terms of these three notional categories, or as in (134), or by a list of the actual words which may appear there--e.g. the various forms of kaan, including its negative ones, and the various forms of pronouns. The list of elements which occur in the constituent would differ in each case, but it is also true that, in each case, we could easily give an exhaustive list. Thus, our analysis of Egyptian Arabic provides an instantiation of the definition given at the beginning of this chapter.

2.5 Japanese[43]

2.5.1 Introduction

Unlike Luiseño, Lummi, or Egyptian Arabic, Japanese is a highly agglutinative, rigid verb-final language. In Japanese (as in other agglutinative languages) it is typical for the main verb of the sentence to be a highly complex fusion of a verb stem plus numerous suffixes, so that on the surface it is not unusual to find a string of suffixlike formatives attached to the main (or, the leftmost) verb:

(135)
Ken   wa   Naomi-ni   hugu-o
Ken   topic   Naomi-dat   hugu:fish-acc

tabe - sase - hazime - ta   - daroo   - ka - ne.
a   b   c   d   e   f   g
eat - cause - begin - past - presume - or - right:?

'I wonder if Ken has begun to make Naomi eat fugu fish.'

The problem is whether or not an argument can be made for the constituency of some (or all) of these suffixes, such that the constituent meets the definition given in section 2.1.

It seems intuitively correct to distinguish such elements as those identified with the letters $\underline{d}$ and $\underline{e}$ in (135)--elements marking tense and modality, respectively--and many Japanese grammarians have in fact done so. However, the grammatical models used so far in the analysis of Japanese have given neither a necessary reason for such a distinction nor criteria to reject it. We will show that in Japanese the distinct status of such elements, as well as the nature of the constituent encompassing them, can be described nicely in a framework of layered syntax. Specifically, we will attempt to motivate, if only as a first approximation, the following phrase structure (PS) rules:[44]

(136)
a. $S^2 \longrightarrow$ (Adv) S^1 Affix^2
b. $S^1 \longrightarrow$ (Adv) S Affix^1

where Affix^1 [Tense]: $\underline{(r)u}$ 'present', $\underline{ta}$ 'past' (e.g. $\underline{d}$ in (135))
Affix^2 [Modality]: $\underline{daroo}$ 'presume', $\underline{mai}$ 'presume not', $\underline{soo\ da}$ 'so I hear', etc. (e.g. $\underline{e}$ in (135))

The constituent which instantiates the definition is best characterized as $\underline{\text{Affix}}$ immediately and exclusively dominated by $\underline{S^n}$ (where $\underline{n} > 1$).

Notice that in this system of PS rules, the category $\underline{X}$ in Japanese is actually a set of S-layers, each layer dominating a sentence-final Affix. For example, S^1 is a constituent which contains S and Affix^1, as shown in (137). This system, like the V-system proposed for English in Akmajian, Steele, and Wasow (1979), allows us to refer to different S-layers in unique fashion. Thus, one could refer to S to the exclusion of S^1, S^2, and so on. In fact, the unique layerings play a significant role in distributional statements in the phrase structure of Japanese. Our strategy will be as follows: we will show that there is independent

(137)

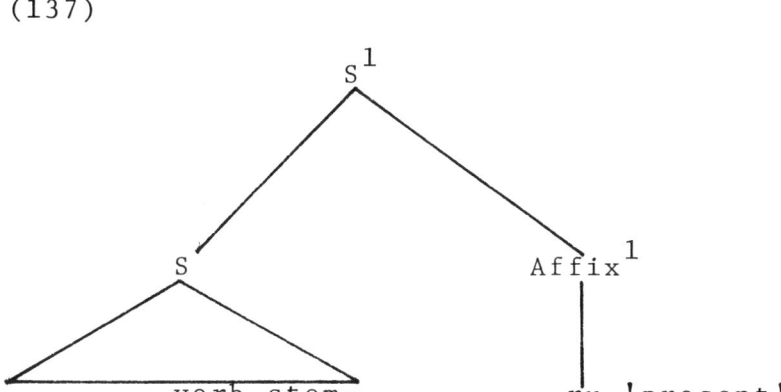

evidence--i.e. language-particular evidence from Japanese--that the layered-S system allows us to state important syntactic generalizations. Having independently motivated the layered-S system, we will present an argument that Japanese offers an instantiation of the definition given in section 2.1.

2.5.2 Layered Analysis of S
2.5.2.1 Tense Affixes ($Affix^1$)
The system of movement rules in English motivated the different layers of the V analysis in Akmajian, Steele, and Wasow (1979), but such evidence is lacking in Japanese. Here, the main evidence for syntactic layering comes instead from <u>subcategorization</u> arguments: we can show that different S-layers occur in different syntactic environments. To illustrate, notice first that certain elements occur only with tenseless complements. For example, <u>nagara</u> 'while', which we will refer to as an adverb, is one such case:

(138)
a. Naomi   wa   piinattu-o   tabe   nagara
    Naomi   topic   peanuts-acc   eat   WHILE

    hon-o   yom-u.
    book-acc   read-present

    'Naomi reads a book (while) eating peanuts.'

b. *Naomi wa   piinattu-o   tabe-ru   nagara
   Naomi topic peanuts-acc eat-PRESENT   WHILE

   hon-o   yom-u.
   book-acc read-present

This fact will fall out automatically if we assume that <u>nagara</u> is syntactically subcategorized as [S___]. In other words, <u>nagara</u> can be preceded by S, but not by S^1; hence, it will never have a tensed complement. The structure for (138a) is as in (139).[45] Only the highest clause in (139), i.e. S^1, has a tense affix; the complement to <u>nagara</u> is simply S. The first piece of evidence for an S-layer, then, is that certain elements (in this case an adverb) cooccur with sentential complements which terminate in a main verb stem without tense morphemes--precisely the composition of what we term <u>S</u>.

The second argument comes from sentence conjunction of the "gerundive" and "infinitive" type, illustrated in (140) and (141).

(140)
Naomi wa   tosyokan-e   it-te,   hon-o   yon-de,
Naomi topic library-to   GOING   book-acc READING

uti-e   kaet-ta.
home-to   return-past

'Naomi went to the library, read a book, and re-
 turned home.'

(141)
Naomi wa   tosyokan-e   iki,   hon-o   yomi,
Naomi topic library-to   GO   book-acc READ

uti-e   kaet-ta.
home-to   return-past

'Naomi went to the library, read a book, and re-
 turned home.'

In (140) <u>it-te</u> and <u>yon-de</u> are tenseless verbs, in a

(139)

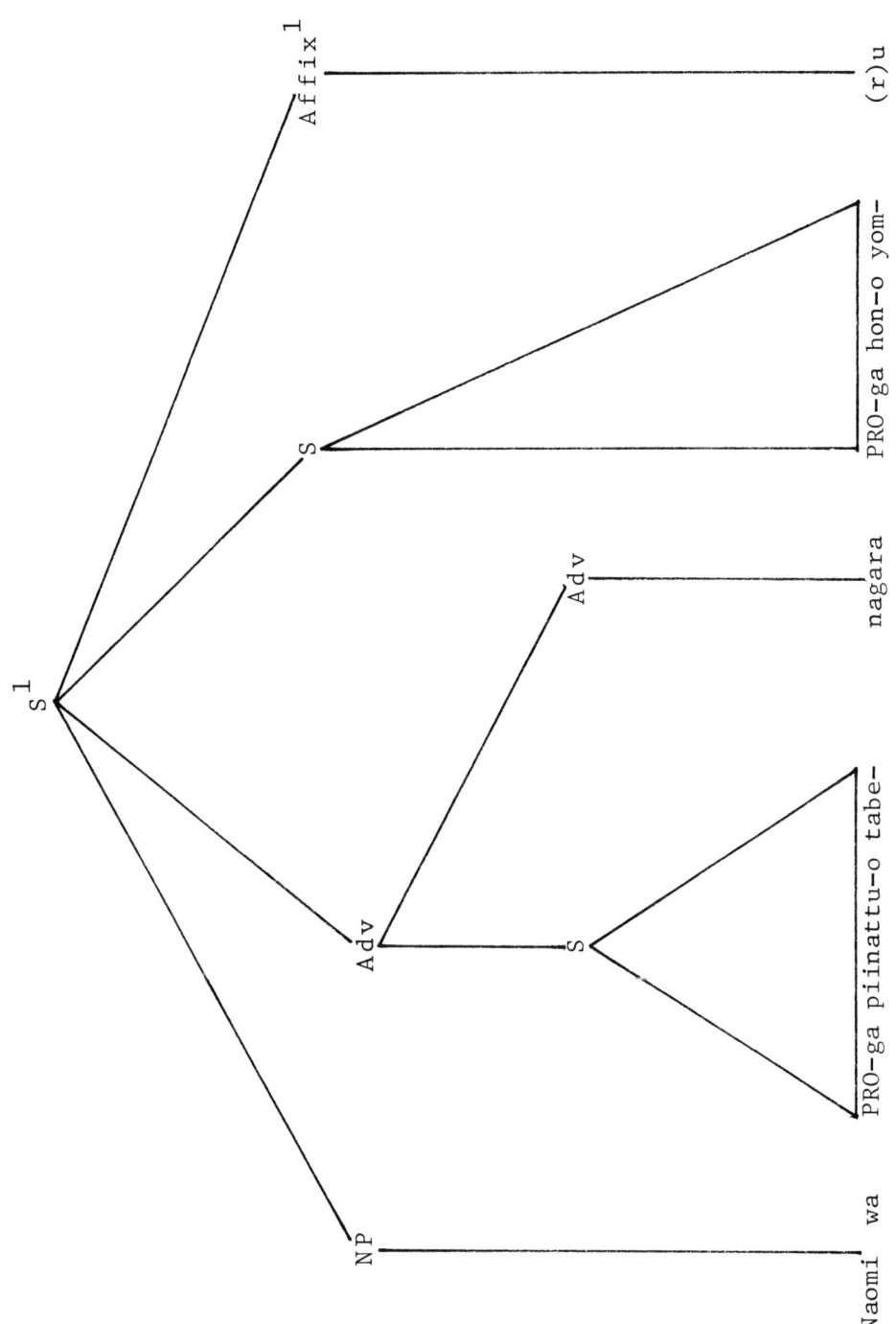

form sometimes referred to as the "continuative", which we have translated with the gerund in English. In (141) iki and yomi are, again, tenseless forms, typically found in conjuncts preceding the final one. In the final conjunct in both examples we do find a tensed verb, kaet-ta; the tenseless verbs in the previous conjuncts are semantically interpreted as past tense, in "agreement" with the final past tense. The structure of this sort of conjunction is quite naturally represented within the layered-S system:

(142)

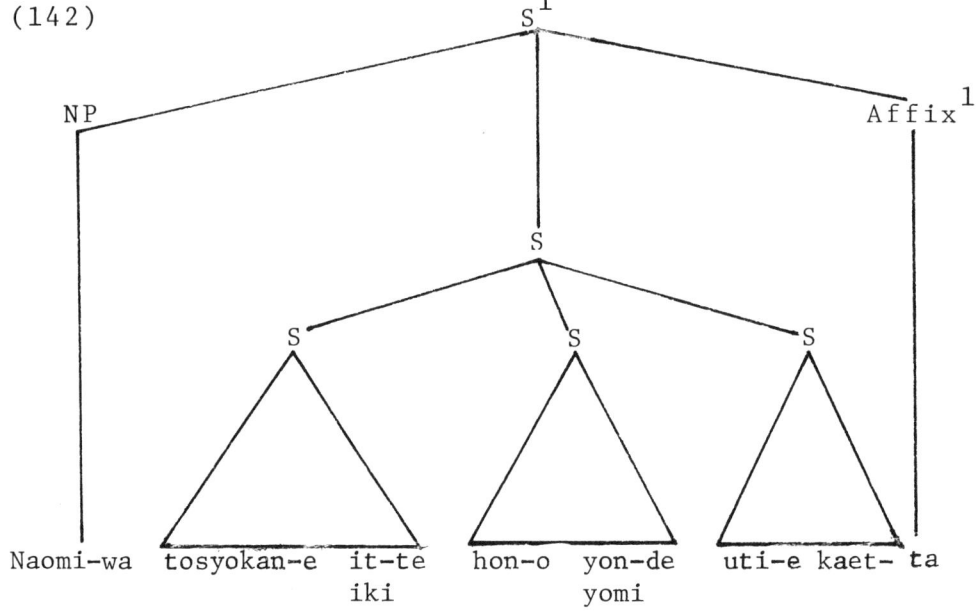

In other words, S^1 contains an S which branches into a series of conjoined Ss; the tense affix, ta, is not dominated by any of the S conjuncts, but is rather the Affix[1] that occurs under S^1. Notice that this syntactic representation lends itself quite naturally to the semantic interpretation of tense as a sentence operator: the scope of ta is the S which it commands (including, of course, the coordinate branching of S, as above). In (142), then, we see another syntactic environment in which the S-layer--and precisely S--is required.

A Definition and Its Instantiations

The third argument for distinguishing S- and S¹-layers concerns the scope of tense in an interesting kind of "containment" phenomenon. Consider examples (143) and (144):

(143)
Sono uti   wa   mada   hito-ga   sun-de
that house topic yet   people-nom   residing

i-   ta/ru   no   ni   minna-de   butikowasi-te
be-PAST/PRESENT   NO   NI   they-all   wrecking

simat-ta.
finish-past

'They demolished the house, even though people were still living in it.'

(144)
Sono uti   wa   mada   hito-ga   sun-de
that house topic yet   people-nom   residing

i-   ta/*ru   keredo   minna-de   butikowasi-te
be-PAST/*PRESENT   KEREDO   they-all   wrecking

simat-ta.
finish-past

'They demolished that house, even though people were still living in it.'

The meanings of (143) and (144) are similar, if not identical, the only difference being that <u>no ni</u> in the former, and <u>keredo</u> in the latter, act as concessive connectives. Nevertheless, present tense <u>(r)u</u> is well-formed only in (143), while past tense <u>ta</u> is acceptable in both. As discussed at length in Kitagawa (1973), this state of affairs suggests that a <u>no ni</u> clause as in (143) falls within the scope of the matrix tense, whereas a <u>keredo</u> clause does not. Structurally, (143) and (144) may be represented, for the present, as in (145) and (146) respectively.[46] In tree (145) <u>ta</u> in the matrix clause commands the <u>ta</u> in the adverbial clause (but not vice versa). In

(145)

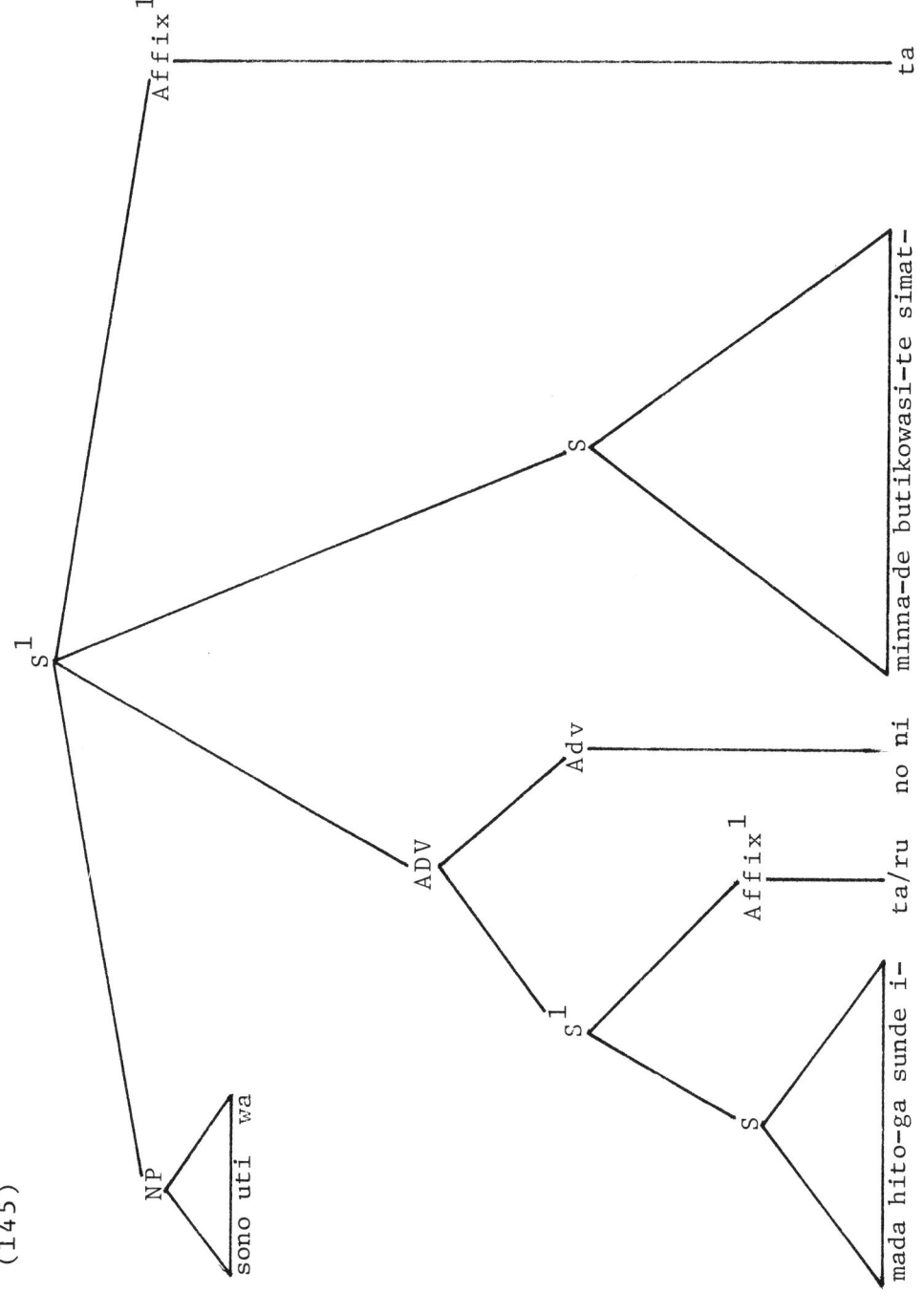

A Definition and Its Instantiations

(146)

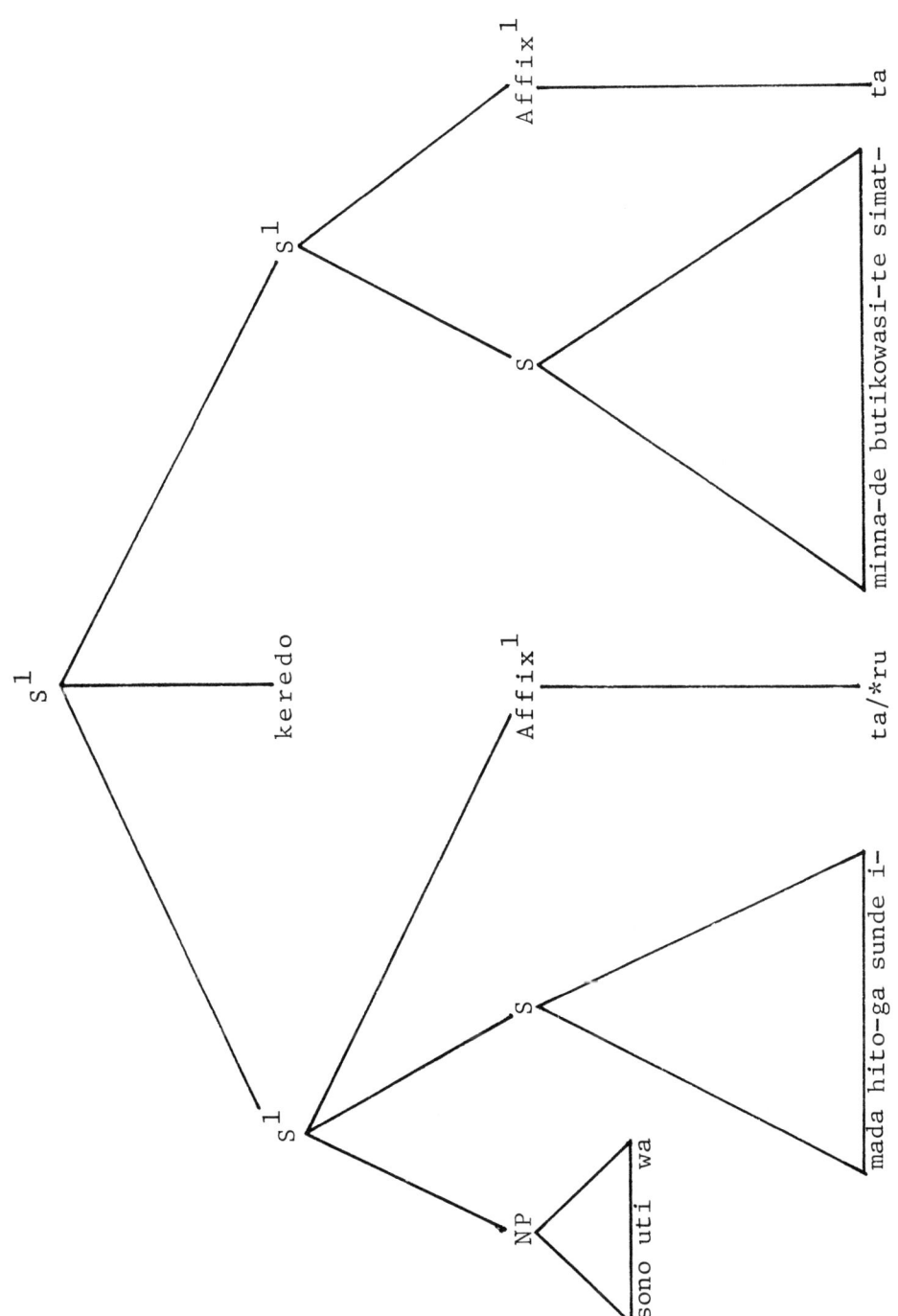

tree (146), in which _keredo_ is represented as a sentence conjunction, neither tense commands the other. A generalization which emerges from these structural representations is as follows: letting T stand for _tense_, if T_1 commands T_2, then T_2 is in the scope of T_1 and in some sense is "subordinate" to T_1. Given these structural representations, how can we explain why _ru_ is ungrammatical in (146), but acceptable in (145)?

The present tense _(r)u_ in (146) is odd because _keredo_ 'although' merely conjoins two clauses, and, as expected in coordinate conjunction, the reference point of tense in each clause is assumed to be that of the time of the speech act. Since, as a matter of fact, the events reported by both S^1 conjuncts of (146) are assumed to have occurred prior to the time of the speech act, the use of _(r)u_ here is bizarre. (That is, the translation (146) with _ru_ is something like 'They demolished (past) that house, even though people are (present) still living in it.') In the case of a _no ni_ clause as in (145), however, using _(r)u_ within the clause merely expresses the fact that the event described by the adverbial clause happened at the same time as, or possibly earlier than, the event described in the main clause, which, of course, does have an acceptable reading here. The use of the past tense _ta_ within the _no ni_ clause is also acceptable, because _ta_ in this case expresses the fact that the event described by the adverbial clause has preceded (whether or not it is also judged to be concurrent with) the event represented by the main clause. And, whether the tense of the _no ni_ clause is represented by _(r)u_ or _ta_, the time reference of the entire event is governed by the _matrix_ tense. In terms of the scope definition established above, the tense of the _no ni_ clause is within the scope of the matrix tense.

The structure of the argument, then, is as follows. First, we have seen that there are well-defined syntactic contexts in which tenseless sentences must occur, namely, as complements to lexical items (such as _nagara_) that are subcategorized for tenseless sentences, and in the context of sentence coordination in which the conjuncts are tenseless. By positing the tense affix in a higher S^1-layer, we are able to specify that the above-mentioned contexts take S, to the exclusion of S^1. Having independently established that the tense affixes should occur in a level higher than S, we then see that the resulting syntactic representations give us just the sort of command relations that we need to distinguish between "dominating" tense and "contained" tense. Thus, the syntactic representations allow us (a) to state important syntactic generalizations, and (b) to provide a natural account of the semantics of "governing" tenses.

2.5.2.2 Modal Affixes (Affix^2) Returning to the contrast between no ni 'although' and keredo 'although' clauses discussed above, we observe that the types of sentences that can be embedded in these two contexts are actually distinct. Thus, consider the following examples:

(147)
a. Mukasi   wa   biiru   mo   non-da   keredo
   old:time topic   beer   also   drink-past   KEREDO

   ima   wa   uisukii   bakari   nom-u.
   now   topic   whiskey   only   drink-present

   'Although he drank beer too in times past, he only drinks whiskey now.'

b. Mukasi   wa   biiru   mo   non-da   no   ni
   old:time topic   beer   also   drink-past   NO   NI

   ima   wa   uisukii   bakari   nom-u.
   now   topic   whiskey   only   drink-present

   'Although he drank beer too in times past, he only drinks whiskey now.'

(148)
a. Mukasi   wa   biiru   mo   non-da-daroo
   old:time topic   beer   also   drink-past-DAROO

```
    keredo    ima    wa       uisukii    bakari
    KEREDO    now    topic    whiskey    only

    nom-u.
    drink-present
```

'Although he must have drunk beer too in times past, he only drinks whiskey now.'

b. *Mukasi   wa   biiru   mo   non-da-daroo
   old:time   topic   beer   also   drink-past-DAROO

```
    no    ni    ima    wa       uisukii    bakari
    NO    NI    now    topic    whiskey    only

    nom-u.
    drink-present
```

What makes the no ni clause of (148b) unacceptable is the presence of daroo, the modality element we glossed roughly above as 'I presume'. The same state of affairs obtains with no de 'because' and kara 'because' clauses, corresponding to the no ni and keredo difference. That is, a modality element like daroo is well-formed in contexts such as [____ keredo] and [____ kara], but not in the contexts [____ no ni] or [____ no de]. This phenomenon can be captured in a straightforward manner by simply specifying that the contexts [____ keredo] and [____ kara] require S^2, whereas [____ no ni] and [____ no de] require S^1.[47]

    A sentence without daroo can, of course, occur in the [____ keredo] or [____ kara] contexts (cf. (147a)). This situation is so far not allowed by the PS rules in (136), which make the Affixes obligatory. However, a natural hypothesis suggests itself within a layered-S system: namely, that contexts that allow S^n also allow S^{n-1}, where $n > 1$. In other words, an item which is subcategorized for S^2, such as keredo, will also allow S^1, but an item subcategorized for S^1, such as no ni, will not allow S^2. (Items which are subcategorized for S^1 generally do not allow a simple S as an alternative subcategorization, which is why we have stipulated above that n > 1.) By adopting a "higher allows lower" principle, then, we can exploit the properties of the layered-S system (as specified in (136)) to account for the kind of variation in subcategorization manifested by elements such as keredo.

Finally, there are additional cases requiring the distinction between S and S. To list some of them:

(i) The contexts that require S^1 include [___ NP] (i.e. the relative clause), [___ toki] 'when...', [___ tame ni] 'in order to..., because...', and [___ nara] 'if...'.

(ii) The contexts that allow S^2, besides the above-mentioned [___ keredo] and [___ kara], also include [___ ga] 'although...'.

These facts, then, clearly point to a significant distinction between S^1 and S^2.

There is also a rather interesting related phenomenon that may be noted here. As is well known, in what is called the "nonreportive" speech style (cf. Kuroda (1973), Kuno (1972)), adjectives of feeling or mental condition normally occur only with the first person "subject", e.g. boku, here marked with the topic marker wa, as demonstrated in (149).

(149)
a. Boku wa   atama-ga   ita-i.
   I   topic head-nom   hurt-present
   'I have a headache.'

b. *Naomi wa   atama-ga   ita-i.
    Naomi topic head-nom   hurt-present

Following Kuroda (1965), we may for the present isolate this particular property associable with emotive adjectives by the arbitrary feature "F". Noteworthy for our purposes is the fact that we can identify this feature "F" as a property of S^2, and not of S^1. In the contexts that allow only S^1, such as the no ni and relative clause contexts in (150), the occurrence of an emotive adjective can be perfectly acceptable with the non-first person "subject", even in the "nonreportive" style.

Surprisingly, though, the oddity returns in the contexts which allow S^2, such as [___ keredo] 'although...' and [___ kara] 'because...'. Thus, observe the following contrasts:

(150)
a. Sono   kodomo   wa   netu-de   kurusi-i
    that   child   topic   fever-with   suffer-present

    no   ni   nak-anakat-ta.
    NO   NI   cry-not-past

    'The child, although suffering with fever, did
     not cry.'

b. Atama-ga   ita-i   kodomo   wa   kono
    head-nom   hurt-present   child   topic   this

    ko   desu.
    child   is

    'The child who has a headache is this child.'

(151)
a. ?*Sono kodomo   wa   netu-de   kurusi-i
     that child   topic   fever-with   suffer-present

     keredo   nak-anakat-ta.
     KEREDO   cry-not-past

b. ?*Naomi   wa   atama-ga   ita-i   kara
     Naomi   topic   head-nom   hurt-present   KARA

     uti-de   ne-te   i-ru   yo.
     home-at   resting   be-present   I:tell:you

     ('Naomi is resting at home because she has a
       headache.')

Clearly, whatever the feature "F" eventually turns out to be, it needs somehow to be identified with S^2 rather than S^1. And this fact is further confirmation for the distinction between S^1 and S^2.

<u>2.5.2.3   Conclusion</u>   Obviously, we have not

discussed all the possible elements which could play a role in the layered system. For example, we have not touched on the difficult issue of negation, nor have we looked at elements such as the formality marker _mas_ and predicational adjectives like _rasii_ 'appear' and _yoo da_ 'seem'. But our task here is not to provide a comprehensive analysis of Japanese syntax, a task which will require considerable future research; rather, it is to show the plausibility of the layered syntax approach to the analysis of Japanese sentences in order to argue that Japanese provides an instantiation of the definition in section 2.1. We will turn to the implications of the layered analysis for this argument shortly.

However, one additional topic worth mentioning here is the set of so-called sentence particles, _na_, _ne_, _yo_, and _sa_. The use of these particles essentially indicates the particular way in which the speaker wishes the addressee to take the utterance. For example, _yo_ indicates that the speaker wishes the addressee to pay close attention to the content of the utterance; _sa_ conveys, generally, a sense that the utterance has to do with something obvious. We will not concern ourselves here with the specific "meaning" of these particles. (Readers are referred to Uyeno (1971) and R. Lakoff (1972) for a detailed discussion of them.) What is relevant to our purpose, rather, is the following fact: notwithstanding the popular term _sentence particles_ given to them, the structural environments in which they occur in an actual discourse context turn out to be those represented in (152):

(152)

a. $[[N^{n-1} \; (Affix)]_N{}^n \; \underline{\quad}]$, where _Affix_ stands for a postnominal particle, e.g. a case particle, a topic marker, etc.

b. $[[V^{n-1} \; (Affix)]_V{}^n \; \underline{\quad}]$, where Affix represents an affix such as _te_ 'continuative' or _(r)eba_ 'if'

A Definition and Its Instantiations

c. $[S^n \rule{1cm}{0.4pt}]$, where n is a maximal expansion

That is, if we assume that syntactic layering is a property of noun phrases and verb phrases, as well as of sentences, the structural context that needs to be specified for na, ne, yo, and sa is simply as follows:

(153)
$[X^n \rule{1cm}{0.4pt}]$, where X = maximal category

Examples (154a-c) correspond to the three contexts (152a-c), respectively.

(154)
a. Naomi-ga   ne,   Ken-to   ne,
   Naomi-nom   YOU:KNOW   Ken-with   YOU:KNOW

   gakkoo-de   yo,...
   school-at   I:TELL:YOU

   'Naomi, you know, with Ken, you know, at the
     school, you see....'

b. Naomi-ga   ki-te   ne,   Ken-to
   Naomi-nom   come-continuative   YOU:KNOW   Ken-with

   hanas-eba   yo....
   speak-if   I:TELL:YOU

   'If, you know, Naomi, coming here, should speak
     with Ken, you see....'

c. Kore   tabe-ro   yo.   Sosite
   this   eat-imperative   I:TELL:YOU   and

   issyo-ni   ik-oo   ne.
   together-dat   go-let's   YOU:KNOW

   'Eat this!' 'And let's go together, OK?'

That the structural context for these particles may be defined elegantly as in (153) is further evidence for the layered syntax approach.

2.5.3 Implications for an Instantiation of the Definition

We have proposed and motivated (in part), a set of phrase structure rules for Japanese, which defines a syntactic layering for the category S. We have provided language-specific evidence from Japanese that the layering--in particular, the distinction among S, S^1, and S^2--allows us to state significant syntactic generalizations of the language, particularly in subcategorization and cooccurrence in phrase structure. Assuming that this system is independently motivated, notice that we have also provided arguments for the constituency of some of those elements which appear as affixes to the verb. That is, if we return to example (135), we have argued that the affix labeled d (the one that contains the notional element tense), the affix labeled e (the one that contains the notional element modality), and the set of affixes labeled f and g (the ones that we have called sentence particles) are each constituents in their own right, as defined in the tree (155).

(155)

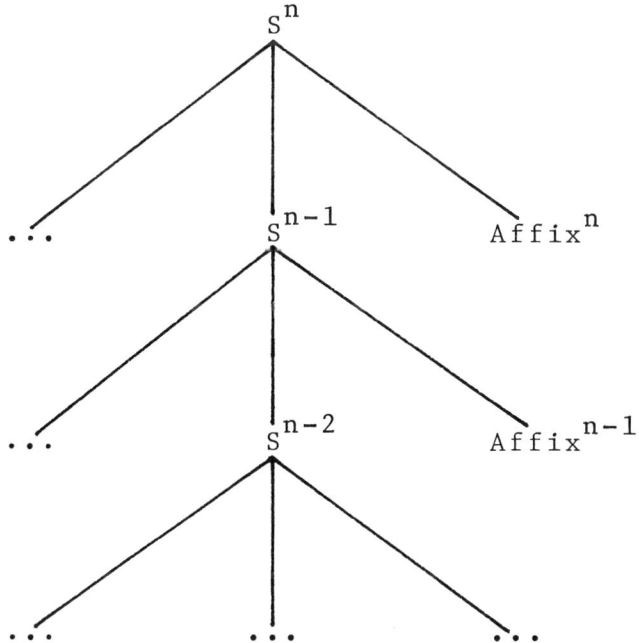

Given (155), there are two constituents in Japanese which meet the definition given in section 2.1: the affix labeled Affix^2 in (136), which contains a specifiable set of elements all of which mark modality, and the affix labeled Affix^1 in (136), which also contains a specifiable set of elements all of which mark tense. Although in Luiseño, Lummi, and Egyptian Arabic, arguments were presented for a single constituent which meets the definition, there is, of course, no requirement that a single constituent in any one language will meet the definition--any more than there is a requirement that each language will have some element which meets the definition. Therefore, given (155), we could conclude that both Affix^1 and Affix^2 in Japanese meet the definition.

However, there is an interesting sense in which the set of affixes which are properties of the sentence in which they may occur do form a single constituent, namely, in the PS rule schema that defines any layered (or $\bar{X}$) analysis:

(156)
$$S^n \longrightarrow (Adv) \; S^{n-1} \; Affix^n$$

In other words, assuming (156), there is a constituent defined by Affix in the PS schema. Therefore, the analysis presented in section 2.5.2 allows us to argue that Japanese provides a single instantiation of the definition, an instantiation which includes both tense and modality, but also the sentence particles discussed in sections 2.5.2.3.

It is not crucial, for our purposes, to decide between these two approaches. Either one will argue that Japanese has some element which instantiates the definition.

2.6 Conclusion

In this chapter, we have given a definition and analyzed an element of each of four languages which instantiates it. To identify these elements in Luiseño, Lummi, and Japanese, we have used language-particular labels: in Luiseño, the Particle Complex; in Lummi, the Enclitic Sequence;

and in Japanese, Affix. In Egyptian Arabic, we used no label, but rather identified the element with an underlined space. Language-internally, such identifications are as good as any; those for Luiseño, Lummi, and Japanese, in particular, are reasonably good descriptive terms. However, since the label of the set of elements identified by the definition was given initially as AUX, each of these elements is a language-particular instantiation of AUX. In the next chapter, we are concerned with the properties of the set AUX.

However, there is one aspect of the analyses just presented which we must address first. The definition with which we began this chapter required any element which is considered an instantiation of it to be a constituent. This requirement is clearly necessary for two reasons. First, and most generally, it is traditionally assumed--and we did not question this assumption--that for something to be identified with a syntactic categorial label, it must be a syntactic constituent. Second, and more specifically, it is clear that simply invoking the notional categories of tense and/or modality would not suffice, since these notional categories can occur outside of the element with which we are primarily concerned; Luiseño clearly illustrates this fact, since tense (and aspect) can be marked by a set of inflections on the "verb".

The discussions of Luiseño, Lummi, and Japanese focus in large part on language-internal arguments for the constituency of the elements under consideration. That the constituency arguments should take such a prominent role follows from the various properties of the elements themselves. The candidate(s) in Japanese for instantiating the definition is/are, on the surface, an affix; the issue in this case is to show that affixation is not a necessary argument against an analysis which proposes a syntactic constituent. The candidate in Luiseño for instantiating the definition is a string of second-position particles; the issue here is to show that, although we can identify each of the various members of this set, it is the entire string--and not its individual members--which is critical to an adequate analysis of Luiseño sentences. The candidate in Lummi is, on the surface, a string of second-position enclitics; the issue here is to show both that obligatory encliticization is not an argument against an analysis which proposes a syntactic constituent and that the various members of the enclitic string are not independent members of the sentence.

Thus, the arguments for constituency in the three cases are somewhat different, and it is an unsettling possibility that the various notions of "constituency" which these arguments center on need not converge. The difficulty which this possibility raises is not a problem specific to the analyses undertaken in this book, but rather a more general issue. For example, many symptoms which are diagnosed as being the result of constituency in a language such as English are often simply absent in other languages. Thus, more general empirical criteria are needed if there is to be a notion of constituency which is universally applicable. We take the analyses here to provide important examples of notions of constituency which are respected in the languages in question. For further remarks, see the discussion of English in appendix A.

Notes
1. The definition which we propose here is different in important respects from the one given in Akmajian, Steele, and Wasow (1979). Most importantly, it adds the requirement that a constituent which meets the definition must contain a specified set of elements. The addition of this requirement meets objections to the original definition raised by Pullum (1981).

2. There is no requirement, however, that an element will mark only one of these notions. Rather, the hypothesis is that there is some "semantic field" which we will call modality, a field which is defined by the notions of possibility, probability, etc. Languages appear to be able to divide up the field in various ways; they also are not obliged to exhaust it.

3. It should not be assumed, however, that universal agreement exists on what are necessary and sufficient conditions for establishing constituency. See Oehrle (1979) for a discussion and refutation of some commonly held assumptions in this regard.

4. In the discussion of the various languages to follow, we will use terms such as Noun and Verb to refer to various elements which are not critically under consideration. However, we take such labels, regardless of whether we use them in all four languages or not, to be defined internal to the specific language under consideration. That is, we could just as easily have given other labels to these categories, and we do not mean to imply by the use of such labels any commitment to the identification of what may be called Verb in Lummi with what may be called Verb in Japanese in the absence of an investigation such as the one we are carrying out relative to the definition given above.

5. This section assumes the discussion of Luiseño in Akmajian, Steele, and Wasow (1979), although it also revises one of the positions taken there. The Luiseño sentences are given in the orthography introduced for Luiseño in Hyde (1971). In general, standard IPA symbols are used; however, a few comments are in order. The sequences sh, ch, and ng represent /š/, /č/, and /ŋ/, respectively; a sequence of two identical vowels, e.g. ee, indicates a long vowel; ṣ is (probably) a retroflex sibilant; and glottal stop is represented as '.

Mrs. Villiana Hyde, a native speaker of the language, is the source of the Luiseño data; her tireless patience, enthusiasm, and generosity are hereby inadequately acknowledged.

6. We write the members of the sequence of particles separately in the example sentences in (1); however, in Akmajian, Steele, and Wasow (1979) it was argued that the particles are members of a single constituent, separated from one another by morpheme boundaries. We continue to hold that position and will provide further evidence for it;

hence, the fact that the members of the particle sequence are given as independent elements in (1) is not to be taken as disputing that position, but simply as a neutral representation, and one which we will immediately dispense with.

Three conventions employed in the literal glosses for the language examples in this and other chapters are worth mentioning here. First, we attempted to keep a one-to-one correspondence between the elements in the language example and the literal English gloss. Therefore, if the literal English gloss for some element is longer than a single word, the words are separated by colons. Second, we want to direct attention in many cases to a particular part of the language example. This we have done by writing the corresponding part in the literal gloss in capitals. Finally, we have abbreviated some of the words used in the literal glosses. The list of abbreviations can be found immediately preceding the bibliography.

7. In Akmajian, Steele, and Wasow (1979), these elements were referred to as <u>clitic pronouns</u>. The term <u>clitic pronoun</u>, like the term <u>pronoun</u>, commonly implies that both number and person are distinguished in the members of the set. However, in certain contexts, subject marking in Luiseño indicates only the number of the subject. The term which we use here is therefore more adequate to the task of labeling these elements. However, it does have the disadvantage of incorporating the term <u>subject</u>; by identifying these elements as subject marking, we do not mean to subscribe to any theory which takes such relational terms as primitive.

8. The following seems a fair summary of Kaisse's position: First, the phonological and syntactic properties of the Luiseño particle sequence are general properties of clitic sequences; thus, "it is...not necessary to invoke any additional explanation for the behavior of the Luiseño particles beyond the uncontroversial observation that they are clitics..." (p.6). (The page numbers given for both the Kaisse and the Pullum articles

refer to prepublication versions.) Second, clitic sequences are not constituents because they are not "functionally or categorially unified elements" (p.4); that is, Kaisse assumes a standard transformational treatment of clitics whereby "clitics can originate in any of several categories..." (p.1). Therefore, "...Luiseño appears to provide an argument for the category AUX only because some of its clitics convey the notions of tense and modality required in ASW's definition, while none of these clitics exhibits the kind of behavior that would lead us to generate them in a place different from their surface position" (p.4).

The first point reveals some confusion over the issue. The Akmajian, Steele, and Wasow article was not, of course, an attempt to "explain" the behavior of the Luiseño particle sequence, rather, it was an attempt to show that, given a definition of the categorial label AUX, such that the label can be applied outside the limits and idiosyncrasies of one language, the Luiseño particle sequence can be identified as an instantiation of the definition. Kaisse's second point seems untenable. Apparently, such properties as forming a word or being a syntactically identifiable unit are arguments for constituency, <u>unless</u> such properties hold over a sequence of clitics. Furthermore, as Kaisse herself points out, "...Luiseño apparently provides no evidence for transformations, particularly transformational movement of clitics out of various underlying constituents" (p.5). Interestingly, she implies that this fact is a problem for Akmajian, Steele, and Wasow: "...ASW have not needed to confront the question of the level at which constituency is to be defined" (p.5). Actually, the problem is hers. If there is no evidence that the members of the particle sequence come from some other constituent(s)--and there is not--then there is no reason to consider some level where the evidence adduced in the Akmajian, Steele, and Wasow article does not hold.

The final point in the above summary, then, is at once a misrepresentation of the argument in Akmajian, Steele, and Wasow and a back-handed recognition that the sorts of arguments against constituency (which Kaisse might adduce in the other examples she presents) do not apply to the Luiseño particle sequence. Luiseño does not "appear to provide an argument for the category AUX"; the Luiseño particle sequence is an instantiation of a definition. And, if "none of the clitics exhibits the kind of behavior that would lead us to generate them in a place different from their surface position", then there is no compelling reason to do so.

Pullum objects to Akmajian, Steele, and Wasow's arguments for the constituency of the Luiseño particle sequence on different grounds. One part of his argument is based on certain presumptions about constituents and categories. He assumes, first, that all constituents, regardless of their label, have certain boundary properties. Therefore, because the particle sequence may form a phonological word with the word immediately preceding it, it cannot be preceded by a # boundary and, therefore, cannot be a constituent. We are quite willing to stipulate--in fact, we will propose in chapter 3--that a constituent which meets the definition will generally have certain possibilities of attachment to adjacent elements which are not common to all categories. Thus, whether the sequence of particles in Luiseño is preceded by a # boundary is orthogonal to the question of whether the particles form a constituent or not. Second, Pullum argues that, if the members of the particle sequence form a constituent, dominated by a single categorial label, it would "introduce an anomaly into the system of syntactic categories implicit in the $\bar{X}$ convention" (p.30), because it is a "peculiar sort of phrase" (p.27). The question of whether all categories conform to some strong version of the $\bar{X}$ convention seems to us an empirical one; thus, the invocation of this convention is not an argument against the constituency of the Luiseño particle sequence. In fact, we will propose in chapter 3 that the set of elements identified by the definition share with Luiseño the property that Pullum finds "peculiar".

The other part of Pullum's argument is an analysis of Luiseño which is meant to capture both the fact that the Luiseño particle sequence occurs in sentential second position and the fact that there are no constituent boundaries internal to it, without identifying the particle sequence as a constituent. That is, since these were the facts that Akmajian, Steele, and Wasow adduced in support of constituency, Pullum is attempting to show that they do not necessarily argue for constituency. A consideration of his proposals, however, reveals that they do not handle these facts, facts which are not in dispute.

Pullum assumes a base rule for S that generates sequences of particles S-initially, with each particle individually dominated by some categorial label. To ensure the correct positioning of the particles, he proposes an obligatory transformation which moves some [+Major] category to sentence-initial position.

(i) = Pullum's (26)
$[_S \; e - [_S \; \ldots - [+\text{Major}]^n - X]]$

$$\begin{array}{cccc} 1 & 2 & 3 & 4 \\ 3 & 2 & \emptyset & 4 \end{array} \Rightarrow$$

Finally, Pullum argues that the members of the particle sequence are successively Chomsky-adjoined to the initial [+Major] category.

(ii) = Pullum's (27)
$[+\text{Major}]^n \; - \; \text{Prt} \; - \; X$

$$\begin{array}{ccc} \mathbf{1} & 2 & 3 \\ 1\&2 & \emptyset & 3 \end{array} \Rightarrow$$

(where "1&2" means "2 is right-Chomsky-adjoined to 1")

This last rule is intended to capture the difference between the two sentences in (iii); in (iiia) the particle <u>up</u> is Chomsky-adjoined to N, and in (iiib), to NP.

(iii)
a. mariyap   heyiq
   mariya-p
   Mary-up   is:digging
   'Mary is digging.'

b. mariya up   heyiq
   Mary   up   is:digging
   'Mary is digging.'

(iv) and (v) represent the proposed structures, respectively.

(iv)
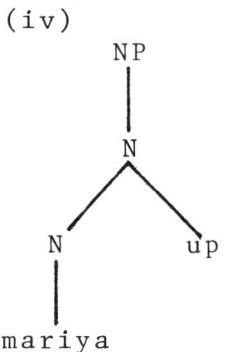

(v)
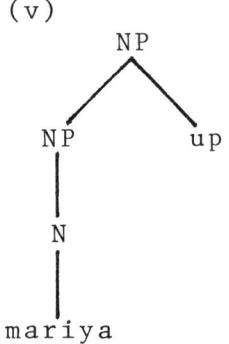

Pullum's analysis does not give the correct position of the particle sequence for all cases. (i) will not satisfactorily account for the fact that the element preceding the Luiseño particle sequence need not be [+Major]. For example, as was pointed out in Steele (1978), the negative qay can precede the particle sequence and be counted as the first element.

(vi)
qay   up   xwaan   yawaywish
negative   particle   John   handsome
'John isn't handsome.'

Thus, the position of the particle sequence is not given an adequate account. It also is not obvious that (ii) will give the correct results for the lack of boundaries separating the members of the particle sequence. Consider the examples in (via,b), sentences which differ from (iiia,b) most importantly in that there is more than one particle in second position.

(vi)
a. mariyapil   heyiquś
   mariya-p-il
   Mary-up-il   was:digging
   'Mary was digging.'

b. mariya   upil   heyiquś
   Mary   up-il   was:digging
   'Mary was digging.'

If Pullum is serious about the application of Chomsky-adjunction and if we assume that all particles are Chomsky-adjoined to the same category, the following structures appear to represent the critical parts of (via) and (vib) respectively.

(vii)
a.

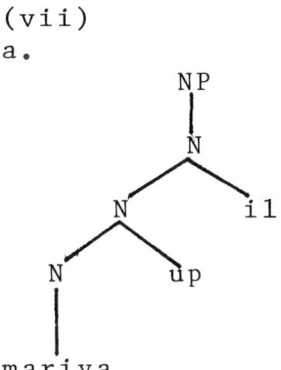

b.

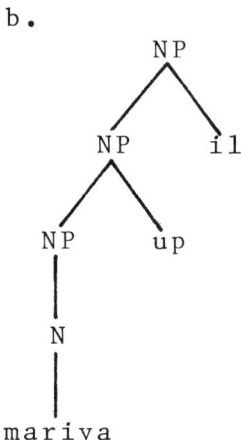

(viic) is reasonably innovative, but it creates no particular problems for (via). However, given Pullum's assumptions about the assignment of boundaries, as evidenced by his (17), each particle in (vib) will be followed by a # boundary, precisely the boundary that is supposed to predict the difference between (iiia) and (iiib) or (via) and (vib).

(viii)
$[_{NP}$ # $[_{NP}$ # $[_{NP}$ # mariya #] up #] il #]

It should be noted that Pullum's X^0 Readjustment will not apply to (viii), since it covers only "a lexical category with 0 bars, i.e. N, V, or A" (p.14). That is, Pullum's analysis predicts that there will be # boundaries internal to the particle sequence, precisely what the Akmajian, Steele, and Wasow analysis argued there are not--and which Pullum does not dispute.

Pullum, however, is inconsistent on the issue of Chomsky-adjunction. For example, in his (15) only the first particle is Chomsky-adjoined to a [+Major] category. These trees cannot be produced by (ii) (Pullum's (27)): they would, however, follow from the revision given in (x).

A Definition and Its Instantiations 125

(ix) = Pullum's (15)
a.

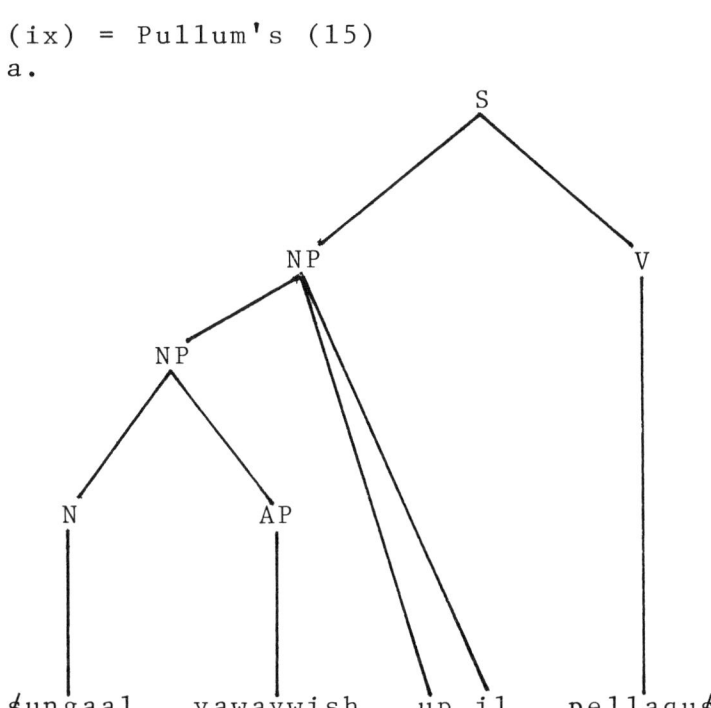

b.

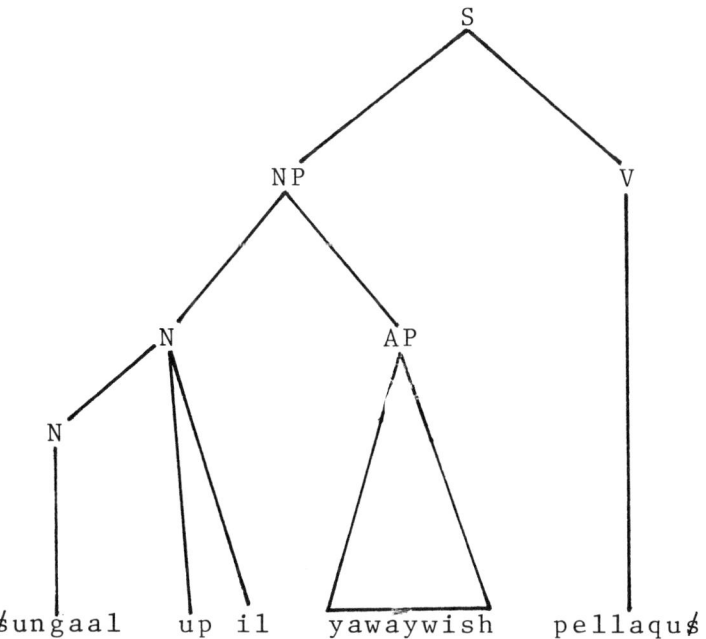

(x)

$[+\text{Major}]^n$ - Prt* - X

| 1 | 2 | 3 | $\Rightarrow$ |
| 1&2 | $\emptyset$ | 3 | |

However, there is no obvious empirical difference between treating the sequence of particles as Prt* and recognizing their constituency.
  In short, Pullum's analysis either fails to account for the properties of the Luiseño particle sequence or must be modified in a fashion that is tantamount to recognizing the constituency of the members of that sequence.

9. $u and xu--the particles which occur in position 1--are mutually exclusive. Il in position 3 is mutually exclusive with either po or kwa. However, po and kwa can cooccur, as the following example illustrates.

(i)
chaam	$ushpokwa	pomoomi	xechiwun
we	$u-cha-po-kwa	them	are/were:hitting
	prt:1-prt:2-PO-KWA		

'Maybe we hit them.'

Since po and kwa can each occur independently in the position immediately following particle 2, we will consider particle sequences having both as containing two particles in position 3.
  One other comment about (4) is in order. Kwa can occur as kwa, ku, or ko, depending, in part, on the quality of other vowels in the particle sequence.

10. An alternative to treating the particle sequences in (3a), (3b), and (3d) as lacking a particle in either position 1 or position 3 or both is to expand the inventory of both sets of particles given in (4) to include $\emptyset$. There are reasons to prefer the statement we have given, which we will discuss at the end of section 2.2.3.

11. Leaving aside quotative speech, two "sentence types" are subsumed in (3d). One, questions, will be discussed below; there would appear to be little problem for our claim that these are not assertions. The other can be roughly paraphrased by English sentences like X better (not) V. Whatever such sentences are in English, in Luiseño they seem not to be modal assertions. That is, the speaker is not ascribing some possibility to the situation which the sentence describes; rather, these constructions have the force of a recommendation, that is, a command which can be ignored with impunity. Formally, they are different from what seems more reasonably called the imperative in Luiseño, but semantically they have more in common with imperatives than with assertions.

12. With the label near nonfuture, we want to express that q/wun or an can indicate both present time and very near past time. That is, this suffix would be used to describe a situation which occurs at the time of speaking or precedes it by a matter of hours.

13. The configuration in (3a), the one lacking a particle in both the first and the third positions in the sequence, is not restricted to sentences containing some form with the suffix q/wun or an. However, the other sentences in which it may occur lack a form with any of the tense/aspect suffixes given in (6). Consider, for example, (ia,b):

(i)
a. noo   n   heyi-lut
   I   ∅-subj:mark-∅   dig-LUT
   'I'm gonna dig.'

b. noo   n   heyi-qat
   I   ∅-subj:mark-∅   dig-QAT
   'I was digging (in the near past).'

Although the Luiseño sentences are reasonably translated here--the first indicating some sort of near future and the second some sort of near past--there are many reasons not to include the suffixes lut and qat with those in (6). Most importantly, these suffixes can occur in subordinate constructions; those in (6) cannot.

14. Wh-questions will also contain a particle sequence of precisely this shape. However, in that wh-words are commonly sentence-initial, although they are not obligatorily so, there is a possible difference between a wh-question and its corresponding statement.

(i)
a. wunaalum ǵu-m   'axiyi   'ariwun
   they   ǵu-subj:mark-∅   who:obj   are:kicking
   'Who are they kicking?'

b. 'axiyi   ǵu-m   wunaalum 'ariwun
   who:obj   ǵu-subj:mark-∅   they   are:kicking
   'Who are they kicking?'

15. It is impossible to have a sequence of two ǵu's as well. However, if we consider sentences like (11) through (13), modal assertions with ǵu, we see that we cannot appeal to this fact as support for the single ǵu position. A modal assertion with ǵu indicates speaker supposition; it may very well be impossible for speakers to question their own suppositions (cf. the strangeness of Do I see that Mary is gonna make a basket?), at least if the speaker is not an actor asking for directions.

16. Either of these two proposals would be difficult to countenance given an analysis of the particle sequence in which its members are independent elements in the sentence, since no other sentence part plays any role in determining their meaning. And, to that extent, even if we attempted to give some one meaning to any of the particles under consideration, we would, in effect, have to recognize the constituency of the particle sequence.
   However, we need not give each of the particles a single meaning to provide that argument, and if we briefly consider the consequences of either of the

suggestions allowed by this proposal, its lack of
appeal is obvious. The first would require us to
decide at the very least that (for example) the
notion "future" is somehow more or less basic than
"unverified" for the particle po, outside
of some context. But that is precisely what cannot
be decided, since the presence or absence of some
other particle conditions its interpretation. The
second suggestion is unsatisfactory on different
grounds. We could give il and po the abstract
glosses 'realized' and 'unrealized', respectively;
these would be modified to 'past' and 'future',
respectively, in the absence of ɣu or to 'verified'
and 'unverified' in the presence of ɣu. (In fact,
Jacobs (1975) suggests precisely these abstract
glosses.) However, applying the same procedure to ɣu
is not nearly so intuitively appealing. The obvious
problem is to find a meaning that subsumes both
'question' and 'supposition', assuming, of course,
that it is reasonable to gloss ɣu as 'question' in
the context where it is unaccompanied by some
particles in the third position.

17. The list (23) assumes an adequate account of
the phonological interaction of the forms given
there and the particles with which they can be
surrounded. First, the first person plural form
always has the phonetic shape sh when it is preceded
by some particle in the particle sequence--a fact
which was noted in Akmajian, Steele, Wasow (1979)
and treated as the result of two independently
needed rules, vowel apocope and ch ---> sh. Second,
any subject marker consisting of a single consonant
will appear as a syllable (that is, a vowel will be
inserted), when the subject marker is initial to the
particle sequence and followed by a particle
beginning with a [-syllabic] segment--with one
exception to be noted below--or when it is final to
the particle sequence and preceded by one particle
ending with a [-syllabic] segment. That is, for
example, n + po is nupo, m + kwa is mokwa (or moko),
and kun + n is kunun. Finally, there are a number of
idiosyncrasies, i.e. combinations which always have

a certain form but which are not the product of more general processes. For example, in (23b), the first person plural form is given as cha with an optional m. However, m is not strictly optional. The alternation here depends in large part on the following particle. Basically, cham precedes a particle beginning with a [+syllabic] segment and cha precedes a particle starting with a [-syllabic] segment; therefore, we find cham-il and cha-po, respectively. It is not possible, however, to treat this alternation as the result of some rule which deletes m, or at least not as the result of some general rule which has that effect, since the sequence xu + m + po is xumpo and the sequence m + po is mo.

18. The sets of subject markers do not include the particle up, a particle which in other publications (including those of Steele, one of the authors of this monograph) has been analyzed as a member of the set of elements labeled subject marking. We will return to a consideration of this particle, and the reasons for excluding it from (23), in section 2.2.3.

19. In footnote 17, we mentioned that a subject marker consisting of a single consonant will appear as a syllable, when it is initial to the particle sequence and followed by another particle. At least the first person singular subject marker n has the possibility of occurring as a syllable if it is unaccompanied by some particle and follows a word which ends in a [-syllabic] segment. The following sentence is illustrative.

(i)
poy   nu   maamayuq
him   1ST:SG   is:helping
'I'm helping him.'

(In (i) the vowel follows n, but there are instances where it precedes; however, the conditions governing the position of the vowel are unclear at present.) We assume that, were (28) possible, it would obey some similar syllabification process, and we therefore give the form as <u>um</u>.

20. The argument for the fourth set of (phonologically unrealized) subject marking follows from the analysis of Luiseño presented in Steele (1981). The discussion is too long and involved to reproduce here; however, its essentials can be summarized. Luiseño "stems" are lexically specified for a particular argument configuration; one argument, however, is excluded--the argument termed, for convenience, the "subject". That is, a "subject" is syntactically, not lexically, specified. There are four different ways in which this syntactic specification is given, but one refers critically to the particle sequence <u>and</u> the presence within it of subject marking. The instances of the particle sequence with what we have termed Set 4 subject marking behave precisely like cases exhibiting any of the other three sets; that is, they behave as if they contained subject marking. On this evidence, we introduce Set 4 subject marking.

21. There is one exception to the schemas in (35c). Between the clitic ¢u and the clitic <u>il</u>, the first person plural marking is impossible. In (ia) below, we find the singular form of the Set 3 subject markers (∅), and in (ib) we find the first person singular form of the Set 2 subject markers (<u>n</u>); however, (id), where we might expect to find the first person plural form of the Set 2 subject markers (<u>cham</u>), is impossible.

(i)
a. noo   ¢il   heelaqu¢
    I   ¢u-∅-il   was:singing
    'Maybe I was singing.'

b. noo   ¢u-n-il   heelaqu¢
    I   ¢u-1st:sg-il was:singing
    'Maybe I was singing.'

c. chaam ¢u-m-il   heelaqu¢
    we   ¢u-pl-il   were:singing

'Maybe we were singing.'

d. *chaam   ŝu-cham-il   heelaquŝ
   we   ŝu-1st:pl-il   were:singing

22. By <u>complement</u>, we mean subordinate constructions which are arguments to some head; by <u>adjunct</u>, we mean subordinate constructions which are not to be construed with some head. In Luiseño, adjuncts are essentially external to the main clause. The term <u>relative clause</u> is used in a traditional, if relatively undefinable, fashion. These may not exhaust Luiseño subordinate constructions, but an attempt to cover the few remaining types would not change the claims about subordination in general and would require a detailed discussion of subordination in its own right. That is, the definitions of the terms above do not obviously cover the Luiseño equivalents of these English sentences:

(i)
a. He went next door to see John.
b. It is raining too hard to go outside.

However, morphologically at least, the former is to be classed with relative clauses and the latter with complements.

23. There are three other particles which, it might be argued, should appear on this list as well: <u>tee</u>, <u>wuŝkapi</u>, and <u>ta'</u>. However, there are clear idiosyncrasies in each case.
   <u>Tee</u> may occur in sentence-initial position and is, thus, generally followed directly by the particles upon which we have focused our attention.

(i)
tee   nupo   'oy   tiiwin
TEE   prt:com   you:obj   will:see
'Maybe I will see you.'

As (i) suggests, <u>tee</u> is the rough semantic equivalent of English <u>maybe</u>; however, with this gloss, we do not mean to identify tee as some sort of adverb, however that category is to be defined. In some cases, like (i), there is no good argument for or against analyzing tee either as a member of the particle sequence or as falling outside of it. In other cases, like (ii), there is a good argument against analyzing tee as a member.

(ii)
tee   upkwa   tiiwi   xwaani....
TEE   up-kwa   see   John:obj
'If you see John....'

Akmajian, Steele, and Wasow (1979) argue that certain demonstrably word-internal processes occur across the boundaries separating the particles; one of those is vowel elision when two vowels are contiguous, so that ɸu + il appears as ɸil. However, in (ii), neither the initial vowel of the particle u nor the final vowel of tee is elided. There is one case that provides evidence for including tee in the particle sequence. When tee is sentence-initial, immediately preceding a sequence of second-position particles which begins with ɸu, tee can form a phonological unit with the sequence. (iii) is a clear example.

(iii)
tespokwa   xwaan   mariyi   xechik
tee-ɸu-po-kwa   John   Mary:obj   used/to:hit
'Maybe John hit Mary.'

The vowel of tee is short, the vowel of ɸu has been elided, and the quality of the initial segment in ɸu is s. It is true that certain phonological processes regularly occur at the boundary between the set of clitics and the word which immediately precedes it, but there are two peculiarities about this particular example. First, we know of no cases other than the one exemplified above where the presence of (some one of) the set of particles affects the final vowel of the immediately preceding word. Second, we know of no other cases where a vowel internal to a string of particles can be

elided, because some word precedes the string.
Hence, it appears that tee, at least in the
environment specified for (iii), may be analyzed as
part of the particle sequence.

Apparently, then, tee can be either inside or
outside the particle sequence; other particles do
not have that option. Furthermore, if tee is inside
the particle sequence in (iii), then the particle
sequence can occur initially.

Examples of the other two particles mentioned
above, wuʃkapi and ta', are given in (iv) and (v),
respectively.

(iv)
wuʃkapi xwaan   popeewi   xexechiq
WUʃKAPI John   his:spouse:obj   repeatedly:hits
'I wonder if John hits his wife.'

(v)
xwaan   up   kopokpamal   noo   ta'   tavulvish
John   prt:com   short   I   TA'   tall
'John is short; I, on the other hand, am tall.'

As the gloss of (iv) suggests, wuʃkapi means
something like 'I wonder'; ta' marks the fact that
the information contained in some clause is to be
contrasted with some other information. That is,
wuʃkapi might not unreasonably be classed
semantically with the elements otherwise shown to be
in the particle sequence, but ta' would extend the
possibilities. On the other hand, ta' occurs in
sentential second position, as (v) suggests, like
the standard particle sequence; wuʃkapi, as (iv)
indicates, occurs sentence-initially. Both wuʃkapi
and ta' are mutually exclusive with all the members
of the particle sequence. We leave the analysis of
these particles as unresolved problems.

24. Both (41) and (42) are to be analyzed as
containing two independent main clauses, although
the English gloss of, at least, (42) might suggest a
different analysis. Noo n takwayaq 'I'm sick' and
noo kunun takwayaq 'I'm sick, I'm told' have all the
characteristics of main, not subordinate, clauses.

A Definition and Its Instantiations

Admittedly, this analysis, which is supported by any generalization which we can make about main clauses, renders the analysis of the first clause mariya pil yaa 'Mary said' somewhat problematic.

25. (50a) is possible in any sentence in quotative speech. That is, although the particle a' can cooccur only with some element inflected for the distant nonfuture, it is not obligatory in such environments. Thus, for example, (i) is an alternate form for (45).

(i)
wunaalum   kun   'oy   'ayali-k
they   kun-Set:4   you:obj   know-UK
'They used to know, I'm told.'

26. It should be noted in regard to ǥu and kun that the linear string ǥu-kun does not represent their internal semantic relationship. For example, we might want to treat ǥu as falling within the scope of kun in (54), but kun as within the scope of ǥu on the (a) reading of (55). Furthermore, if the linear string directly reflected the semantics, we might expect a sequence of ǥu's in the (b) reading of (55).

27. Sentences of possession are not the only sentential constructions which require a possessive marked form. Another marks certain types of aspect or modality.

(1)
a. noo   p   no-ngeepi   miyq
    I   UP   POSSESSIVE-leave:future   is
    'I have to leave.'

b. noo   p   no-ngeevo   miyq
    I   UP   POSSESSIVE-leave:past   is
    'I have left (already).'

c. noo   p   no-ngee   miyq
    I   UP   POSSESSIVE-leave   is
    'I have left (many times).'

A third might be characterized as "emotive".

(ii)
noo   p   'oy   no-ma'max
I   UP   you:obj   POSSESSIVE-like
'I like you.'

A fourth indicates some sort of capacity of the subject.

(iii)
noo   p   no-tooyax
I   UP   POSSESSIVE-laugh
'I'm good at laughing.'

See Steele (1981) for discussion of an analysis of Luiseño which includes such sentences.

28. Up is possible, in sentences such as those in (59) and footnote 27, but some of these allow subject marking as well.

29. Lummi is a member of the Salish family of languages and is now spoken natively by only a handful of people. The Lummi Reservation is located in the northwest corner of Washington State. The language data were provided by Mr. Al Charles, a speaker of Lummi who has patiently contributed his time and his intelligence to the study of his language. The Lummi examples are written in the orthography adopted by the Lummi people. With minor exceptions, the symbols are drawn from the IPA. We therefore mention only two orthographic conventions. First, ł represents a voiceless lateral fricative. Second, a consonant with an apostrophe above it, e.g. č, is glottalized. (Glottal stops are, however, represented by the standard symbol ʔ.)

30. The -s third person marker does not pattern in all cases with the other subject marking enclitics. For the purposes of this discussion, however, it can be considered one.

31. Although there are several different language families in the Northwest, they share structural features. Thus, one can speak of the grammatical properties of Northwest languages in general, referring to languages in nonrelated families. For an excellent assessment of the controversy over categories in Northwest languages, see Jacobsen (1976).

32. The particle kʷ also functions as a definite particle indicating remoteness. Thus, kʷ swəy?qə? refers to a man (not present) and may even be used metaphorically to indicate that he is deceased. The s-prefix is the most common nominalizer in Lummi. Thus, whereas ?iłən is 'to eat', s-?iłən is 'food'.

33. In (71b) the connective particle ?u? is absent. This particle interacts with λ'el in a fashion not totally understood at present; minimally, however, we can state that, in a sentence with λ'el, the connective particle is present only when λ'el is initial.

34. The sentences in which the subject marker is attached to λ'el imply that the subject has a greater degree of responsibility or control over the situation than is the case when the subject marker is attached to the verb.

35. In dependent clauses, possessive pronouns will appear on the sentence-initial element, regardless of its basic category. In (70), for example, the first person possessive prefix nə is found on a (nominalized) verb.

36. Certain aspect markers may appear in sentence-initial position, but nevertheless do not have enclitics attached. The category C in (73) must thus be specified as a major lexical category.

37. See Selkirk (1978) for an excellent study of the relationship between syntactic structures and prosodic phrasing.

38. The transliteration of Egyptian Arabic sentences uses standard symbols. We therefore mention only three which might be unfamiliar. 9 indicates a voiced pharyngeal fricative; H, a voiceless pharyngeal fricative. The subscript , indicates a pharyngealized consonant.

The data upon which this section is based were provided by Professor Adel S. Gamal, who teaches Classical Arabic language and literature at the University of Arizona, and his wife Suad. Thanks are due to them for their patient and constructive answers to questions on their language. We also thank Trandil El Rakhawy and Nagwa Younes for their comments.

39. Arabic verbs are traditionally referred to by the third person masculine singular of the perfect paradigm. The verb kaan is rarely inflected in the bi-imperfect; when such inflections occur, they seem to be in free variation with the Ha-imperfect.

40. Kaan marking past tense is used as irrealis in Egyptian Arabic in conditional sentences and in modal constructions that express a failed obligation. In such constructions, kaan appears with the imperative inflection of some other verb, but these sentences are not imperatives. For example:

(i)
kunt   ruuH   šuufu
PAST   go:imperative   see:imperative:him
'You should have gone to see him.'

(See Steele (1975) for a discussion of past tense and irrealis.)

41. These predicates, like all other predicates in finite sentences in Egyptian Arabic, are preceded by kaan:

(i)
kaanit   biddaha   tifaaHa
she:was   wish:her   apple

'She wanted an apple.'

(ii)
kunt   9andi   tifaaHa
I:was   with:me   apple
'I had an apple.'

These constructions thus differ from sentences having an initial NP subject followed by <u>kaan</u>:

(iii)
giddaha   kaan   Hakiim
her:grandfather   was   doctor
'Her grandfather was a doctor.

42. (126a) is given as a variant of (126b) rather than the reverse, because there are sentences in Egyptian Arabic which do not allow a subject. Specifically, in existential sentences in Egyptian Arabic, no subject may precede the predicate of the sentence. (See example (92).) Thus, existential sentences are sui generis in Egyptian Arabic, as is often the case across languages.

43. The Japanese examples are romanized in the National orthographic system, a system which is reasonably phonemic.

44. The glosses we have given for the affixes are only rudimentary. See Martin (1975) for a much more detailed discussion.

45. Notice that in tree (139) we have included the topic phrase, <u>NP wa</u>, as a constituent of S^1 which binds the <u>PRO</u> subject of S. This is not specifically provided for in the PS rules in (136), but represents our hypothesis that topic phrases, like tense affixes, are in a level higher than S. The evidence for this is too detailed to present here.

46. Tree (145) illustrates an adverb, <u>no ni</u>, which is subcategorized to occur with an S^1; that is, it has the feature $[S^1 \_\_\_\_]$. This provides an interesting contrast with <u>nagara</u>, which takes only S.

47. Given the closeness of meaning between <u>keredo</u> and <u>no ni</u> and between <u>kara</u> and <u>no de</u>, it is difficult to see how their differential behavior with respect to complement type could be explained on the basis of semantic facts. Indeed, the closeness of meaning provides further support for the structural explanation we are proposing here.

Chapter 3

EQUIVALENCE

3.1 Introduction

In chapter 2, we presented a definition and considered analyses of aspects of four languages which instantiate it. Thus, the definition which we proposed there is a "good" one--it is (widely) instantiated--and we have fulfilled the first requirement of a theory of cross-linguistic equivalence: we have identified a set of elements which are similar in that they share certain criterial properties. Now we must consider whether or not this identification is linguistically interesting.

The critical issue is whether or not it is possible to specify properties--other than those given in the definition--of the set of elements it identifies. There is, of course, no logical necessity that any properties other than the definitional ones be found to hold across the individuals which comprise the set. However, the elements which are identified under the definition will be taken to form an equivalence class only if we can establish, for the set, such nondefinitional properties.

The issue is, necessarily, an empirical one. The nondefinitional properties which we will propose are empirical generalizations based on the analyses of Luiseño, Lummi, Egyptian Arabic, and Japanese presented in chapter 2, the analyses of the languages discussed in appendices A and B, as well as (less complete) analyses of a large number of other languages (cf. Steele (1978a) and (1978b)). Therefore, while we do not, and could not, deny the possibility of some revision in the statements concerning the properties of the set, we fully expect that they will hold for any expansion of the sample.

In this chapter, then, we are simultaneously establishing cross-linguistic equivalence and giving the properties (other than those specified in the definition) of the label which identifies the equivalence, the category which we have called AUX.

Now that we have adequately characterized the category, it is reasonable to attempt an explanation of the set of properties associated with it, a set of properties possibly intuitively quite unrelated. The categorial equivalence will not be invalidated if we cannot satisfactorily accomplish the task, but its interest will be substantially strengthened if we can. Thus, in the final section of this chapter, we are concerned with such second order questions.

3.2 Nondefinitional Properties

We will consider four properties of the members of the set identified by the definition: their positions, their compositions, their internal orders, and their relationships to adjacent elements. In each case, clear generalizations about the set are possible. Briefly, the members of the set (a) occur in one of only three positions; (b) contain elements marking a certain limited number of notional types; (c) have a fixed internal order which is (d) not predictable from any other property of the language; and (e) generally are attached--or can be attached--to some adjacent element. There are important distinctions to be drawn among these generalizations, and the organization of this section is based on these distinctions. The fifth property given above holds probabilistically across the set; that is, it is generally true of the aggregate but may not hold for any individual member. The other four generalizations are not probabilistic. The first and second, those concerning positions and composition, specify a limited number of possibilities within which any member of the set will fall. While no member of the set need exhibit the entire range of possibilities, the position and composition of any given member are necessarily included in the specification for the set. Finally, the third and fourth generalizations, those involving internal order, hold absolutely across the set. Every member of the set will exhibit both properties.

3.2.1 <u>Attachment: A Probability</u> We begin with the characteristic that differs from the other four in that it holds probabilistically across the set: if some element is identified by the definition (i.e. if some element is a member of the set AUX), there is a reasonable likelihood that it will be bound to some adjacent element.[1]

Of the four languages discussed in chapter 2 two--Japanese and Lummi--have an instantiation of AUX which is necessarily bound to the word which precedes it. The Lummi instantiation of AUX is enclitic to the word that precedes it, regardless of its category; the Japanese instantiation of AUX is an affix to the word that precedes it, and that word is commonly, although perhaps not necessarily, what we can term, internal to Japanese, a member of the category Verb.[2]

The other two languages discussed in chapter 2--Luiseño and Egyptian Arabic--exhibit some attachment possibilities as well. Although not every member of the element which instantiates Aux in either case may attach to some adjacent element, some may. Consider, for example, the following alternations in Luiseño.

(1)
a. mariya   up   tooyaq
   Mary   prt:com   is:laughing
   'Mary is laughing.'

b. mariyap   tooyaq
   mariya-up
   Mary-prt:com   is:laughing
   'Mary is laughing.'

In (1b) <u>mariya</u> and <u>up</u> form a phonological word, as indicated by the deletion of the initial vowel of <u>up</u>. Luiseño has a regular process of vowel deletion when two vowels come together across a morpheme boundary, that is, word-internally. Not all forms of the Particle Complex exhibit the alternation shown in (1); the point is simply that it is possible for some of its members to be attached to the word which precedes them. In Egyptian Arabic, the negative may attach to the following predicate, under conditions specified in chapter 2--essentially when it is the only member of the Constituent and is followed by a particular predicate type. Other forms of the Egyptian Arabic Constituent do not obviously attach.

We leave open the question of precisely how such attachment possibilities are best handled language-internally. The critical consideration is that each language discussed in the preceding chapter exhibits, relative to the element under consideration, either obligatory attachment or attachment possibilities. Obviously, given Luiseño and Egyptian Arabic, we cannot claim that the set which is AUX will necessarily be attached, but it is clear that this is a property that its members commonly exhibit.

The property of attachment may very well follow from some other property of the set. That is, it appears that the members of AUX will commonly be either necessarily stressless or able to occur without stress. The former is true of all instantiations of the Lummi Enclitic Sequence and the Japanese Affix; some of the forms of the Particle Complex in Luiseño are incapable of taking stress--none can take primary stress--and others can occur without stress. Even if the possibility of attachment follows from stresslessness and the statement about the set AUX should refer instead to the latter, we cannot claim that stresslessness or the possibility of lacking stress is an absolute property of AUX; it is generally true of the members of the set, but not necessarily true of all members.

The definition under which the elements are identified as members of the set AUX specifies nothing about their relationship to adjacent elements; thus, there is no reason to expect that some generalization about the set can be made in this regard. Therefore, the fact that we can give the above generalization about attachment is the first indication that the identification is linguistically interesting. We turn now to other, nonprobabilistic, generalizations.

3.2.2 Limits and Possibilities While the definition in chapter 2 specified elements expressing the notional categories of tense and/or modality, it otherwise left open the composition of the constituent which contains them; furthermore, it did not specify the constituent's position in a sentence. Logically, then, it is possible that the set of elements identified as AUX could contain, in addition to tense and modality, elements marking a random collection of other notional categories or that it could occur in any number of positions. Neither logical possibility is realized, however; each has clear limits. In fact, we can precisely specify the positional and compositional possibilities for any instantiation of AUX.

Elements expressing the notional categories of tense and modality are criterial to the identification under the definition. But it is obvious from the instantiations for the definition discussed in chapter 2 that elements expressing other notional categories can be included. The Luiseño Particle Complex, the Lummi Enclitic Sequence, and the Egyptian Arabic Constituent all contain subject marking.[3] The Luiseño Particle Complex and the Lummi Enclitic Sequence indicate question marking, the former by a certain particle configuration and the latter by the presence of a particular particle. The Luiseño Particle Complex indicates what we called in chapter 2 "quotative speech". The Egyptian Arabic Constituent contains negation.

As at least the first two facts on this list suggest, there is some similarity among the elements identified by the definition, in terms of notional categories, a similarity which the definition itself does not require. That is, three of our four example languages exhibit subject marking as part of the element which is identified by the definition, and two of the four exhibit question marking. In fact, an examination of a larger sample suggests that these two notional categories are commonly an integral part of the members of AUX; furthermore, neither the Luiseño Particle Complex nor the Egyptian Arabic Constituent is unique in containing what we might call <u>evidential markers</u> and <u>negation</u>, respectively.

These similarities suggest that some generalization can be made across the set regarding composition. An examination of the set of elements identified under the definition reveals a limited and specifiable set of notional categories which may be marked there, in addition, of course, to tense and modality. These include elements indicating: subject marking, subject agreement, aspect, question marking, emphasis, evidential, object marking, object agreement, and negation. That is, any element identified by the definition may include items marking some subset of these notional categories, but it is limited to these. Thus, the list above, with the addition of tense and modality, specifies the possible notions that can be expressed by any element which is part of the set AUX; furthermore the list exhaustively characterizes the composition of the set.[4]

The empirical generalization about composition is not meant to apply simply to the analyses of the elements included in the set, but also to its surface manifestation(s), assuming that we allow items to be moved into (or out of) the element under consideration. Thus, for example, common treatments of the English Aux, which instantiates the definition, do not generate the negative in Aux, although it can occur there.[5]

Just as we can specify the compositional possibilities for the set AUX, so also there are a specifiable and limited number of positions in which the members of the set may be found. They occur in one of only three positions in the sentence: first, second, or final. Egyptian Arabic exemplifies the first and second possibilities; Luiseño and Lummi the second; and Japanese the last.

The element under consideration in each of these languages is analyzed relative to a sentence. If such an analysis can be presented for any instantiation of the definition, logically the set of elements identified thereby could occur in any position in a sentence. Furthermore, if it were possible to analyze some instantiations of the

definition as depending for their position on some
other element in the sentence--say, as specifier to
Verb--there is no logical reason to expect the three
positions we have recognized, and only these. Thus,
the restriction to these three positions is
significant.

A point similar to one made in the immediately
preceding discussion of the possible composition of
the elements identified by the definition is in
order. The restriction to first, second, and final
positions is meant to hold for the position for this
element in any sentence, not simply for some
abstract level from which strings of any variety can
be derived. However, to maintain this view, we will
have to admit the possibility that certain elements
are transparent to the determination of these
positions. For example, in Luiseño, a topicalized element occurs initially, but is not
immediately followed by the Particle Complex. (We
should note concerning topicalization in Luiseño
that the topicalized element, xwaani in (2), is
necessarily followed by an intonation break.)

(2)
xwaani   noo nil   chaqalaqiquś
John:obj I   prt:com   was:tickling
'John, I was tickling.'

Similarly, if the two-constituent analysis of
Japanese is correct, the imperative and "speaker
attitude" markers occur in absolute sentence-final
position, following the instantiation(s) of AUX.[6]

(3)
Ken   wa   Naomi-ni   hugu-o
Ken   topic Naomi-dat   hugu:fish-acc

tabesasehazime-ta-daroo-ka-ne.
eat:cause:begin-AFFIX^1-AFFIX^2-OR-RIGHT

'I wonder if Ken has begun to make Naomi eat
 fugufish.'

It would be relatively easy to remove these apparent counterexamples by arguing that the offending elements are outside the sentence of which the Particle Complex or the Affix, respectively, is a part. For example, (2) could be analyzed as follows:

(4)
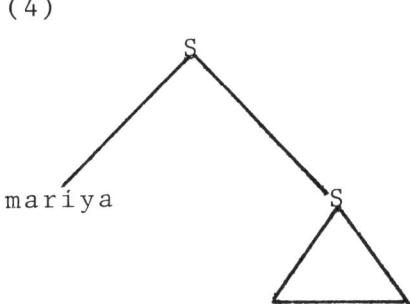

The analysis of Japanese presented in chapter 2 is consistent with such a proposal. However, this solution does not obviously accord with the claim that the restriction to first, second, and final positions applies to the surface string. A second solution--a more consistent one--recognizes a particular characteristic of the elements which can disturb the positional properties of the constituents identified by the definition and plays on it. Such elements can be recognized as having sentential scope; thus, they are essentially limited to topicalized elements, sentential adverbs, conjunctive elements, or elements such as the imperative and the "speaker attitude" affixes in Japanese. We propose that such elements do not count for--are transparent to--the determination of first, second, and final positions.[7] We will return in footnote 11 to a brief justification of this proposal.

We have presented, then, two empirically-based generalizations about the instantiations for the definition: they will contain elements expressing a limited number of notional types, and they will occur in one of three positions. It follows from this discussion that the instantiations can differ dramatically from language to language, but within definite parameters. That is, based on empirical evidence, we have established certain limits to AUX, limits which are not given in advance by the definition which identifies its membership.

3.2.3 The Absolute Properties

We have discussed a probabilistic property of the set AUX. We have also noted that certain limits can be placed on the possible instantiations of AUX regarding composition and position and that, therefore, certain possibilities can be associated with the set which is AUX, some number of which will be exhibited by each member of the set. We will now consider the internal order of the members of the set AUX. There are two generalizations which can be made about the members of the set in this regard; both hold absolutely across the set, although with somewhat different results.

First, every instantiation of AUX has a fixed internal order. That is, if the units of analysis occur in a particular order in one language-particular case of an instantiation of AUX, they will occur in the same order in all cases (in which the units cooccur). Thus, for example, in the nonquotative Particle Complex of Luiseño, we can distinguish particle 1, particle 2, and particle 3 positions, and we find that the members of these various sets always occur, relative to the members of the other sets, in the same position. A similar statement could be made for any of the analyses presented in chapter 2.[8] Thus, every member of the set of elements identified by the definition exhibits the property of having a fixed internal order, and the set AUX will have this nondefinitional property associated with it.

This generalization about relative order eliminates certain logically possible types of AUX, but it makes no systematic statement about the relative order of the various notional types within the constituent. That is, assuming that we can identify some piece of an instantiation of AUX in language L_1 and some piece of an instantiation of AUX in language L_2 as both marking modality (or any of the other notional types listed in section

3.2.2), the question is whether or not this piece will occur in some particular order relative to the other notional types found in the instantiation of AUX in either. The answer is no. While the internal order of AUX is fixed, the relative order of elements does not follow from any known principle(s). This is the second generalization about internal order in AUX. It has the interesting consequence that the order exhibited by any language-particular instantiation of AUX is a language particular idiosyncrasy; insofar as we can similarly identify the various pieces of the members of the set, as a set their internal arrangement is essentially random.

Numerous arguments have been made that the linear order of elements in a word or a clause reveals something about their semantic relationships. As it pertains to the internal arrangement of the set of elements under consideration here, this hypothesis would suggest that the internal order of subparts (or notional categories) reflects their relative scope. It is easy to show that such a hypothesis is false.

If the internal arrangement of the elements identified by the definition reflected the relative scope of their component parts, it would follow that the items with the most limited scope would be at one end and those with the widest at the other. From this, we could entertain one of a number of expectations about the cross-linguistic patterns of relative order. We could expect that the (pieces which express the) various notional categories might occur in a certain necessary order. For example, they might be ordered from left to right or from right to left; elements expressing modality might always occur either to the left or the right of those expressing tense, but one order or the other would be precluded out of hand. A comparison of Lummi and Japanese shows this expectation to be false; the relative order of tense and modality in Lummi is precisely the reverse of the order in Japanese. With this hypothesis falsified, we might consider a second, weaker, position: whether the order of pieces is from left to right or right to left follows from and is correlated with some other fact about a language (for example, the basic order of elements). A comparison of Lummi and Luiseño argues against this expectation. Lummi might reasonably be characterized as a verb-initial language; Luiseño, clearly, cannot be. Nevertheless, in both, the elements that express modality--in Luiseño the particles that impart the particular modal force to a modal assertion--precede elements marking subject and tense.

We could continue in this vein, weakening our expectations--and our predictions--about relative order. However, it would be pointless to do so. First, certain elements of the various instantiations have no obvious scope relations with respect to the others with which they occur. Subject and object marking are clear examples. Second, and more important, the discussion of Luiseño in chapter 2 provides a clear counterexample to the hypothesis. In the discussion of the Luiseño particle sequence in quotative speech, we considered the order of the particles ṣu and kun. Like all the members of the Particle Complex, these two particles occur in a fixed order relative to the others; however, they can have different scope relationships. The sequence ṣu-kun can indicate that the speaker is asking about some report, an interpretation which could be argued to mirror the linear order, or that the speaker is reporting a question, an interpretation which would require precisely the reverse linear order, if linear order reflected their semantic relationship.

In sum, the various ordering relationships within the set of elements identified by the definition cannot be argued to follow from some general semantic principle, such as relative scope.[9]

A second hypothesis about the order of elements within a constituent is to be found in the X-Bar Convention and in certain expansions of that convention. Specifically, for instance, Jackendoff (1977a) applies the hypothesis directly to the English Aux, one instantiation of the definition given in chapter 2. The X-Bar Convention claims that phrasal categories within any one language have parallel structures. As Jackendoff (p. 250) puts it,

"... each lexical category X defines a set of syntactic categories X', X'', ... X^p, the supercategories of X, related by phrase structure rules of the form (1): [Jackendoff's numbering; footnote omitted]

(1) $x^n \longrightarrow \ldots x^{n-1} \ldots$

(1) is a phrase structure rule schema provided by universal grammar. It results in phrase structure configurations of the form (2).

(2)

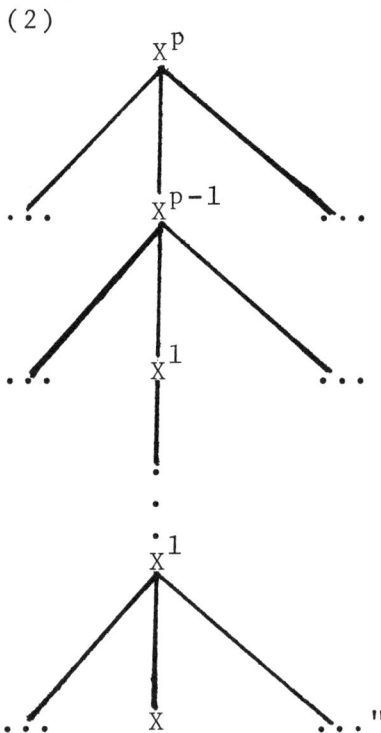

The value of n in Jackendoff's (1) differs depending on the particular formulation of the X-Bar Convention. For example, Jackendoff adopts what he calls the Uniform Three-Level Hypothesis, which states that no phrase structure rule for X contains a level of fewer than three, except for V''. Following from the hypothesis of phrase structure rules like Jackendoff's (1) is the assumption that each nonlexical category has a head--and specifiers to that head.

Jackendoff specifically states the application of these hypotheses about categories to the English Aux. He analyzes Modal as the head, with Tense as a specifier at the double bar level, and claims that an Aux is a three-level structure labeled M(odal)'''.

(5)
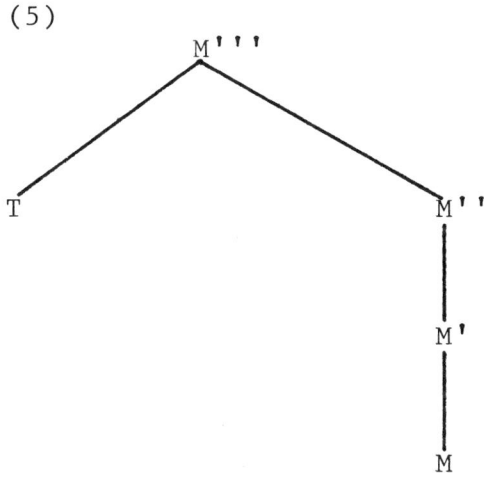

Whether the X-Bar Convention is in general a reasonable theory of categorial structure or not is beside the point here. However, with respect to the set of elements which are the various instantiations of AUX, it appears obviously incorrect. Jackendoff's analysis of the English Aux follows simply from the formalism he adopts. If N''' is the phrasal category which minimally contains the lexical category N, the lack of parallel with the analysis in (5) is striking: M(odal) is not obviously obligatory to all cases of M'''. Furthermore, it is impossible to extend an analysis such as the one in (5) to the other elements subsumed under the definition: assuming that we can apply the term outside of English and assuming that it involves those elements which mark modality, M(odal) is not even present in all members of the set AUX (cf. Egyptian Arabic). More importantly, there is no single lexical category which is obviously pivotal to all instantiations of AUX.[10] This claim is implicit in the definition which established the set. The definition requires that elements marking <u>either</u> tense or modality or both be present, but neither alone is obligatory. While all the analyses discussed in chapter 2 contain elements marking tense, there are instantiations of AUX which display modality alone. Classical Nahuatl is an example (cf. Steele (1978a)).

Finally, there is no reason to assume that because (other) phrasal categories are headed structures, instantiations of AUX must be as well. None of the analyses presented in chapter 2 offers evidence for proposing a headed structure. Although there is a dependency among the elements found in any particular instance of the Particle Complex in Luiseño, for example, this dependency is not unidirectional in the sense that some one element might be considered a head and the others its specifiers or complements.

In short, we can generalize across the set with the statement that insofar as various notional categories can be identified across languages, the order of elements expressing them does not follow from any other obvious, known linguistic principles. The characteristic of fixed internal order is an absolute property of the set AUX; thus, all its various instantiations will exhibit it. Similarly, this generalization about the relative order of elements is an absolute property of the set; any principle which might be proposed to account for the relative order of elements within an instantiation of AUX does not extend beyond the language at issue and thus is simply language-particular.

Our discussion of composition and position suggested certain empirically-based limits on the instantiations of <u>Aux</u>, while the last generalization states that there are no limits on internal order. However, the fact that generalizations about internal order can be made across the members of the set argues that the identification given by the definition is linguistically interesting.

3.3 The Equivalence Class

We have now shown that there are properties other than those specified in the definition which hold across the elements it identifies. Given the framework outlined in chapter 1, we have fulfilled the second requirement for establishing cross-linguistic equivalence and we have, therefore, established an equivalence class AUX.

It is important to note, however, that we have accomplished something else as well. Insofar as a theory of a category is a statement of its properties, we have given a theory of the category AUX, a theory which is language-independent. That is, if (6) represents the equivalence class AUX, then (7) is a statement of the properties which hold across the set.

(6)
$$\left\{\begin{array}{llll} \text{Luiseño} & \text{Lummi} & \text{Egyptian} & \text{Japanese}\ldots\text{Language}_n \\ \text{Particle} & \text{Enclitic} & \text{Arabic} & \text{Affix} \quad\quad\quad\text{Y} \\ \text{Complex} & \text{Sequence} & \text{Constituent} & \end{array}\right\}$$

(7)
AUX = a set of language-particular properties Aux_L such that:

a. Aux_L is a constituent.

b. Aux_L occurs in first, second, or final position.

c. For most choices of L, Aux_L may attach to some adjacent element.

d. Aux_L contains a specified, i.e. fixed and small, class of elements.

e. These elements occur in a fixed order.

f. Aux_L <u>must</u> include elements marking tense and or modality.

g. Aux$_L$ <u>may</u> include, as well, elements indicating subject marking, subject agreement, question, evidential, emphasis, aspect, object marking, object agreement, and negation.

h. Insofar as these notional types can be indentified across languages, their relative order does not follow from any general principle(s).

The list of properties in (7) holds across the set and thus specifies the properties of the set. But, this is quite different from specifying the properties of some one of its members. For example, (7b) and (7g) list possibilities which limit the set as a whole but which nonetheless offer choices to any individual member. Furthermore, if we formalize (7c), it may not be true of any individual instantiation. Consider the following formalization:

(8)
P (X ε AUX & X attaches) > (perhaps) 70%

We are not committed to the precise percentage given in (8); however, it is probably roughly accurate. While (8) holds for the set which is AUX, it need not hold for any of its members. In Lummi, for example, statement (9) appears to be true.

(9)
P (X ε Enclitic Sequence & X attaches) > 100%

Thus, (7) is a theory of the set and not of any individual found therein, although the properties of the set were established through an empirical examination of its members.

3.4 Second Order Questions

List (7) gives the properties of AUX in language-independent terms. That is, it provides a characterization of the cross-linguistic category within which its various language-particular instantiations will fall; the category is so characterized that the linguistic phenomena which instantiates it may vary considerably, but must nonetheless respect definite parameters. It is worth asking, however, <u>why</u> these characteristics, which have no obvious necessary connections with one another, should cluster together. In this section we will provide a (first) answer to this question. To do so, we must step up one level of abstraction; we must first consider the category we have called AUX in somewhat different terms.

The most attractive hypothesis is this: Aux is that part of a sentence which makes possible a judgment regarding its truth value. That is, the presence of the sentence element which we have labeled AUX is a necessary (but not sufficient) condition for the sentence to be a "speech act" which expresses a truth value. We will return in chapter 4 to the various distinctions which are implicit in this hypothesis and to certain problems it faces. For now, we note simply that it suggests that every language will have a set of elements which meets the definition.

If the point of linguistic argumentation is to bring coherence to apparently disparate phenomena, this hypothesis about AUX deserves serious consideration. It explains a substantial number of the properties of AUX: the positional property specified in (7b); the possible compositions specified by the combination of categories given in (7f) and (7g); and the restrictions on internal order given in (7e) and (7h).

<u>Property (7b)</u>: AUX occurs in first, second, or final position. Given the above hypothesis, there is an obvious, if somewhat simple-minded, explanation for the appearance of AUX in, at least, sentence-initial or sentence-final positions. An AUX occurring at either end of the sentence would not interrupt the part of the sentence upon which the judgment is imposed; thus, the surface order of elements would have some relationship to a more abstract representation of the sentence. But there is another, somewhat more satisfactory explanation which also includes sentential second position. A

sentence necessarily has an initial position, a
final position, and a second position. For example,
even a sentence in a language in which the entire
sentence can be (except for the instantiation of
AUX) a "verb" has these three positions, although
final and second positions are collapsed. Thus, AUX
occurs in some position which is always and
necessarily available; if AUX makes possible some
judgment about the truth value of a sentence, it
should be specified to occur in precisely such a
position.

In this light, we must note that a fourth
position is also necessarily available: second from
the end. However, certain considerations make this
fourth logically possible position for AUX at least
exceedingly rare, given the above discussion.
First, if an instantiation of AUX is cliticized, but
not affixal, it must abide by certain properties
otherwise general to clitics. Although clitics may
be enclitic to whatever precedes them, regardless of
its category (cf. Lummi), we are aware of no
element that is necessarly proclitic to the one
following it, regardless of its category. Thus, for
an instantiation of AUX to occur in penultimate
position in a sentence would require that the
language have rigid word order and also that the
same category be last in every sentence. Therefore,
that category, to which this instantiation of AUX
could attach, would have to appear in all
sentences--or at least in all sentences containing
the instantiation of AUX. The only obvious
candidate, then, is a "verb"; however, even here
certain problems arise, for example, the possibility
of copular sentences which lack "verb". Furthermore,
the beginning of the sentence--i.e. initial or
second position--is favored for instantiations of
AUX. Instantiations of AUX which occur
sentence-finally (in surface order) are limited to
languages such as Japanese which are commonly termed
"rigid verb-final". No similar typological
considerations appear to constrain instantiations of
AUX which occur initially or in second position.
Taken together, these two considerations will
obviously militate against the penultimate position

for AUX.

They do not obviously rule this position out altogether, though. If it turns out that there are in fact languages whose instantiation of AUX occurs in penultimate position in a sentence, the explanation offered above--i.e. that AUX should occur in some position which is always and necessarily available--will still hold, although the list of properties given for AUX in (7) will need minor revision. However, if it turns out that there are no languages whose instantiation of AUX occurs in penultimate position in a sentence, we will be obliged to consider another explanation. That is, it may be that we will simply have to stipulate that first, second, and final positions are the ones which allow sentential access, where the elements which provide a judgment about a given sentence's truth value will necessarily occur. This stipulation is, at least, consistent with our hypothesis concerning AUX.[11]

Properties (7f) and (7g): AUX may include elements marking tense, modality, subject marking, subject agreement, question, evidential, emphasis, aspect, object marking, object agreement, and negation. We should note that this list does not make the distinction given in (7f) and (7g) between criterial notional categories and optional ones. However, all of the notional types, except subject marking or agreement and object marking or agreement, can have what is commonly termed sentential scope. Tense and modality must; question, evidential, aspect, emphasis, and negation may, although their scope can also be more restricted. If AUX makes possible a judgment about the truth value of a sentence, it follows that it should include precisely such elements.

The fact that AUX may contain subject marking or agreement and object marking or agreement does not follow obviously from the appeal to sentential scope. However, it is worth noting that the existence of, at least, subject marking or object marking in a language by definition allows the absence of an independent subject or object. To that extent, such elements have sentential properties. The inclusion of such elements thus at least does not obviously contradict the hypothesis about the category. We must admit, however, that we have at the moment no explanation for the inclusion of subject or object agreement.

Properties (7e) and (7h): AUX is a category with a fixed internal order and, insofar as the notional types which these elements express can be identified across languages, their relative order does not follow from any general principles. Although it may be possible to decompose an instantiation of AUX into morphemes, insofar as each of these expresses a notional category which has sentential scope or otherwise is sentential in some broader sense, property (7h) suggests that AUX has no parallel syntactic or semantic decomposition. Thus, it is the unit which applies directly to the sentence and not its individual members independently. This possibility follows from the hypothesis that AUX supplies a (single) judgment about the truth value of the sentence. Were there a series of independent judgments, we might expect AUX to exhibit some general organizational strategy corresponding to their interrelationships. On the other hand, were there some general organizational principles for AUX which reflected those judgments, AUX would not be intimately connected with the judgment about truth value; presumably a sentence, on a single interpretation, can have only a single truth value.

The fact that AUX has a fixed internal order--property (7e)--follows indirectly from the discussion of property (7h). Given the existence of property (7h), the only alternative to a fixed internal word order is free order. We suggest that this logically possible characteristic would directly contradict the general hypothesis about the character of AUX; that is, it would then be impossible for AUX to express a judgment about the truth value of a sentence. It is clear that there are languages in which the order of elements in a sentence is absolutely free (except for the position of the instantiation of AUX). Therefore, there appears to be no special perceptual problem in putting elements together which occur randomly relative to one another. However, in such languages, it is also the case that the instantiation of AUX occurs in a fixed position and contains much of the information which allows those pieces to be composed. So, for example, Walbiri (Kenneth Hale (personal communication)) has absolutely free word order, except for its second-position instantiation of AUX; and its instantiation of AUX contains, in addition to tense, subject marking and object marking. However, if the AUX had free internal order and if AUX expresses a judgment about the truth value of a sentence, there would be nothing "higher" to specify how its pieces were to compose. Thus, the other logical possibility for AUX's internal arrangement is rendered impossible by our hypothesis about its character.

We have concentrated in this discussion on a subset of the properties given in (7). We have suggested that these properties reasonably follow from the hypothesis about the character of AUX; that is, if AUX provides a judgment about the truth value of a sentence, it might be expected to exhibit this set of properties. Conversely, since these properties hold for AUX, regardless of what hypothesis we might have about the category, the fact that they can be argued to follow from the proposed hypothesis is an argument for the hypothesis. We have not considered properties (7a), (7c), and (7d), or the distinction between criterial and noncriterial notional categories represented by (7f) and (7g). At the moment we see no obvious reason why these properties should also hold for AUX, at least in terms of our hypothesis. However, it is interesting to note that, except for (7c), these are the properties given by the definition which established the set AUX in the first place: a constituent (7a) which contains a specified, i.e. fixed and small, set of elements (7d), crucially containing elements marking tense and or modality (the difference between the lists in (7f) and (7g)). The very fact that these properties do not obviously follow from the hypothesis offers it support of a somewhat different kind--and at the same time validates the definition with which we began this investigation, thereby supporting the linguistic interest of identifying those elements which fall within it.

An examination of the set of elements that meet the definition produces a set of nondefinitional properties; the hypothesis about the character of AUX provides a reasonable explanation for essentially the same set of properties. Conversely, this result indirectly supports the linguistic interest of both the definition and the hypothesis. (10) represents these conclusions schematically.

(10)
Definition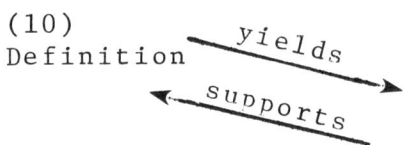

Nondefinitional Properties

Hypothesis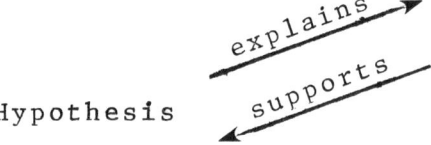

(10) suggests that the definitional properties and the hypothesis simply represent the same linguistic fact, but at different levels of abstraction. The definition depends on, and assumes, a syntactic analysis; the hypothesis is a semantic characterization of an element identified in the syntax.

We assume that there are certain properties of language which cannot be "explained" simply because they are defining properties. As we have noted, there is no a priori reason that the definition which allowed the identification of the elements discussed in chapter 2 should have any instantiation or, if it does, that this fact should be linguistically interesting. Similarly, it is not logically necessary that the hypothesis regarding the character of AUX be linguistically interesting. And, in fact, we can argue for the linguistic interest of either only indirectly, by showing that certain otherwise unexpected consequences follow from them. Thus, we would suggest that the fact that languages exhibit some element which conforms to the definition and the possibility that this element will express a judgment about the truth value of a sentence are simply irreducible properties of language--or better yet that they are the same property viewed from different perspectives.

3.5 Conclusion

The discussion of the previous section is speculative. Nevertheless, we must repeat a point made at the beginning of this chapter: what is critical from our point of view is not whether or not the immediately preceding discussion ultimately turns out to be correct in all of its essentials. Rather, the important point is that the framework within which this investigation has been carried out allows language-internal properties to be specified on a relatively free basis; we seek definitions of, and common ground for, the similarities we find in comparing a variety of languages with one another. A major result of this study is that it is possible to frame a definition of a cross-linguistic category AUX whose instantiations have much in common apart from the criterial properties. This nontrivial fact demands attention. Theories of language which can accommodate the facts given in (7) on general grounds are to that extent well-corroborated; those that are only consistent with such facts--but also consistent with other possible facts concerning the results of this and similar investigations--are weak; and those which are inconsistent with these facts are thereby falsified. It is in this sense that the method of cross-linguistic equivalence is a powerful theoretical tool, as well as a device revelatory of the degree of consistency among the languages whose grammars we have access to. Finally, it must be recognized that the result of applying this method specifically to the AUX has allowed us to ask interesting questions--essentially the issues raised in section 3.4--questions which could not have been asked prior to this investigation.

Notes

1. The elements which compose a particular instantiation of AUX are also commonly bound to one another. However, we concentrate in this discussion on the attachment properties of the entire constituent.

2. This generalization is true, regardless of which of the two possibilities we choose in section 2.5. The "speaker attitude" particles may follow, and attach to, categories other than "verb", but then they are not members of the constituent under consideration. Further, we should note that we treated the set of Japanese affixes as affixes to S^n (where $n > 1$), but since they follow S^n, they attach to the final element in it, an element which is generally "verb".

3. A language is said to have <u>subject marking</u> if the elements indicating the number and/or person of the subject regularly take the place of an independent subject. We use the term <u>subject agreement</u> to refer to a distinct phenomenon whereby the elements that mark the number and/or person of the subject do not take the place of an independent subject but rather necessarily cooccur with it. We use <u>object marking</u> and <u>object agreement</u> in parallel fashion, relative to the interaction between elements so labeled and an independent object.

4. This list assumes the identification of two constituents in Japanese which meet the definition in chapter 2. If the second possibility suggested for Japanese--i.e. the one represented by schema (153) in chapter 2--turns out to be the correct one, the list will necessarily be expanded to include elements marking the imperative or some notion that we might generally characterize as "speaker attitude".

5. Although the presence of any one of these elements in some instantiation of AUX depends, of course, on its presence in the language in question, it does not follow that they will necessarily occur

there when they are present. For example, the negative element in Luiseño is not a part of the Luiseño Particle Complex, a fact which was discussed in Akmajian, Steele, and Wasow (1979). Nor is object marking in Lummi a part of the Lummi Enclitic Sequence, as was noted in chapter 2. These are only two examples among the elements which can occur in AUX, but similar ones could be given for all other possible elements.

6. If the single-constituent analysis of Japanese is correct, of course, this problem for absolute sentence-final position does not exist. We should note, further, that if the two-constituent analysis is correct, the constituent which includes only tense will precede the one which includes only modality and thus will not appear in absolute sentence-final position. This fact falls together with the other apparent exceptions to our claim about first, second, and final positions, and we take it up briefly in footnote 10.

7. Obviously, the problem involving second and final positions does not arise in regard to first position. If some language's instantiation of AUX occurs initially and yet may be preceded by something (e.g. a topic), then it will occur in second position and, thus, offer no problem for the generalization.

Languages like German and English apparently contradict the claim that instantiations of AUX are limited on the surface to first, second, and final positions, since tense elements which in either language can be argued to be part of the language-particular instantiation of AUX can appear on the surface to be in third position, following the verb.

(i)
John died.

(ii)
Hans lächelte.
John laughed.

'John laughed.'

In either case, we should note that it is only the finite verb (the verb with tense attached) which occurs in second position. Further, the verb stem itself can indicate tense.

(iii)
John wrote a letter.

(iv)
Hans schrieb.
John wrote
'John wrote.'

Therefore, the facts of English and German do not necessarily contradict the claims about the three possible positions for instantiations of AUX.

8. We assume, then, that the elements of analysis of the Lummi Enclitic Sequence are the two units specified in (79) in chapter 2, each of which can be further analyzed and within which the order is not fixed.

9. This claim necessarily contradicts any analysis of the members of the set which we have termed AUX which calls some or all of their various pieces "main verbs" or "higher predicates". Such analyses depend on the hypothesis that we have just argued to be false.

10. We left open in chapter 2 whether the lexical items for the Luiseño Particle Complex or the Egyptian Arabic Constituent are the elements which compose any particular instantiation or the particular instantiations themselves. Either choice is consistent with this objection to the application of the X-Bar Convention to AUX.

11. We can now consider the reasons for the proposal made at the end of the discussion of the possible positions for AUX. If initial, second, and final positions are positions with sentential

access, it is possible that other elements which similarly "pertain" to the sentence will occur there as well as AUX. That is, these positions are not reserved exclusively for AUX. However, if AUX expresses a judgment about the truth value of a sentence, that judgment need not extend to other elements which are also "sentential" in their scope. Thus, such elements will be transparent to the determination of first, second, and final positions.

Chapter 4

FURTHER EXPLORATION

4.1 Introduction

In chapter 1, we gave a framework within which cross-linguistic equivalence can be decided. In chapters 2 and 3, we gave an extended example of that framework, specifically as it applies to the cross-linguistically identifiable category AUX. This, the concluding chapter, will not summarize the preceding arguments. Rather, given that each of a number of typologically diverse and genetically unrelated languages provides an instantiation of AUX and given that we can extract from those instantiations a list of properties which allow a language-independent characterization of the category, we are concerned here explicitly with a new way of considering the linguistic phenomena we have isolated.

In section 3.4, we proposed that AUX provides a judgment about the truth value of a sentence. In this chapter, we will present a semantic classification which both refines the proposal of chapter 3 and gives it more substance. First, the semantic classification we propose defines the term sentence in a relatively precise fashion and crucially distinguishes it from subordinate clause. Second, this classification provides a framework within which the language-particular instantiations of AUX can be compared. The list of properties of AUX given in (7) of chapter 3 places certain limits on the language-particular instantiations of the category, but it also allows for substantial differences among the various instantiations. While the discussion here approaches the phenomena from an entirely different perspective, it has precisely the same result. That is, even within the semantic classification we will suggest, it can be shown that there is no one-to-one correspondence among the various members of the set AUX. Finally, the semantic classification provides a framework which allows different instantiations of AUX within a particular language to be distinguished from one another.

While the proposals in this chapter presume the foregoing investigation, they are not meant to supplant it. The results of that investigation stand or fall on their own merits. This chapter, then, essentially considers the insights afforded by those results--insights we feel can and should be profitably explored. The framework itself is a "working framework", in the sense that one can have a "working definition." In fact, it shares with most working definitions the fault that it is not entirely adequate to the task at hand. Nevertheless, there is heuristic value in imposing it on the facts and relations which are known, for by doing so we gain a clear separation of problems which are otherwise inextricable from one another, and, at the same time, we are able to raise in a concrete fashion questions about the function or functions of the members of AUX which would otherwise remain unknown or uninvestigated. If the (intentionally) provocative speculations of this chapter lead to deeper results, its aim will have been satisfied.

4.2 Diagrams and Postulates

Our goal is to investigate the relations which hold between four classes of objects which we refer to as $\underline{S}$, $\underline{P}$, $\sqrt{\underline{P}}$, and $\underline{C}$, and which we characterize below.

We use the symbol $\underline{S}$ to refer to the sentences of a given language which may be used to perform speech acts whose analysis depends on propositional satisfaction conditions. We take this class to include declarative sentences, (relative to asserting), interrogative sentences (relative to asking questions), imperative sentences (relative to issuing orders and requests), and perhaps a few others. Outside this group fall such expressive utterances as <u>uh-oh</u>, <u>nice doggie</u>, <u>wow</u>, and whatever speech acts are involved in the practice of articulation, the singing of popular songs, and so forth.

The propositional basis of the three above-mentioned types of sentences in S varies: we may say that the propositional basis of an assertion is satisfied if it corresponds to the way the world is (and an assertion is true if its propositional basis is satisfied); the propositional basis of a question is satisfied if a positive answer to the question is a true assertion; and the propositional basis of an order is satisfied if the order is carried out. These distinctions, crudely stated though they are, indicate that the propositional basis of assertions and questions is in an abstract sense the same: in either case, we take the propositional basis to be complete and responsible to fact. The propositional basis of an imperative sentence is, in contrast, incomplete and responsible to deed.

We use the symbol $\overline{P}$ to represent the (abstract) propositional basis of assertions and questions, and the symbol $\sqrt{P}$ to represent the propositional basis of imperatives.

We also introduce the following postulate:

(I)
Tense is a function from $\sqrt{P}$ to $\overline{P}$.

This yields the following diagram:

(1)

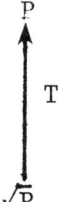

Finally, the object represented by C is the class of subordinate clauses, which we shall restrict here to (propositional) arguments in some functional structure (e.g. subject and object "sentential" complements).

Further Exploration

We may now raise the fundamental issue of this chapter: given the assumption that <u>tense</u> is a syntactic and semantic function from $\sqrt{P}$ to P, is it possible to analyze other grammatical elements in a language as functions defined over the class of objects $\sqrt{P}$, P, S, C?

Relative to one assumption, the characterizations we have given above of these four objects immediately restrict the set of functions definable over them. This assumption is:

(II)
'Functions are always additive semantically and never non-additive syntactically.'[1]

The consequences of this postulate are:

a. If there is a function from X to Y, there is no function from Y to X.
b. If the interpretation of members of Y depends on the interpretation of members of X, then there is a function from X to Y.

An immediate result of this assumption is the following fundamental structure:

(2)

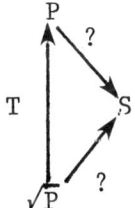

Moreover, no diagram can contain the subdiagrams given below:

(3)
P ——> $\sqrt{P}$ C ——> P
S ——> P   C ——> $\sqrt{P}$
S ——> $\sqrt{P}$

Further Exploration   172

   Although examples can be found which might be taken to exemplify functions from S to C (direct quotation) or from C to S (such desiderative expressions as <u>O! that I weren't such a nitwit!</u>), we shall not consider such possibilities here.

   As a result, only four possibilities remain:

(4)
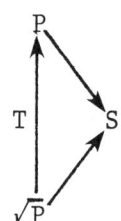

(5)
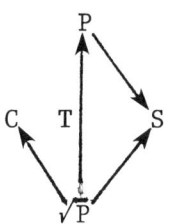

(6)
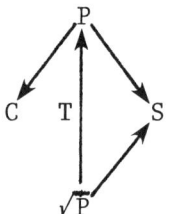

(7)
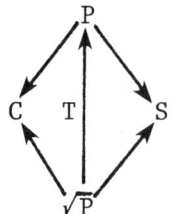

Two remarks are in order concerning (4) through (7).

a. (4) applies only to languages which lack syntactic subordination entirely, if there are any. (Seneca is a possibility.)
b. Note that of the four basic objects, two represent either complete utterances (S) or proper subparts of complete utterances (C), while the other two (P and $\sqrt{P}$) represent an abstract basis from which elements of C and S may be formed.

Assuming the soundness of our characterizations of the objects S, P, $\sqrt{P}$, and C, and the correctness of postulates (I) and (II), the four diagrams given above provide in principle a new classification of the ways in which languages treat the relation between sentence and subordinate clause. Moreover, they allow considerable refinement in the analysis of properties of language-particular instantiations of AUX and provide a means for further comparison with respect to these refinements. We now apply this analysis to two cases: Luiseño and English.

4.3 Examples

4.3.1 Introduction

The languages to be examined here will exemplify schemas (5) and (7). Whether or not schemas (4) and (6) may be instantiated among the world's languages, we leave open. Obviously, it is not possible to exemplify all four schemas on the basis of two languages, since a single language can be associated with exactly one schema.

4.3.2 Luiseño

We begin the discussion of the various mappings in Luiseño with the one between $\sqrt{P}$ and P, since our decision in this regard has certain necessary consequences for the other mappings. Postulate (I) above defines this mapping: tense is a function from $\sqrt{P}$ to P. In Luiseño there are two apparent choices for the elements which provide this mapping, but one can be shown not to apply. First, in chapter 2 we noted that Luiseño has a set of suffixes which mark tense (and aspect). We repeat them here for ease of reference:

(8)

	Nonfuture	Future
Distant	Near	
quş	q/wun or an	an
uk		
'ya or ax		

Second, we noted that the set of particles in position 3 in the (nonquotative) Particle Complex might be argued, when there is no particle in position 1, to mark tense.

(9)
```
wunaalum   m-il                heyiquş
they       ∅-subj:mark-PRT:3   was:digging
```
'They were digging.'

However, the discussion of Luiseño in chapter 2 also demonstrated that none of the particles in either position 1 or position 3 can be given a single meaning. Rather, the interpretation of a particular particle depends on the configuration in which it occurs.

(10)
```
wunaalum   şu-m-il                  heyiwun
they       prt:1-subj:mark-prt:3    are:digging
```
'They are digging (but I didn't know it until just now).'

Furthermore, we argued that the Particle Complex determines "sentence type". Thus, when there is no particle in position 1, as in (9), the configuration does not simply indicate some tense notion, but rather indicates that the sentence is a nonmodal assertion. Finally, we characterized the symbol P above as representing the (abstract) propositional basis of assertions and questions, <u>not</u> as representing the distinction between the two. As we noted in chapter 2, the distinction between questions and assertions in Luiseño is carried by the absence of particles in position 3, relative to the presence or absence of some particular particle in position 1. Compare (11) to (9) and (10), for example.

(11)
wunaalum ⌀u-m   heyiqu⌀
they   prt:1-subj:mark-⌀   was:digging
'Were they digging?'

In the light of these considerations, it is obvious that we must choose the first alternative given above for Luiseño; that is, we must choose the set of suffixes shown in (8) as providing the mapping between $\sqrt{P}$ and P.

The initial delimitation of the elements which provide the mapping between P and S is clear from the above discussion, as well as from the discussion of the Luiseño Particle Complex in chapter 2, given the characterization of S in section 4.2. As stated there, we use the symbol S to refer to the sentences of a given language which may be used to perform speech acts whose analysis depends on propositional satisfaction conditions, and we defined this class as including interrogative, declarative, and imperative sentences. The distinction between the first two is carried entirely by the shape of the Particle Complex. That is, while both an interrogative and a declarative sentence may contain a "verb" with precisely the same tense (and aspect) inflections, the addition of some particular particle sequence allows the determination of some sentence as either interrogative or declarative. Compare (11) and (9), for example.

On the basis of these various considerations, we could propose the mappings for Luiseño given in (12). However, the mapping between $\sqrt{P}$ and P is incomplete and the mapping between P and S is too broad.

Concerning the possibility that the tense/aspect suffixes do not exhaust the mapping between $\sqrt{P}$ and P, consider the sentences in (13) and (14).

(12)

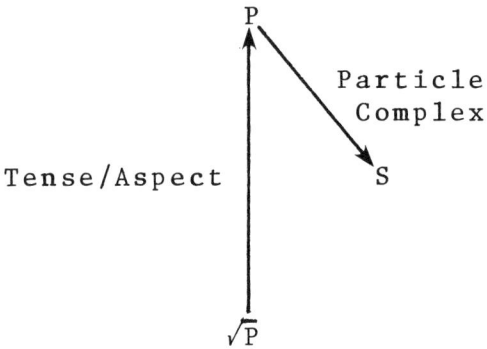

(13)
a. noo   p   'oy   no-ma'max
    I   Prt:Com   you:obj   POSSESSIVE-like
    'I like you.'

b. noo   p   no-tooyax
    I   Prt:Com   POSSESSIVE-laugh
    'I'm good at laughing.'

(14)
a. noo   n   heyi-lu-t
    I   Prt:Com   dig-temporal:reference-ABSOLUTIVE
    'I'm gonna dig.'

b. noo   n   heyi-qa-t
    I   Prt:Com   dig-temporal:reference-ABSOLUTIVE
    'I dug (in the immediate past).'

None of the sentences in (13) and (14) contains any of the suffixes given in (8). Rather, the form to which we might expect them to be added, insofar as the English translation is any guide, has in (13) a possessive prefix and in (14) a suffix indicating temporal reference and what we have labeled, in accordance with traditional Uto-Aztecan terminology, the <u>absolutive</u>. On various grounds which are beyond the scope of this discussion, the suffix marking temporal reference can be shown to be a part of the "stem" to which the absolutive is added. The term <u>absolutive</u> is simply a label for a set of suffixes

Further Exploration

in Luiseño which are mutually exclusive with possessive prefixes and tense/aspect suffixes. They are listed in (15):[2]

(15)
la	cha	ta
l	sh	t

(We should note that possessive prefixes are also mutually exclusive with tense/aspect suffixes. That is to say, there are clear restrictions on cooccurrence among these affix types, although various Luiseño stems can--in fact, must--take some subset of the three.

(16)
"Stem"	+Possessive	+Absolutive	+Tense/Aspect
a. na	nona 'my father'		
yo	noyo 'my mother'		
b. muu		muuta 'owl'	
ŝungaa		ŝungaal 'woman'	
c. heela			heelaquŝ 'was singing'
pella			pellaquŝ 'was dancing'
d. too	notoo 'my rock'	toota 'rock'	
kutapi	nokutapi 'my bow'	kutapish 'bow'	

Steele (1980) and (1981) discuss this particular aspect of Luiseño.[3])

The critical points for our purposes are two. First, these three affix types can be shown to be syntactic operators, in the sense that the syntax of Luiseño can be specified in terms of them.[4] Second, in general, any sentence which lacks a tense/aspect-marked form will contain either a possessive-marked or an absolutive-marked form, critically appearing on what we might label the "head of the predicate". In short, in sentences like (13a,b) and (14a,b), the possessive and the absolutive are the syntactic parallel to the tense/aspect suffixes, and we can therefore add them to the mapping between √P and P. (17) is a more satisfactory specification of the mapping between √P and P in Luiseño than (12).[5,6]

(17)

P
↑
| Tense/Aspect
| Absolutive
| Possessive
|
√P

We can turn, then, to refining the mapping between P and S. In arguing for the association of the Particle Complex with the mapping between P and S, we focused on the fact that the Particle Complex, and it alone, marks the difference between questions and declaratives. It is critical to remember, however, that the statement of the configurations included within the Particle Complex allows at once finer and coarser distinctions than the one between interrogative and declarative. We repeat an abbreviated version of the final statement of the possible configurations for the Particle Complex in nonquotative speech in (18). (18) suggests that, within assertions, there is a distinction between nonmodal and modal assertion, and that, within nonmodal assertions, there is yet another distinction. Furthermore, (18) recapitulates only the form of the Particle Complex found in nonquotative speech. On the other hand, each of at least (18b), (18c), and (18d) subsumes a set of possibilities,

(18)

a. $\emptyset - \left\{ \dfrac{up}{\text{Subject:Marking}} \right\} - \emptyset$ ⎫
⎬ Nonmodal Assertion
b. $\emptyset - \left\{ \dfrac{up}{\text{Subject:Marking}} \right\} - \text{Particle:3}$ ⎭

c. Particle:1-Subject:Marking-Particle:3   Modal Assertion

d. Particle:1-Subject:Marking-∅   Nonassertion

depending entirely on the particular particles in either position 1 or position 3. Thus, for example, there is no configuration in (18) which is to be identified only with questions; questions are a subtype of (18d), depending entirely on the presence of ṣu in position 1.

From the point of view of determining the association of certain elements in Luiseño with various mappings, the interesting aspect of this last fact--the fact that a statement like (18) obscures some of the important distinctions within the Particle Complex--is that we must distinguish two subsets of the particle sequences identified by (18c) and (18d). Specifically, the particle sequences with ṣu in position 1 necessarily occur in sentences which otherwise contain (some subset of) the elements specified for the mapping between $\sqrt{P}$ and P; the particle sequences with xu in position 1 do not. Consider, for example, the following sentences.

(19)

a. wunaalum   ṣu-m-po   heyi-wun
   they   ṣU-subj:mark-prt:3   dig-TENSE/ASPECT
   'They are digging (but I didn't know it until just now).'

b. wunaalum   ṣu-m   heyi-wun
   they   ṣU-subj:mark-∅   dig-TENSE/ASPECT
   'Are they digging?'

(20)
a. wunaalum   xu-m-po   heyi
   they   XU-subj:mark-prt:3   dig
   'They should dig.'

b. wunaalum   xu-m   heyi
   they   XU-subj:mark-∅   dig
   'They better dig.'

(19a) and (20a) are both examples of (18c); the sentence with ǵu includes a form marked with one of the tense/aspect suffixes, but the sentence with xu does not--nor is heyi marked with the absolutive or possessive. (19b) and (20b) are both examples of (18d); again the sentence with ǵu includes a form marked with one of the tense/aspect suffixes, but the sentence with xu does not--and again, heyi is not marked with the absolutive or possessive.[7]

If we assume that each mapping is syntactically additive, along the lines of the strong form of postulate (II) discussed in footnote 1, the simplest hypothesis concerning these facts is that the particle sequences with xu provide the mapping between √P and S, but that all the other particle sequences are added to P. Thus, we can revise statement (12) and add another mapping as well.

(21)

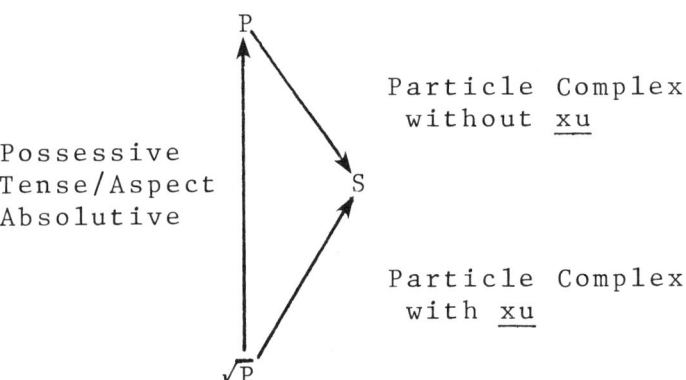

The mapping between √P and S is a natural consequence of postulate (II) and the specification of the mapping between √P and P (taken together).

Further Exploration

The mapping between $\sqrt{P}$ and S is not exhausted, however, by the particle sequences with <u>xu</u>. We noted in chapter 2 that imperatives lack both the Particle Complex <u>and</u> the tense/aspect suffixes. (22) illustrates both claims.

(22)
heyi-yam
dig-PL:IMPERATIVE
'Dig (plural)!'

(22) is an example of a plural imperative, i.e. an imperative addressed to more than a single individual; an imperative addressed to a single individual is given in (23).

(23)
heyi
dig
'Dig!'

The fact that the "verb" in singular imperatives appears without an affix seems to pose a problem for the strong form of postulate (II). However, since the absence of a suffix in singular imperatives alternates with the suffix <u>yam</u> (or <u>am</u> with certain "verbs") in plural imperatives, we will treat singular imperatives as adding a ∅ affix.

Negative imperatives similarly share no formal properties with the set of declaratives and questions which result from the mappings between $\sqrt{P}$ and P and between P and S.[8]

(24)
a. tuǵǵu   heyi
   NEG:IMPERATIVE dig-SG:IMPERATIVE
   'Don't dig!'

b. tuǵǵu   heyi-yam
   NEG:IMPERATIVE dig-PL:IMPERATIVE
   'Don't dig (plural)!'

Given that imperative sentences are included among the elements identified by the symbol S, given

Further Exploration   182

that $\sqrt{P}$ is the propositional basis of imperatives, and given the peculiarities of imperatives (both positive and negative) relative to the other members of S, we can add the various elements given in the imperative examples above--**∅/yam** and **tu¢¢u**--to the mapping between $\sqrt{P}$ and S in (21).

(25)

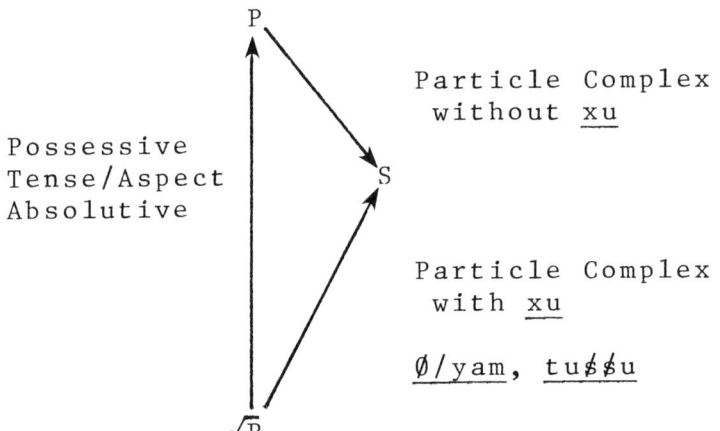

Finally, we can consider Luiseño subordinate clauses. The definition of the symbol C included only subordinate clauses which fulfill some propositional argument structure. However, in Luiseño, we can extend C to include relative clauses and what we called in chapter 2 "adjuncts". As noted there, subordinate clauses in Luiseño share with imperatives the property of lacking both any instantiation of the Particle Complex and any of the various tense/aspect suffixes given in (8). All, however, will contain some "stem"--the "head of the predicate" of the subordinate clause--which is marked for aspect and/or temporal reference. Consider, for example, the complements in (26), the relative clauses in (27), and the "adjuncts" in (28).

(26)
a. noo   n   wingeeq   po-waaqi-qala-y
   I   Prt:Com   think   possessive-sweep-ASPECT-obj
   'I think that he is sweeping.'

b. noo   nil   tiiwik   moyil
   I   Prt:Com   saw   moon:obj

   kari'a-qal
   rise-qala-l
        ASPECT-absolutive

   'I saw the moon rising.'

(27)
a. noo   n   chaqalaqiq   hengeemali
   I   Prt:Com   is:tickling   boy:obj

   po-'ayali-vo-y
   possessive-know-TEMPORAL:REFERENCE-obj

   'I am tickling the boy that John knew.'

b. noo   n   chaqalaqiq   hengeemali
   I   Prt:Com   is:tickling   boy:obj

   tooyax-lu-t-i
   laugh-TEMPORAL:REFERENCE-absolutive-obj

   'I am tickling the boy who will laugh.'

(28)
a. po-tooya-qala   mariya   upil
   possessive-laugh-ASPECT   Mary   Prt:Com

   heelaquɬ
   was:singing

   'While he was laughing, Mary was singing.'

b. tooya-a-t   mariya   upil
   laugh-ASPECT-absolutive   Mary   Prt:Com

   heelaquɬ
   was:singing

   'While laughing, Mary was singing.'

(For the argument that these various affixes are part of the "stem", we refer the reader to Steele (1980).) The critical point for correctly characterizing subordinate clauses in Luiseño is that the "head of the predicate", the form which is marked for aspect/temporal reference, also has a possessive prefix in the (a) sentences in (26) through (28) and an absolutive affix in the (b) sentences. All complements, except for the complements to perception "verbs", take a possessive prefix, on the form which is marked for aspect/temporal reference; all complements to perception "verbs" take an absolutive on the parallel form. For all relative clauses which have a possessive prefix on the form under consideration, the head of the relative clause must not also be its subject; for all relative clauses which have an absolutive suffix on the form under consideration, the head of the relative clause must also be its subject.[9] All adjuncts in which the subject is referentially distinct from the subject of the main clause take a possessive prefix, on the form which is marked for aspect/temporal reference; all adjuncts in which the subject is referentially identical to the subject of the main clause and in which the time of the adjunct does not precede the time of the main clause take an absolutive. (We will return later to the temporal restriction given in this last generalization.) In short, there is a set of subordinate clauses which require a possessive prefix on the "head of the predicate" and a set of subordinate clauses which require an absolutive suffix on the "head of the predicate".

We have specified that the mapping between $\sqrt{P}$ and P includes the possessive and absolutive. However, we cannot include the subordinate clauses which also necessarily take one or the other of these two elements in that mapping, <u>if</u> we wish to maintain postulate (II), (the requirement that any mapping will be semantically additive). That is, if we were to propose that subordinate clauses in Luiseño--those clauses represented by C--are a result of some mapping from a subset of the elements in P, specifically those lacking any of the tense/aspect suffixes in (8), there is no obvious (semantic or syntactic) difference between the elements in P and those in C. (29) cannot be correct, given the assumptions under which we are conducting this investigation.

(29)

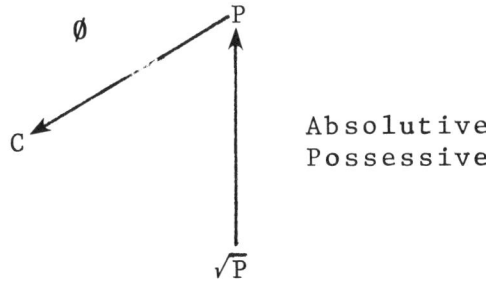

Absolutive
Possessive

Therefore, Luiseño subordinate clauses (C) are mapped directly from $\sqrt{P}$ by the addition of the absolutive and possessive.

(30)

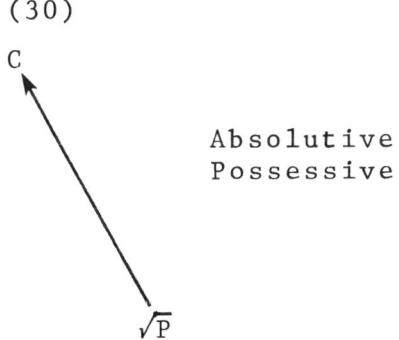

Absolutive
Possessive

We return, then, to the temporal restriction in the final generalization about adjuncts given above. There is one type of adjunct which contains neither an absolutive nor a possessive. It also contains none of the tense/aspect suffixes given in (8); rather, the "head of the predicate" is always marked with <u>nik</u> (and it is always interpreted as having a time reference preceding the time of the main clause).

(31)
heela-nik   xwaan   upil   heelaquş
sing-NIK   John   Prt:Com   was:dancing
'After singing, John was dancing.'

We will therefore add <u>nik</u> to the mapping between $\sqrt{P}$ and C. With this addition, we have completed the specification of the various mappings in Luiseño.[10]

(32)

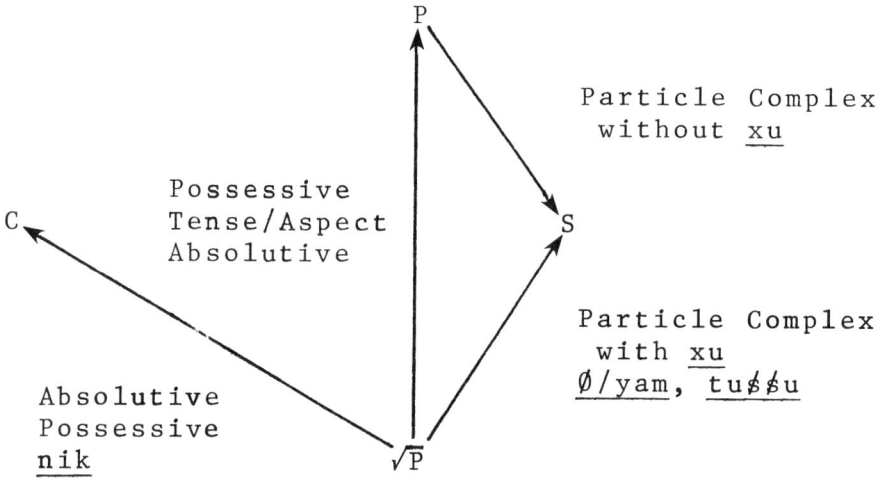

In section 4.2, we gave four possible mapping configurations. We now see that Luiseño is an example of the configuration specified in (5)--it lacks any mapping between P and C.

4.3.3 English

Since English contains a subordinate clause type which may be identified with $\sqrt{P}$, it is convenient to take this clause type as a starting point. The type in question is the so-called tenseless <u>that</u>-clause which appears underlined in the following examples:

(33)
It isn't required <u>that he come</u>.

(34)
Is it necessary <u>that I be in court tomorrow?</u>

Further Exploration

We assume such subordinate clauses to be formed by the application of that to a member of $\sqrt{P}$. Thus, we have (35) and (36):

(35)
that: $\sqrt{p}$ ──> that $\sqrt{p}$, where $\sqrt{p}\ \varepsilon\ \sqrt{P}$ and that $\sqrt{p}\ \varepsilon\ C$

(36)
he come $\varepsilon\ \sqrt{P}$

Imperative sentences are formed from members of $\sqrt{P}$ having the form you + VP by adding do or don't to the left, with the stipulations that do is always emphatic, you is always emphatic, and don't is not always emphatic. In addition, at most one emphatic element may appear. This yields the following possibilities.[11]

(37)
a. He may go, but don't yóu go.
b. You may want to go, but dón't (*you) go.
c. If you want to go, then dó (*you) go.
d. If you want to go, then you gó. (not an imperative)
e. If you want to go, then (*do) gó.

We shall denote imperative formation by Imp and add the following (imprecise) formula to our list:

(38)
Imp: $\sqrt{P}$ ──> S

Together with our first rule, this yields the following representations:

(39)

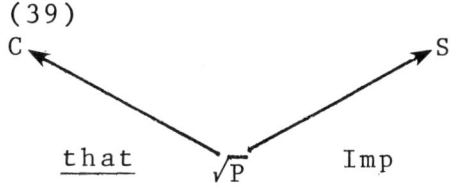

Consider now the relations between $\sqrt{P}$ and P. By assumption, one of these relations is the function tense. In addition, we assume that there is a set of aux-elements which includes the modals, the (tense-carrying) do of Do Support fame, IS (= all tensed forms of be), and HAS* (= all invertible tensed forms of have), each of which we identify with a syntactic function whose domain is a subset of $\sqrt{P}$ and whose range lies in P. Collectively, these elements may be regarded as particular instantiations of the cross-linguistic equivalence class AUX, either on syntactic or on semantic grounds, a view which is justified in appendix A.

Although we cannot consider here the details of the analysis proposed in appendix A, we can sketch the way in which these functions apply. In particular, since more than one position is in general possible in the case of the aux-elements themselves (either preceding or following the subject), we shall identify the addition of each of the aux-elements with a mapping from $\sqrt{P}$ to P, and we shall treat the placement of the aux-elements by mappings from P to S. More precisely, the functions associated with each of these elements may be characterized as follows:

(40)
a. tense: subj be predicate $\longmapsto$ {IS, subj predicate}
subj have* XP... $\longmapsto$ {HAS*, subj XP...}
subj V ... $\longmapsto$ subj V_{tensed}...

(where IS, HAS*, and V_{tensed} agree with subj in person and number)

b. do: subj V... $\longmapsto$ {DOES, subj V...}
(where DOES agrees with subj, and V ≠ be or have*)

c. modal: subj V... $\longmapsto$ {modal, subj V...}

d. 1st position: {aux, subj...} $\longmapsto$ aux subj
(where aux stands for any aux-element in the sense given above)

e. 2nd position: {aux, subj...} ⊢→ subj aux
   subj V_{tensed}... ⊢→ subj V_{tensed}...

It should be pointed out that the semantic categories $\sqrt{P}$, P, and S do not fully determine the characteristics of this family of mappings. For example, it is possible to treat the tense mapping and the do mapping in ways which collapse their common properties, to the extent that they exist. We have not tried to bring out here either the semantic similarities which they share in certain cases or the fact that differences between them arise when we consider negation, emphasis, and ellipsis. To see whether or not the framework proposed here is capable of resolving such issues would require much fuller treatment of the semantic and syntactic properties of these operators than we are able to provide here. Nevertheless, granting the existence of the mappings proposed above, their addition to the diagram (39) yields (41):

(41)

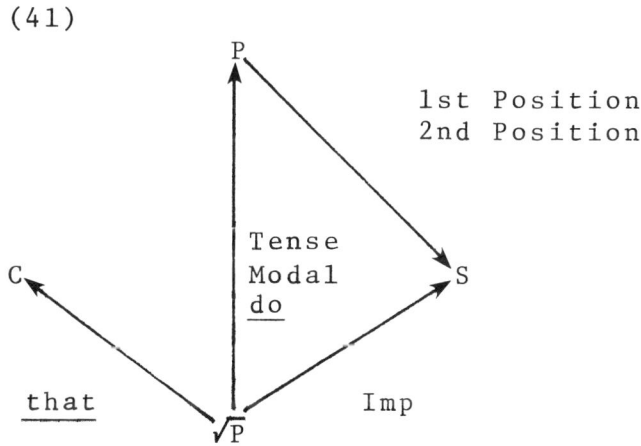

The identification of the (obligatory) mapping from $\sqrt{P}$ to P accords very well with the fact that in English the expressions we have identified with $\sqrt{P}$ always lack tense or modal. The identification of the mapping from P to S with aux-position raises at least two intriguing problems.

First, consider the following cases:

(42)
John is bald

(43)
Is John bald

We find that the second, depending on intonation, can be construed as either a question or an exclamation. Suppose that we associate the continuum of cases ranging from (final) rising intonation to (final) falling intonation with a corresponding continuum whose poles we dub Subjective Doubt and Subjective Nondoubt. In the cases considered, we shall say that the noninverted case is representational, whereas the inverted case is nonrepresentational. The combination of a postsubject aux-element with falling intonation combines a representational form with (intonational) Subjective Nondoubt. We identify this combination with Assertions.

The combination of a postsubject aux-element with rising intonation combines a representational form with (intonational) Subjective Doubt. We identify this combination with what we shall call conjectives or suppositions. They are not to be identified with inverted aux-element yes-no questions, since they resist the presence of such negative polarity items as any or budge:

(44)
a. Does he know any Iranians?
b. *He knows any Iranians?

(45)
a. Did it budge?
b. *It budged?

When we consider cases involving inverted aux-elements, the situation is somewhat more complicated. Questions may have either rising or falling intonation. The falling intonation case (nonrepresentational form and Subjective Nondoubt) seems to be used in circumstances in which the questioner has little personal concern in the

Further Exploration

answer, as for example, in elicitation ("quiz show") questions. Rising intonation in these cases (nonrepresentational form and Subjective Doubt) betrays the utterer's personal interest in the answer (or at least the appearance of it).

Sentences with inverted aux-elements can at times be interpreted as both (falling intonation) questions and exclamations. Intonational characteristics can in some cases resolve this ambiguity. For example, if the intonational phrase contains two falls joined by a slight rise, as represented below, the utterance is construed as an exclamation.

(46)

```
        J
Is    o        t
      h        a
       n        l
                1.
```

When we consider the role of inversion in such examples as (47) and (48), we find that the intonational facts are rather different.

(47)
What mistakes I have made.

(48)
What mistakes have I made?

Rising intonation on the first forces the interpretation that it is a (fragmentary) echo question, as in the following discourse:

(49)
A: We want to know what mis... made,
B: (quizzically): What mistakes I have made?

Falling intonation forces an exclamatory interpretation.[12]

Case (48) can easily be construed as either a rising-intonation question or a falling-intonation question, but is rather peculiar as an exclamation on either (simple) intonation (or on more complex intonational contours, for that matter).

While we will not attempt here to resolve in complete detail the rather interesting relations which hold among assertions, questions, and exclamations, the existence of the problems discussed above suggests that the English manifestations of the mapping from P to S include intonation.

In fact, this addition suggests immediate extensions. Intonation also affects the way in which imperatives are construed (e.g. the distinction between commands and (cookbook) instructions). Moreover, tags appear only on members of S, whether they are derived from P or from √P:

(50)
It's hot, isn't it.

(51)
Is John tall, isn't he.

(52)
What a mess I've made of things, haven't I.
(cf. *What a mess have I made of things, haven't I.)

(53)
Be quiet, can't you.

Based on these extensions, we revise our diagram as in 54.

(54)

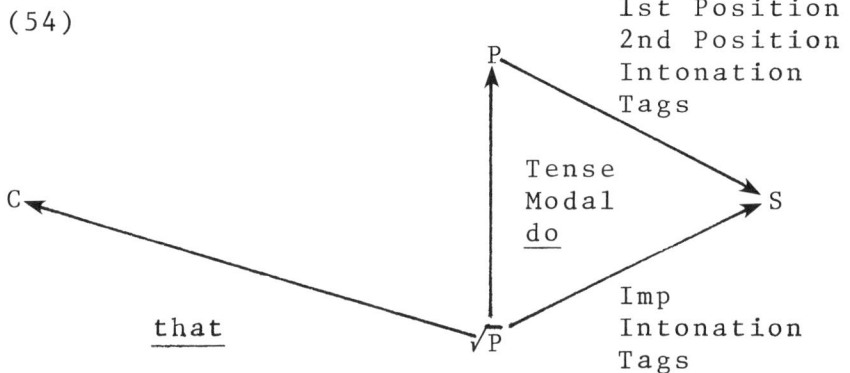

This ends our discussion of the first problem alluded to above concerning the possibility of identifying the mapping from P to S with aux-position.

The second problem we alluded to is this: in certain environments, the position of aux-elements is fixed. Most characteristically, these involve cases in which an "affective" element with maximal scope occurs before the subject (cf. Klima (1964), Liberman (1974)), as in the following examples:

(55)
a. Not once did John arrive on time.
b. With no job is John happy.   (from Liberman)
c. ≠With no job, John is happy.
d. With no job, is John happy.
   [question or exclamation corresponding to (c), not to (b)]

How to treat this problem is not clear. First, note that inversion is obligatory in sentences which tolerate the embedding of this construction.

(56)
a. We know that not once did John arrive on time.
b. *We know that not once John arrived on time.

In contrast, to the extent that the constructions with inverted aux-elements discussed above are embeddable at all (questions are, while exclamations are not, though there are verbs which take noninverted "exclamatory" <u>wh</u>-complements; cf. Grimshaw (1979)), the position of aux-elements is fixed.

Accommodation of these cases depends primarily on how non subject phrases containing an "affective" element are introduced. While we shall take no stand on this issue here, we may consider two possibilities. Notice first that instances of the construction at issue are extremely difficult to exemplify in the tenseless <u>that</u>-clause construction: <u>*It is required that with no job be he happy.</u> Hence, it is reasonable to suppose that $\sqrt{P}$ contains no such constructions. Since we know that they occur in S and also, under rather special circumstances, in C, then there are basically two possibilities, though each one admits various refinements. First, suppose that such constructions exist in P. Regardless of how they arise (two possibilities are: either (a) as a result of a mapping from $\sqrt{P}$ to P; or (b) as the result of a mapping from P to P), the formation of such constructions may be taken to fix the location of invertible aux-elements in second position, namely between the initial constituent containing the "affective" element and the subject. On this view, the domain of the 2nd-position mapping from P to S would be extended to this case and, with respect to this extension, would leave the position of 2nd-position aux-elements unaffected. At the same time, such cases would be considered to fall outside the domain of the 1st-position mapping from P to S, with the satisfactory result that there exist no questions corresponding to such cases.

Alternatively, one might assume that "root" operations in the sense of Emonds (1976) are all added in mappings from P to S. This would require a mapping from S to C by which such constructions could be embedded. The choice between these two possibilities or between either of them and some other possibility depends, then, on how these matters are to be treated. We leave the issue open.

Now let us consider in more detail the syntactic form of subordinate clauses, which we divide into those based on P and those based on $\sqrt{P}$. To the first class belong only indicative that-clauses, that-relatives, and tensed wh-complements. We assume that these are all the result of mappings from P to C. The exact formulation of these mappings depends on how one treats the variable binding problems of wh-movement and relativization. Aside from this question, certain facts concerning tense and modality warrant attention.

First, the position of modals in such contexts is always fixed. We could take this to be a property of the various mappings from P to C or, in accordance with one of the alternatives mentioned above, assume that modals in members of P have a fixed position.

Regardless of how this issue is to be resolved, it is also a fact that under certain circumstances, the interpretation of tense and modals in members of C may differ from their interpretation in main clauses. (57) and (58) provide examples of this:

(57)
John said that I might use his car.
(report of John asserting, "You may use my car.")

(58)
John said that Bill would be here on the third.
(report of John saying, "Bill will be here on the third.")

This phenomenon has often been described by invoking a "sequence of tense" rule which converts a subordinate present tense form to a corresponding past tense form when the immediately dominating verb is also past. This seems correct with respect to the environment; but if there is such a rule, it is neither obligatory nor purely syntactic, for both of the following sentences are good, yet (at least pragmatically) distinct.

(59)
a. John said that Bill will be here at six.
b. John said that Bill would be here at six.

However this phenomenon is to be analyzed, it is not necessarily an isolated one. Even in members of S, the "deontic space" of modals such as must, may, and shall is identified with the speaker in assertions, but with the addressee in questions.

These observations suggest that modals are interpretable only relative to indices which specify an individual and a time. We shall assume that these indices may be variable in P, but must be fixed in any interpretable occurrence of tense or modality. Mappings from P to S fix the interpretation of these indices: tense may be specified relative either to the indices associated with the utterer (at the time of utterance) or to those of the addressee (at the time of interpretation);[13] modality is associated with the answerer of questions rather than the utterer, but with the utterer in the case of assertions. Finally, in certain subordinate contexts, tense and modality may be (but need not be) associated with the indices of the event designated by the superordinate clause. We shall leave open how this is to be done.

We turn now to a more complete specification of the mappings from $\sqrt{P}$ to C. We have already assumed that tenseless <u>that</u>-clauses are formed from members of $\sqrt{P}$ by simply adding <u>that</u> on the left. In addition, we need to recognize the formation of various types of infinitive and possibly of various types of participles and gerunds.

Obviously, we cannot do justice in a short space to the full complexity of the interesting issues which investigation of these problems has brought to light. Rather, we shall comment here on those problems in which issues concerning the instantiations in English of AUX are particularly salient.

There are two crucial, interrelated questions which arise at the very outset: namely, what are (a) the syntactic relations and (b) the semantic relations between complement-types which contain a recognizable complementizer and a subject and complement-types which lack a subject and/or complementizer. In its syntactic guise, the question may be posed by asking whether <u>to go</u> and <u>for him to go</u> belong to the same syntactic type (at some stage of derivation). In its semantic guise, this question may be illustrated by considering whether or not the expressions following <u>want</u> in the contexts ...<u>want to go</u>... and ...<u>want for him to go</u>... are of the same logical type.

While it is easy to conflate these two problems, they are really independent of each other, theoretical predispositions aside. Thus, in the following two cases, the expression <u>that John left</u> seems to be syntactically the same, though clearly its evaluation may be taken to be distinct.

(60)
a. That John left is annoying.
b. That John left is obvious.

Similarly, such cases as (61a) and (61b) at least raise the possibility that the interpretation of subjectless infinitival complements need not be taken to be identical to the interpretation of subject-containing complements.

(61)
a. John expects himself to quit.
b. John expects to quit.

For, even assuming that in (61a) we interpret expect as a relation between entities with a (possibly collective) will and a propositional representation of some kind, it is still possible in principle to interpret (61b) either analogously or as a relation between such entities and an action.

The semantic side of this issue thus depends in part on whether or not every instance of a subjectless complement can be explicated in terms which apply to comparable complements endowed with subjects. Yet, as we shall see, even if there are significant differences between the interpretations assigned to subjectless complements and to those with subjects and/or complementizers, these differences need not be attributed to the logical type of the complement expression.

On the syntactic side, there seem to be three possibilities:

(62)
a. In subjectless complements, there is always a syntactic expression which is deleted in the course of the derivation of the sentence containing the complement.

b. In subjectless complements, there is a phantom variable expression which has no phonological shape, and whose value is specified in the analysis of sentences in which it appears.

c. In subjectless complements, there is never
any syntactic subject present at any stage
of the derivation.

There are certain conditions under which alternative (62b) collapses with one of the other two--namely, where the syntax does not require that there be a subject in order to countenance the existence of a verb phrase of some kind. Under these conditions, the grammatical behavior of a phantom syntactic variable may either be identified with the behavior of an actually existing element or not. If so, then there is no reason to assume the existence of a variable. If not, its behavior may be taken to be a purely semantic problem.

The view that we shall adopt on these questions is this: subjectless VP-complements are always to be assessed as propositional representations; subjectless VP-complements always lack a syntactic subject; any possible semantic difference which arises between contexts in which subjectless complements may alternate with complements containing subjects is attributable to different ways in which the "subject" of the propositional representation is specified.

The justification for these views is that: (a) we shall show how it is possible to provide a syntax for English complementation which does not require the syntactic presence of subjects; (b) the assumption that subjectless complements are not evaluated as propositional representations of some kind leads to unnecessary metaphysical complications; and (c) any semantic difference which arises between subjectless complements and analogous complements which contain a subject may be attributed to other factors.

The last claim is entirely analogous to the fact that differences in interpretation may arise in simple transitive sentences of the form $\underline{NP_1 \; V \; NP_2}$, when we compare cases in which NP_2 is a reflexive pronoun with those in which it is not--differences in interpretation which are not attributable solely to referential distinctions. This is particularly obvious in cases which, like many of the cases which embed VP-complements where such differences may be observed, involve concepts having to do with physical sensation or mental consciousness. As an example, in the following cases, the pairs of sentences are not fully semantically compatible in their range of readings if we make allowance only for referential differences.

(63)
a. I cut John.
b. I cut myself.

(64)
a. I don't know John.
b. I don't know myself.

Thus, it is reasonable to assume that if a verb, for example, carries with it the requirement that it obligatorily specify some binding relation between its arguments, then it may carry a different value than it carries in cases in which no such binding relation is forced.

It is perhaps worthwhile to illustrate how these claims are distinguished from other possible accounts. Some researchers (for example, Fodor (1975)) have concluded that complements without subjects are always formed from clauses containing a subject, and have identified the subject with a reflexive pronoun. Yet there are many cases that differ by having either a reflexive pronoun (possibly preceded by <u>for</u>) or ∅ in which the interpretations can easily be distinguished. For example, consider the following sentences:

(65)
  a. I want to sneeze.
≠ b. I want myself to sneeze.

(66)
  a. I expect to get as far as Mile 20.
≠ b. I expect myself to get as far as Mile 20.

(67)
  a. I remember giving the speech about blood, sweat,

and all that.
≠ b. I remember myself giving the speech about blood, sweat, and all that.

In (65), for example, if one wants to experience what it is like to sneeze, (b) is rather inappropriate, for it seems to emphasize that what one wants is merely that a certain state of affairs (i.e. "my sneezing") exist. Similarly, in saying (66a) one is reconciled with fate, whereas in uttering (66b) one states that one's body may be in conflict with one's spirit. Finally, (67b) might be true if one's memories were based solely on the recollection of a television broadcast of the speech, whereas (67a) would not be true under such circumstances--to say (67a) requires that the experience of actually giving the speech be recalled.

Although all of these cases trade on <u>Ich-Spaltung</u> (that is, there is a split induced between ego and body), it is nevertheless the case that there are differences in the uses of reflexives (which allow Ich-Spaltung and in some cases require it) and the uses of the null element (which never allows Ich-Spaltung).

In order to make Fodor's view responsible to the facts, then, it is necessary to suppose two things: first, that a distinction may be made between cases where the reflexive pronoun is present and those where it is not, in which case some of the original motivation for assuming that the subject is to be identified with a reflexive pronoun disappears; second, that it must be possible in some cases (e.g. <u>try</u>) to ensure that a reflexive pronoun which must be deleted occurs in the subject position of the infinitival expression. Since there is no reason to expect that these two suppositions are dependent, we should find verbs which require the presence of a reflexive in such a position but do not require that it be deleted. To our knowledge, no such cases exist. Moreover, as we shall see, there is a natural and general restriction which prohibits a verb from restricting the properties of a subject of a complement within the domain of a complementizer.

If this restriction is imposed, then the approach to complementation advocated by Fodor cannot be correct.

Let us assume then that there are higher predicates in English which embed infinitives having intrinsically bound subjects. We include among these both the cases of obligatory Equi (like <u>try</u>, <u>persuade</u>, and <u>promise</u>) and the cases of Raising (like <u>seem</u> and <u>believe</u>). The conflation of these cases raises the second salient question which we should like to address: namely, what is it that is bound in these cases?

The standard treatment, insofar as it is workable at all, assumes that the problem to be solved is the subject-binding problem. This is inadequate for two reasons. First, the "bound" subject may have to play a specific "thematic" role with respect to the propositional structure of the complement. Second, assuming as we did above that the embedded clauses are propositional in some sense, there is always a temporal relation specified between the temporal structure of the embedding predicate and the (relative and perhaps unrealized) temporal structure of the embedded propositional clause. We shall illustrate both of these points in some detail.

First, it is well known that many verbs seem to embed "action"-infinitival complements (i.e. those whose propositional structure requires that the bound variable in the complement's subject position be construed as a volitional agent relative to the way in which the satisfaction conditions of the complement are construed with respect to the verb). Nevertheless, no standard way of expressing this fact has evolved. Thus, while one may say <u>John broke the glass</u> under a variety of circumstances, including those in which John inadvertently broke the glass (perhaps by closing the dishwasher door on it in the dark by mistake), still, if one says <u>John tried to break the glass</u>, then it must be the case that he endeavored to bring it about that actions of his performed with the intention of breaking the glass would succeed. It would be rather odd to say that John tried to break the glass under circumstances in which he asked his friends to hurl him at the glass, even if he asked them to hurl him at the glass in such a way as to break it.

Thus, one cannot adequately describe the interpretation of the structures in which <u>try</u> occurs by simply referring to a certain binding condition which holds between the subject of <u>try</u> and the assumed subject of the embedded infinitive phrase. More is obviously necessary. One might suggest that the propositional whole of the embedded infinitive be construed as an action, in whatever sense one might use that term, or one might say that <u>try</u> embeds only an infinitive VP which is construed as an action. But it is equally simple to require that the intrinsically bound subject of the embedded infinitival complement be construed as a volitional agent[14] relative to the rest of the (infinitival) proposition. Thus, suppose we allow a mapping from $\sqrt{P}$ to C, the result of which is expressions of the following kind:

(68)

$\underline{x}$ to   VP
volitional
   agent

The verb <u>try</u> is one that embeds such expressions to its right, identifying the intrinsically bound variable $\underline{x}$ with its subject.

In this regard, it is useful to compare a certain problem of Kajita's (1968), whose solution is due to Higgins (1973). Kajita was concerned with certain questions raised in Chomsky (1965) concerning the depth of subcategorization. He noted that there were verbs which seem to embed only transitive infinitival complements. Among his examples were sentences like (69a,b):

(69)
a. The ice served to chill the beer.
b. *The ice served to melt.

Clearly, both of the following sentences are good:

(70)
a. The ice chilled the beer.
b. The ice melted.

As a result, it is evident here (as in the case of _try_ discussed above) that further information is necessary. Kajita suggested that the requisite added information was that the embedded infinitive be a transitive verb phrase. But this is too general, for it would allow such sentences as (71):

(71)
*John served to meet Max for dinner.

Instead, the correct requirement seems to be that the intrinsically bound subject of the infinitival phrase be (thematically) an instrument. Since there are no intransitive sentences in which the subject can be construed as an instrument, this restriction accounts for Kajita's observation: he was correct in pointing out that there are certain verbs which embed only transitive infinitival complements, but he was incorrect in suggesting that this fact could be expressed in terms of subcategorization.
  If we assume that _try_ binds an embedded volitional agent to its subject and that _serve_ binds an embedded instrumental agent to its subject, we account completely for the "selectional" restrictions on the subjects of these two verbs. Note that these restrictions are independently necessary, for we cannot account for the facts by assuming that only the binding relation is required. Thus, grammars are considerably simplified if they do not need to state these requirements independently. As a result, we may ask how those verbs which bind an intrinsically bound subject may differ with respect to the "thematic" role of the intrinsically bound subject of the infinitival phrase. In English, it appears that only three thematic relations are called for: volitional agent, instrument, and free. The free cases are the so-called Raising verbs. In the system addressed here, these three types embed clauses of the following kinds:

Further Exploration

(72)
a. try to VP ⊢→ $\underline{x}$ try' ($\underline{x}$ to VP')
                          volitional
                          agent

b. serve to VP ⊢→ $\underline{x}$ serve' ($\underline{x}$ to VP')
                              instrument

c. seem to VP ⊢→ $\underline{x}$ seem' ($\underline{x}$ to VP')

For all three types, there also exist transitive counterparts:

(73)
a. persuade np$_{\underline{x}}$ to VP ⊢→
   $\underline{y}$ persuade' $\underline{x}$ ($\underline{x}$ to VP')
                                volitional
                                agent

b. use np$_{\underline{x}}$ to VP ⊢→
   $\underline{y}$ use' $\underline{x}$ ($\underline{x}$ to VP')
                          instrument

c. believe np$_{\underline{x}}$ to VP ⊢→
   $\underline{y}$ believe' $\underline{x}$ ($\underline{x}$ to VP')

(where $\underline{x}$ and $\underline{y}$ are semantic variables which range over individuals, and where we use the notation $\underline{e}$ to represent the interpretation of a syntactic expression $\underline{e}$)

There are two alternatives to stating the requisite relations in this fashion. First, we could assume that there are "agentive propositions", "instrumental propositions", and possibly "free propositions" (if no distinction is made between equi phenomena and raising phenomena), on the further assumption that semantically such verbs as <u>try</u>, <u>serve</u>, <u>seem</u>, <u>persuade</u>, <u>use</u>, <u>believe</u>, etc., have access only to the value of the constituents that they embed and that these are propositional constituents ("S"). Second, adopting the same assumptions about semantic composition, we could consider that such verbs embed only VPs and we could distinguish among "agentive VPs" (i.e. phrases which denote "actions"), "instrumental VPs" (i.e. phrases whose denotation is anything but obvious), and "free VPs" (phrases which denote functions from properties to truth values). Thus, insofar as there is any reason to think that various arguments to verbs may be distinguished according to thematic relations of any sort, the alternative we have adopted seems to be the most reasonable, as it relies only on access to the thematic role of various arguments within a proposition, information which seems to be independently justified to some extent.

However this phenomenon is to be treated, it intersects with the second problem mentioned above concerning the adequacy of standard assumptions about the syntax of infinitival complements, namely, the problem of the temporal relation between embedding predicate and embedded proposition. Consider first a sentence such as (74):

(74)
John wants to open the door.

Suppose that we construe the infinitival complement propositionally in some sense (it would be more accurate to say $\sqrt{\text{propositionally}}$ or $\sqrt{P}$ -ly). If John wants at the present moment to open the door, his (stated) desire will be satisfied if in fact he opens the door sometime in the future. Similarly, if one were to utter (75),

(75)
John wanted to open the door.

John's (stated) desire would be satisfied if he opened the door in the future relative to the tense referent, i.e. future relative to the moment when the desire is said to occur. Violation of this temporal relation induces strangeness:

(76)
*John wants to open the door yesterday.

With respect to the classification of verbs according to the thematic properties of the subject of the embedded proposition discussed above, want is free: it embeds clauses in which the subject may play any thematic role. In this way, it differs from try, which binds only volitional agents. In fact, want seems to require of its own subject that it be capable of desire, but there is no obligatory relation between the subject of want and the subject of the infinitival proposition that it binds. Yet want does impose relative temporal restrictions on the realization of the embedded infinitival propositional complement: namely, that its realization (if it is realized) is relatively future to the time at which the desire indicated by want holds.

Suppose that every member of $\sqrt{P}$ contains a temporal variable whose value is fixed by any operation which maps a member of $\sqrt{P}$ to either P or S. Moreover, suppose that this variable is carried over into C by any mapping from $\sqrt{P}$ to C and that whenever a member of C is embedded this temporal variable must be given a value relative to the value of the temporal variable of the embedding symbol. Assuming that for all members of S it is possible to specify a temporal coordinate at which the propositional content within S is judged, it follows that every embedded member of C within S will inherit some relation to this temporal coordinate.[15] Let us use the following notation to represent such relations: to the left of every verb of a propositional radical, we shall attach a symbol of the form t_x, which is to be construed as a temporal variable. When a member of C is embedded under a given symbol (here we deal for the most part only with verbs and in some cases adjectives), the temporal variable attached to C will be specified relative to the temporal variable attached to the head of the embedding member of $\sqrt{P}$ in which it is embedded. To illustrate this notation, we represent the embedding of an intrinsically bound infinitive phrase under want as in (77).

Just as different infinitive-embedding predicates may vary with respect to the thematic function

(77)
want to VP $\longmapsto$ $\underline{x}$ $\underline{t_y}$ want' ($\underline{x}$ $\underline{t_z}$ VP')

(where $t_y < t_z$; that is, the temporal coordinate of the embedded infinitive is future with respect to the temporal coordinate of the clause under which it is embedded)

obligatorily assigned to the bound subject of the infinitive, so they may vary with respect to the relations between the temporal coordinate of the embedding clause and the temporal coordinate of the embedded clause. Consider the verb <u>manage</u>, for example. It is well known that if one asserts (78), then one is committed to the truth of (79):

(78)
John managed to win the game.

(79)
John won the game.

In fact, if it is true that John managed to win the game, then it becomes true as soon as the sentence <u>John won the game</u> is true. We can describe this fact by assuming that in this case, the temporal coordinates of the embedding clause and the embedded clause are identified, which we represent as:

(80)
manage to VP $\longmapsto$ $\underline{x}$ $\underline{t_y}$ manage' ($\underset{\text{volitional agent}}{\underline{x}}$ $\underline{t_y}$ VP')

One consequence of this assumption is the strangeness of such sentences as (81a,b):

(81)
a. Yesterday, John managed to win the match whose outcome was decided two weeks ago.
b. John managed to leave tomorrow.

If these sentences make sense, they must be construed in such a way that, in the first case,

John managed to change the outcome of the match yesterday or, in the second, that he managed to arrange things so that he leaves tomorrow.

In principle, similar relations between temporal coordinates should account for the well-known fact that <u>seem</u> and <u>believe</u> constrain the temporal coordinates of the infinitival phrases embedded beneath them. Thus, compare the following cases:

(82)
a. John wants to hit Bill.

b. John seems to hit Bill.

   (= either It seems to be the case that John hits Bill (generically), or It seems that John hits Bill (as used for example to provide running commentary to a videotape))

   (≠ It seems that John will hit Bill.)

c. I believe John to hit Bill.

   (= I believe that John hits Bill.)

A complete analysis of such cases requires a deeper inquiry into the relation between temporal coordinates and the various <u>Aktionsarten</u> by which the standard interpretations of various verbs may in part be classified.

There is at least one other way in which verbs that embed intrinsically bound infinitival phrases may differ: the binding relation between an element in the higher clause and the bound element in the lower clause is not a homogeneous one. In particular, we can distinguish several different relations of "nondistinctness" which may hold. The most well-known example of such distinctions involves sentences such as (83), (84), and (85):

(83)
Senator Eastland moved to adjourn.

(84)
John wanted to meet at noon.

(85)
John voted to disperse.

In such cases the selectional restrictions of the infinitival phrase are incompatible with an individual subject. Hence, on semantic grounds, if such infinitival complements are to be construed propositionally, they must be endowed with a subject which does not designate an individual. Moreover, such a subject is clearly not completely independent of the binding NP of the embedding clause; in fact, the referent of the matrix subject in each of these cases must be construed as belonging to the plurality relative to which the interpretation of the infinitival complement is assessed. Suppose that we represent these cases as follows:

(86)
$\underline{x}\ \underline{t}_{\underline{y}}$ move to VP $\longmapsto$ $\underline{x}\ \underline{t}_{\underline{y}}$ move' $(\underline{X}\ \underline{t}_{\underline{z}}\ VP')$
$\underline{t}_{\underline{y}} \leq \underline{t}_{\underline{z}}$, and $\underline{x} \in \underline{X}$

(87)
$\underline{x}\ \underline{t}_{\underline{y}}$ want to VP $\longmapsto$ $\underline{x}\ \underline{t}_{\underline{y}}$ want' $(\underline{X}\ \underline{t}_{\underline{z}}\ VP')$
$\underline{t}_{\underline{y}} \leq \underline{t}_{\underline{z}}$, and $\underline{x} \in \underline{X}$

(88)
$\underline{x}$ vote to VP $\longmapsto$ $\underline{x}\ \underline{t}_{\underline{y}}$ vote' $(\underline{X}\ \underline{t}_{\underline{z}}\ VP')$
$\underline{t}_{\underline{y}} \leq \underline{t}_{\underline{z}}$, and $\underline{x} \in \underline{X}$

It is worth noting here that in every case in which a matrix variable binds a superset in the embedded clause, there is a fixed relation between the temporal coordinates of the embedding structure and the embedded structure. Moreover, in all these cases the embedded propositional structure denotes a collective action. Whether these regularities have deeper significance or are only accidental, we will not attempt to decide here.

On the assumption that infinitives occur only when the temporal coordinate associated with the propositional structure they represent is bound, we can easily conclude that infinitives may never contain an independent aux-operator such as Tense or Modal. For insofar as the value of Tense or Modal fixes the temporal coordinate in the propositional structures in which they occur, if a propositional structure contained both a bound instance of to and Tense or Modal, its temporal coordinate would be doubly specified. We assume that this is as meaningless as a sentence which is supersaturated with arguments, such as *John died the mule, on an interpretation in which died is a one-place predicate. In this sense, it is possible to count to as a kind of surrogate aux-element, one which bears functional affinities with tense and modals, but whose distribution is completely disjoint from them. Thus, it is not surprising that Tense and Modal belong to an entirely different branch of our diagram for English than does the infinitival marker:

(89)

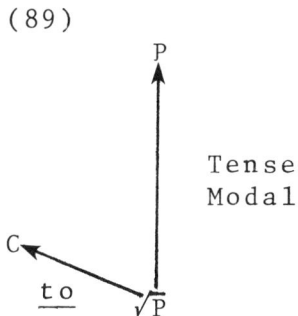

   Although the remarks we have made concerning infinitival complementation touch on only a few of the problems of subordination in general, and while we shall neither elaborate on the general problem here nor attempt to work out in more detail the consequences of pursuing this program of research, we have nevertheless tried to show that the general diagram of English propositional structures yields an interesting perspective in which to view certain questions concerning the behavior of English aux-elements. We may summarize the preceding discussion in the diagram in (90).

(90)

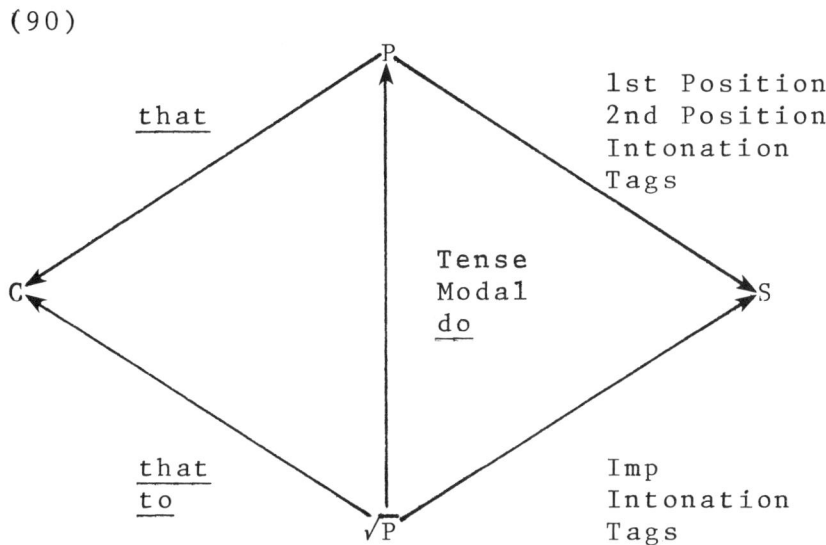

If a more complete account along these lines can be achieved for English, we may gain new insight into classical problems of English syntax, and we will have done so in a way that allows interesting comparisons to be made between certain operators in English and the operators of other languages which can be described in an analogous way. Regarding the distinctions which exist among S, P, $\sqrt{P}$, and C, English is obviously typologically distinct from Luiseño, both with respect to the form of the diagram itself and with respect to the distribution of those of its elements which instantiate Aux in it.

4.3.4 Conclusion We are well aware that the proposals of section 4.2 and the analyses of Luiseño and English in this chapter are less a completed picture and more like the preliminary sketches which precede it. Yet the final shape is clear. Luiseño and English exemplify two of the four possible schemas given in section 4.2; furthermore, the schemas provide an elegant way of distinguishing among a variety of phenomena in either language--and predicting some of these distinctions. In short, the discussion of this section at once supports the proposals of the preceding one and opens up a new avenue for investigation.

However, our major concern is the category AUX. The distinctions which we have proposed and the distribution of the instantiations of AUX within them are consistent with the hypothesis presented at the end of chapter 3: that AUX provides a judgment about the sentence. They symbol $\underline{S}$, as defined in section 4.2, identifies both sentences with a truth value (questions and declaratives) and sentences without (imperatives). As pointed out in the discussion of both Luiseño and English, this division must be amplified, perhaps in language-particular ways. However, the Luiseño facts suggest the following generalization:

(91)
($\forall$ S)   (S has truth value —> S contains AUX)

This generalization may also hold for English; however, as discussed in appendix A, the decision as to precisely what comprises the English Aux depends on the definition of <u>constituent</u>. Therefore, it is possible that generalization (91) does not hold for English; if not, the English facts suggest instead the following one.

(92)
($\forall$ S)   (S has AUX —> S has a truth value)

Whether we are required to posit both of these generalizations or only the first, we have given substance to the hypothesis proposed at the end of chapter 3.

We have shown in chapters 1, 2, and 3 how to provide equivalence across languages. We have argued that equivalence is the required notion, since there is no identity across the elements and categories of languages. The preceding discussion of Luiseño and English argues that even when we provide a classification which depends entirely on semantic criteria--and try to predict syntactic (and morphological) facts from it--what we have argued to be language-particular instantiations of AUX retain some differences. English and Luiseño share a

Further Exploration

number of mappings, since the difference between the two schemas which represent them is the presence in English of a mapping between P and C and its absence in Luiseño. The material which represents the mapping within the two languages is different--in both a trivial and a nontrivial sense. Clearly, the morphological material is different; for example, English has no <u>nik</u>. Much more critically, the mappings are not isomorphic. That is, while the mapping between $\sqrt{P}$ and P in English is the addition of some member of the English instantiation of AUX, the same mapping involves no members of the instantiation of AUX in Luiseño. And while the mapping between P and S in Luiseño is the addition of a member of the Luiseño instantiation of AUX, in English the same mapping does not add a member of the English instantiation of AUX, but rather fixes its position or gives an intonation contour. Thus, although both Luiseño and English can be shown to have an instantiation of AUX--see chapter 2 and appendix A--there is no isomorphism between the two in terms of the schema we have proposed.

However, the schemas in (4) through (7) of this chapter and the discussion of Luiseño and English do suggest certain hypotheses concerning the category AUX and the proposed semantic classification. First, the English instantiation of AUX is added only on the $\sqrt{P}$ to P mapping and the Luiseño instantiation of AUX is added on either the P to S or the $\sqrt{P}$ to S mapping. We hypothesize that AUX may be added only on these mappings and that these two languages therefore exhaust the universal possibilities.

Hypothesis I:

Any instantiation of AUX is restricted to $\sqrt{P} \longrightarrow P$
                                            $\sqrt{P} \longrightarrow S$
                                    and $P \longrightarrow S$

(Alternatively, we could state that AUX will never be the mapping between $\sqrt{P}$ and C, or P and C.) Second, in English all the aux-elements are confined to a particular mapping, and were English the only language under investigation, we might propose the following hypothesis.

Hypothesis II:

There is a single mapping to which all instantiations of Aux in a particular language are restricted.

However, in Luiseño the instantiation of AUX is distributed across two mappings, and therefore hypothesis II is immediately invalidated. The interesting thing about Luiseño is that no single element which falls within AUX--no single member of the Particle Complex--occurs on more than a single mapping. Hypothesis II is consistent with the English facts, but is not valid for Luiseño; hypothesis II' is consistent with the facts of both languages, and we suggest that it holds more generally across the set AUX.

Hypothesis II':

Any element which is a member of some instantiation of Aux is restricted to a single mapping.

Should these hypotheses hold across a wider sample--and they appear to be supported in the other languages discussed in chapter 2--there is at least preliminary evidence that they uniquely identify AUX among the various possible elements which give the mappings. First, English and Luiseño both provide examples of mappings, other than the language-particular instantiations of AUX, which do not conform to hypothesis I. There are elements in both languages which occur only on those mappings where the elements of AUX will not (for example, that in English and nik in Luiseño). There are elements in Luiseño, the possessive and the absolutive, which occur on the mapping from to P but are not restricted to the mappings given for AUX in hypothesis I. Finally, there appear to be elements (for example, certain English intonation contours and English tags) whose mappings are a proper subset of those available to an instantiation of AUX.

Second, both English and Luiseño provide examples of various elements, other than the language-particular instantiations of AUX, which do not conform to hypothesis II'. Neither intonation nor tags are unique to a particular mapping in English; more important, it is not the case that intonation and tags can each be divided into two subsets, one of which is exclusive to the mapping between P and S and the other exclusive to the mapping between $\sqrt{P}$ and S. Similarly, in Luiseño, neither the possessive nor the absolutive is unique to a particular mapping; more significantly, all possessive prefixes and all absolutive suffixes can occur on both the $\sqrt{P}$ to C and the $\sqrt{P}$ to P mappings.

Obviously, the claim that the AUX can be uniquely identified (in regard to the various mapping possibilities) by hypotheses I and II' ultimately depends on a more exhaustive consideration of the other types of elements which can provide some mapping and their various distributional properties with respect to schemas (4) through (7). However, the Luiseño and English data are fully in accord with this result of the hypotheses above.

Corollary I:

Aux (and other elements which provide mappings) are uniquely identifiable relative to their distribution among the possible branches.

This discussion raises a number of interesting questions, and it is with these that we will conclude our investigation. If AUX can provide the mapping between $\sqrt{P}$ and P, between P and S, and between $\sqrt{P}$ and S (hypothesis I) and if, language-internally, AUX is not limited to a single mapping, but rather can be distributed among these three mappings, in a manner consonant with hypothesis II', then the seven possibilities given below in (93) are logically possible. That is, logically, a language could represent one of seven types, with respect to its instantiation of AUX.

(93)
a. $\sqrt{P} \longrightarrow P$

b. $P \longrightarrow S$

c. $\sqrt{P} \longrightarrow S$

d. $\sqrt{P} \longrightarrow P$, $P \longrightarrow S$

e. $\sqrt{P} \longrightarrow P$, $\sqrt{P} \longrightarrow S$

f. $P \longrightarrow S$, $\sqrt{P} \longrightarrow S$

g. $\sqrt{P} \longrightarrow P$, $P \longrightarrow S$, $\sqrt{P} \longrightarrow S$

Whether all of these logically possible types are in fact realized is an open question at the moment. Clearly, (93a) and (93f) are realized; on the other hand, we have serious doubts that (93c) will be. We need not speculate about the realization of these seven possibilities, however; it is an empirical question, and the procedure by which it can be resolved is obvious. The answer is clearly of linguistic interest; that is, if some of these logical possibilities are not realized, we have to ask why.

The classification in (93) raises another interesting possibility. In (7) in chapter 3, we listed a set of properties which provide a language-independent characterization of the category AUX. Although an explanation may exist for at least some of those properties, as we discussed at the end of that chapter, we left open the question of whether it was possible to predict when a language-particular instantiation of AUX might exhibit some subset of them. In fact, in terms of any standard typological considerations, it is generally impossible to predict some property of a language's instantiation of AUX from some other one of its properties. The classification in (93) is not a standard typology; but we see at least a promising possibility that it will afford some insight into the distribution of the properties listed at the end of chapter 3.

4.4 Final Remarks

The basic distinction between the cross-linguistic equivalence class AUX and its language-particular members can arise only within the kind of framework for cross-linguistic investigation that we have proposed in chapter 1. In later chapters, we have shown that this framework produces significant results: the definition of AUX with which we began need not have been instantiated, but it is; the language-particular instantiations of AUX need not have shared any properties aside from the definitional ones, but they do. Nevertheless, we cannot regard these results as definitive and final: obvious questions arise, although in many cases they are questions which could not have been clearly formulated prior to this investigation.

First, investigations of languages beyond our sample might require that the set of properties which are associated with the category AUX be revised. More importantly, it might be possible, especially in view of the proposals made in this chapter, to provide a better definition of the phenomenon we have labeled AUX. Finally, and most importantly, our definition rests on the notions "tense", "modality", and "constituent". Insofar as these notions are clear, our results are solid. If our results are not clear, the lack of clarity is transmitted to our inability to pick out elements of language which satisfy these notions. To the extent that these notions are clear and clearly applied in this work, they provide fertile ground for further investigations of the abstract basis of the notions "tense" and "modality". By the same token, to the extent that the language-particular expressions which we have taken to fall under our definition are tendentious choices, then our results make it equally possible to clarify such notions as "constituent" and "category", notions which are, after all, equally as abstract as (or more abstract than) "tense" and "modality", since they are defined only relative to theoretical assumptions and are not intrinsically given by the phenomenon under investigation.

Notes

1. Whether this is the right assumption to adopt is not at all clear. One would like in some simple fashion to constrain the possible mappings which relate members of the objects S, P, $\sqrt{P}$, and C, for otherwise the problems rapidly become intractable. As a result, we have tried to construct a postulate which entails that there are never mappings both from X to Y and from Y to X. One difficulty is that the notion "semantic additivity" is far from clear on intuitive grounds alone. This suggests that a syntactic condition be incorporated as well; among the possibilities are a strong form (mappings are always syntactically additive) and a weak form (mappings are never syntactically nonadditive). We have chosen the middle course by including the weaker of the two syntactic conditions. However, we have done so with reservations, in part because everything hinges on one's characterization of the members of $\sqrt{P}$. The impact of these issues will be seen in the discussion of English. Where they make themselves felt, we have briefly touched on the relation of the problems at hand to the problems which arise in formulating the correct postulate. This has led to various inconsistencies which we take to be manifestations of the fact that our approach is relatively new and not as evidence of inherent weakness. Our goal is to show that this point of view opens new and promising avenues of research. And to the extent that this is the case, we have been willing to tolerate a somewhat fluid position at various points.

2. The Luiseño absolutives obviously form three pairs, as suggested in (15), where one member of the pair has a final vowel /a/ and the other does not. However, there is no obvious way to predict which member of a pair a particular "stem" will take, any more than there is an obvious way to predict the initial consonant of the absolutive. That is, "stems" must be lexically specified for the particular absolutive they will take.

3. (16) is meant to illustrate that, relative to these three affix types, some "stems" take only the possessive, other only the absolutive or only tense/aspect, and still others only the possessive and the absolutive. Some "stems" may take other affix types as well (some of which will be discussed below), but these other affix types are always secondary in the sense that there is no set of "stems" which takes one of them and only that one. That is, any "stem" which takes one of these other affixes will also allow at least one of the three affix types given in (16). While Steele (1980) discusses the interaction of "stems" and affixes, the position taken here represents a significant revision of that earlier paper.

4. This is a relatively complex aspect of Luiseño which we have only recently begun to understand. It is quite clear that "stems" can be formally specified for which of these three affixes (and a few others) they allow. However, every "stem" must also be lexically specified for the arguments it allows or requires in terms of these affix types. For example, _miy_ 'be' requires an absolutive-marked or a possessive-marked form.

(i)
ya'ash   up   paapavi-sh   miyq
man   Prt:Com   thirsty-ABSOLUTIVE   is
'The man is thirsty.'

(ii)
ya'ash   up   po-ngeepi   miyq
man   Prt:Com   POSSESSIVE-leave:future   is
'The man has to leave.'

This last fact (that the argument structure of Luiseño can be specified in terms of the affixes--and not in any other terms) supports our characterization of them as syntactic operators.

5. There are sentences which appear to lack any of the three, specifically sentences in which the "head of the predicate" takes the aspectual suffix _ma_.

(i)
xwaan   up   heyi-ma
John   Prt:Com   dig-MA
'John digs (often or habitually).'

However, there is good reason to treat this suffix in (i) as complex, as ma + a, where a is a variant of the q/wun or an suffix given in (8). The vowel sequence aa is shortened word-finally; long unstressed vowels do not occur word-finally in Luiseño. The otherwise irregular form qala is to be analyzed in the same fashion.

(ii)
noo   p   notoonav   qala
I   Prt:Com   my:basket   QALA-A
'I have a basket.'

The suffix ma (without the a tense suffix) can also precede quś, uk, and an in (8):

(iii)
xwaan   po   heyi-ma-an
John   Prt:Com   dig-MA-AN
'John will be digging.'

Therefore, ma can precede any of the suffixes in (8) which admit the possibility that the action described in the sentence continues over an extended period of time; 'ya/ax alone of the suffixes in (8) does not--and ma does not cooccur with it.

6. The absolutive suffixes and possessive prefixes are different from the tense/aspect suffixes, however, in that there may be elements within $\sqrt{P}$ which include the former; the latter are always added on the $\sqrt{P}$ to P mapping. This point concerning the absolutive and possessive was implicit in footnote 4, since we noted there that "stems" can be lexically specified in Luiseño to take an absolutive-marked or a possessive-marked form.

7. Sentences like (13a,b) and (14a,b) in which the "head of the predicate" is marked with the

possessive and the absolutive, respectively, also do not allow a Particle Complex with xu.

(i)
```
*noo   xu-po              no-tooyax
 I     XU-Subj:Mark-prt:3 POSSESSIVE-laugh
```

(ii)
```
*noo   xu-n-po
 I     XU-Subj:Mark-prt:3

heyilu-t
dig:temporal:reference-ABSOLUTIVE
```

8. The negative imperative form tuṣṣu may mark number, so (24b) can also be expressed as (i):

(i)
```
tuṣṣu-m              heyi-yam
neg:imperative-PL    dig-pl:imperative
'Don't dig (plural)!'
```

Also, when tuṣṣu is marked with m, the plural imperative suffix on heyi can be absent.

(ii)
```
tuṣṣu-m              heyi
neg:imperative-PL    dig
'Don't dig (plural)!'
```

9. There may be relative clauses in which the "head of the predicate" of the relative clause is marked with a postposition, rather than with a possessive or an absolutive. However, we have not yet resolved the intricacies of this particular aspect of Luiseño, and we must leave this possibility open.

10. (32) correctly represents the various elements we have discussed; however, there is one aspect of Luiseño which it does not specify. The indeterminateness on this point results from the fact that we have not given any precise characterization of what we take $\sqrt{P}$ to be in Luiseño.

In brief, the question is whether a subject must be included in $\sqrt{P}$ or whether subjects can be added as part of some mapping. We mentioned in footnote 4 that "stems" in Luiseño--i.e. those forms which lack any of the various affix types--must be lexically specified for the arguments they allow or require in terms of these affix types. Thus, <u>miy</u>, for example, can be given the following lexical specification.

(i)
[X + Absolutive_____]
[X + Possessive_____]

This excludes one argument, what we will call the "subject". In Steele (1981) it is argued that the subject can be syntactically specified. For example, a Particle Complex which contains subject marking will sanction a subject which is compatible with it. Or, a possessive prefix may sanction a subject which is compatible with it. In fact, each of the elements given in (32) is involved in the specification of the subject.

Two possibilities therefore present themselves. What we characterize as $\sqrt{P}$ in Luiseño could lack, in addition to the various elements specified in (32), a "subject". A subject would be added in conjunction with the mapping between P and S, between $\sqrt{P}$ and C, or between $\sqrt{P}$ and S. On this account, the semantic object $\sqrt{P}$ is closely approximated by what is commonly termed "VP". The second possibility is that $\sqrt{P}$ contains a variable, the reference of which is fixed by a particular mapping. (We should note, in this regard, that the interpretation of the "subject" of any absolutive-marked subordinate clause is fixed. An absolutive-marked adjunct must be interpreted as having the same "subject" as the main clause; the head of an absolutive-marked relative clause must be interpreted as being its "subject"; and the object of the embedding "verb" must be interpreted as the subject of an absolutive-marked complement.) We will not attempt to decide this issue here.

11. This formulation conflicts with the principles of section 4.2 in two ways. First, while it is clear that imperatives may be taken to be derived from members of √P, the rule given here is not a function, but a partial function, since it is defined only over a subset of √P. Second, although imperative formation can add the elements <u>do</u> or <u>don't</u>, since the appearance of <u>you</u> depends on emphasis (of some sort), it is not clear that imperative formation is an additive function in the sense required by postulate (II) of section 4.2.

12. Whether on this construal the utterance should be considered a sentence or simply a noun phrase is not clear. Compare:

(i)
What mistakes I have made!

(ii)
(0!) The mistakes (that) I have made!

The fact that tag questions distinguish the two cases, as in (iii) and (iv), suggests that (i) is not a noun phrase.

(iii)
What mistakes I have made, haven't I.

(iv)
*(0!) The mistakes (that) I have made, haven't I.

13. Fillmore (1971) contains an interesting discussion of cases in which these may nontrivially diverge.

14. We distinguish between agents (or causes) and volitional agents. Nonvolitional agents cause unintended changes of state to occur through their actions. Volitional agents cause intended changes of state to occur. This is the difference between interpretations of <u>John broke the glass</u> in circumstances in which he inadvertently stepped on it as opposed to circumstances in which he hurled

the glass against a brick wall. Instruments are causal agents which do not act in bringing about the change that they effect.

15. When a modal occurs, the question of temporal coordinates becomes somewhat complicated, for there can be more than one. Without going into the rather complex details of this problem, let us simply point out that _may_ and _must_ differ in this regard on their "epistemic" interpretations. Compare the following cases:

(i)
John may be there.

(ii)
John must be there.

"Epistemic" interpretations are possible for each case, but the first sentence seems to have two different "epistemic" interpretations, while the second sentence seems to have only one. The first may be interpreted either as (a) 'It is possible that he is there' or as (b) 'It is possible that he will be there'; but the second seems to have only the interpretation 'It must be the case that he is there'. If this is correct, then there should be a distinction between the following two sentences, with respect to interpretations of the modals as "epistemic":

(iii)
John may be there tomorrow.

(iv)
John must be there tomorrow.

And, in fact, the second seems to have no "epistemic" interpretation. Further complications arise when we consider sequences consisting of _modal_ + _have_, but we defer their discussion. Considerable insight into the interpretations of the various modals may be gained by considering the temporal properties of the different interpretations of modal structures of this kind. For discussion, see Oehrle and Shiman (1980).

All that is necessary here is the assumption that, on a given interpretation, tense and modals fix the temporal coordinates by which the relative temporal coordinates of subordinate clauses embedded within their scope may be constrained.

Appendix A

AUX IN ENGLISH

A.1 Introduction

Struck by the similarities one can find among the most diverse human languages, and urged on by the ever-recurring dream of a universal grammar, many scholars have sought a set of categories and relations definable over them which can be applied unambiguously and without restriction to all those systems of human experience to which we commonly apply the term <u>language</u>. The method of establishing equivalence classes of grammatical properties expounded in chapter 1 is a means by which these scientific aspirations can be placed on a relatively sound empirical basis. It is sound to the extent that it allows objective assessment of the degree of similarity and difference between languages with respect to some defined grammatical property, and it is relative in the sense that it depends on the well-definedness cross-linguistically of the particular vocabulary in which the definition of the grammatical property is couched.

    There is no conflict in principle between the method of equivalence adopted here and the a priori postulation of universal grammatical properties, for, since equivalence is a generalization of the concept of identity, any demonstration that grammatical phenomena in distinct languages have an identical abstract basis can be easily translated into a comparable demonstration of their equivalence. Thus, any conflict between the two approaches can arise only in practice. Moreover, it is important to recognize that the method of equivalence rests in fact on the assumption that there exists a common basis of properties across languages. In the absence of a common vocabulary applicable to the linguistic phenomena we seek to characterize, comparative grammar of any sort would not be possible. Ideally, one seeks a common vocabulary whose terms are well-defined over any possible linguistic experience, in which case the relativity mentioned above vanishes--at least with respect to the phenomena that can be characterized in terms of this ideal vocabulary. This stringent criterion is not always easy to satisfy, and it is common practice to apply terminology developed in the analysis of one language to the analysis of another without specifying precisely the grounds which justify its application.

In fact, such is the case with the definition of the equivalence class AUX which we have provided, for it rests crucially on the concepts "tense", "modality", "category", and "constituent", concepts which we assume as given and attempt to characterize only minimally. Relative to the possibility of identifying the above properties with respect to the grammatical phenomena found in a given language, however, the resulting definition is a precise one. Yet it is a rather remarkable fact that it is possible for linguists to disagree radically on the analysis of particular cases, even when they involve such basic concepts as "constituent".[1] A well-known example of such disagreement is the various analyses which have been proposed of aux-phenomena in English.

A.2 English Aux-Phenomena

The existence of aux-phenomena is a particularly salient feature of English grammatical structure: there is a set of sentential properties and relations (aux-operations) which crucially depend in central cases on the analysis, in the sentence or sentences under consideration, of a relatively small set of aux-elements. The aux-operations are: negation, inversion, contraction, agreement, (sentential) emphasis, certain kinds of ellipsis (i.e. "VP Deletion"), "VP-Fronting", tag questions, specification of sentence type (declarative, interrogative, imperative, etc.), characterization of sentence mood, differentiation of subordinate clauses, certain problems concerning the position of quantifiers and adverbs, certain problems concerning word order and its relation to interpretation, and questions concerning morphological dependency. The aux-elements are: <u>not</u>, <u>can</u>, <u>can't</u>, <u>could</u>, <u>couldn't</u>, <u>shall</u>, ?<u>shan't</u>, <u>should</u>, <u>shouldn't</u>, <u>will</u>, <u>won't</u>, <u>would</u>, <u>wouldn't</u>, <u>may</u>, ?<u>mayn't</u>, <u>might</u>, <u>mightn't</u>, <u>must</u>, <u>mustn't</u>, <u>ought (to)</u>, <u>oughtn't</u>, <u>better</u>, <u>be</u>, <u>been</u>, the tensed forms of <u>be</u> (= <u>am</u>, <u>is</u>, <u>isn't</u>, <u>are</u>, <u>aren't</u>, <u>was</u>, <u>wasn't</u>, <u>were</u>, <u>weren't</u>), <u>have</u>, the tensed forms of <u>have</u> (= <u>have</u>, <u>haven't</u>, has, <u>hasn't</u>, <u>had</u>, <u>hadn't</u>), the tensed forms of <u>do</u> (= <u>do</u>, <u>don't</u>, <u>does</u>, <u>doesn't</u>, <u>did</u>, <u>didn't</u>), <u>need</u>, <u>needn't</u>, <u>dare</u>, <u>used to</u>, and the inflectional feature <u>tense</u>.

We recognize an occurrence of an aux-element in an analysis of an utterance under a wider than usual variety of nontrivial phonetic circumstances, including reduction of /wıl/ to /1/ or /l/, /hæz/ and /ız/ to /s/ or /z/, and other well-known cases. But under what circumstances shall we recognize an occurrence of an English category Aux which falls under the definition of AUX given in chapter 1?

A.3 Categories

A.3.1 Optimal Categorial Solutions

The standard approach to this problem is to assume the existence of a set C of categorial symbols, associate each aux-element with a subset of C, and specify the combinatorial properties of the members of C in such a way that every instantiation of a well-formed combination of members of C is a well-formed English expression and every aux-operation can be defined over these categorial combinations.[2] Relative to this simple application of the hypothetico-deductive method, an optimal solution would be one in which the number of categories is minimal, each aux-element is associated with a unique category, and every aux-operation is defined over the same set of categories. Call this a <u>common categorial solution</u> to the problem of defining the aux-operations. A solution which is categorial but nonoptimal still exists if it is possible to assign each aux-element to a set of categories such that on any good analysis of a sentence in which an aux-element <u>e</u> occurs, <u>e</u> has a unique categorial analysis, and every aux-operation which has <u>e</u> in its domain analyzes it as such in virtue of its categorial assignment.

Many proposed analyses of the English aux-phenomena are not categorial solutions in this sense, for they contain operations which are not defined over categories. A case in point is the analysis provided in Chomsky (1957), which includes rules having the following structural description:

(1)

$$\text{NP} - \text{C} + \left(\left\{\begin{array}{c}\underline{M}\\ \underline{have}\\ \underline{be}\end{array}\right\}\right) - \ldots$$

On Chomsky's analysis, <u>have</u> and <u>be</u> are lexical elements and not categorial symbols; as a result, any rule with the above structural description is not purely a categorial operation.

The point of making such distinctions is a simple one: they allow us to assess the extent to which, on any given analysis, the treatment of aux-phenomena depends on the assignment, under that analysis, of aux-elements to categories. This distinction is relevant to two problems: the general case being whether or not a categorial solution exists at all; the special case being whether or not, given two distinct categorial solutions, it is possible to choose between them.

<u>A.3.2 Remark</u> Why this should be important in the current context is easy to clarify. Many of the proponents of the "main verb" analysis of the English aux-elements have been motivated by the desire to restrict the theory of grammar by restricting the available inventory of categories. Given this methodological principle, attempts have been made to account uniformly for the properties of the English aux-phenomena by assuming that there is no category or constituent other than "Verb" to which aux-elements are assigned--attempts which invariably lead to the introduction of syntactic features, rule features associated with particular lexical elements, or aux-operations defined over particular aux-elements (and not categories).

There are two reasons to be skeptical of the success of these endeavors. First, it is not at all clear in what sense the proposed reduction of aux-phenomena to a class of phenomena defined over the notion "Verb" and its projections succeeds, if it is invariably necessary to abandon a categorial solution. In words, it is not at all clear what aspects of aux-phenomena follow strictly from the assumption that aux-elements are verbs. Second, it is not clear that the principle which motivates the reduction in the first place is sound. Standardly, no definition of the notion "Verb" is provided. Nor is it merely tendentious to raise the issue; there are languages in which there is apparently no class of words that can be identified with the class of verbs in English; any word which one might choose to call a verb may stand independently as a sentence, a fact which may have considerable ramifications for the syntactic properties of the languages in question. Thus, the empirical claims of the reduction are not obviously well-defined. Moreover, restricting the available inventory of categories does not obviously result in restricting the class of available grammars compatible with a given corpus of linguistic data, particularly if features of various kinds spring up to replace the missing category or categories.[3] In fact, just the reverse argument is often given: requiring the presence of linguistic structure rather than its absence constitutes a strengthening of linguistic theory, if it is possible as well to specify how such structure is to be identified empirically and what role it can play in grammatical operations and relations over distinct sentences.[4] Thus, even were we to grant the possibility of empirically adequate accounts of English based on the "main verb" assumption, there is no reason to think that, simply because of the paucity of categories they employ, they are to be preferred a priori to accounts in which the "main verb" assumption plays no role.

A.4 Finite Character of Aux-Phenomena
Relative to one assumption, the English aux-phenomena are <u>finitely characterizable</u>, in the

sense that the aux-operations are limited in number and each has a narrow domain. The necessary assumption is that the number of ways in which the complement of the aux-element(s) in the domain of any given aux-operation may affect its behavior is narrowly restricted. It is obvious and widely recognized that the occurrence of an aux-element may constrain the form which the members of its set-theoretic complement may assume. The more subtle issue of whether or not the aux-operations must be sensitive to nonsyntactic properties is rarely raised. Oehrle and Shiman (1977; 1979; 1980) have provided both theoretical and empirical grounds for taking the issue seriously (cf. section A.8 below and, for fuller discussion, the Oehrle and Shiman papers just cited).

The finite character of the English aux-phenomena and aux-elements makes it possible to attempt a constructivist approach to the problem. Assuming access to the elements in question, we can attempt to specify for each one (up to the limits of intuition, of course) the set of grammatical environments in which it occurs. The aux-operations, then, constitute relations over these environments.

Given such a procedure, there is no a priori reason to expect that any two operations will be defined over identical domains. Moreover, given the finite character of the aux-operations and aux-elements, it is consistent with accepted psychological assumptions that no regularities do in fact exist. If regularities do exist, their existence will emerge in the form of relations definable over the domain and range of the aux-operations. This approach, then, makes it possible to decide whether or not an optimal categorial solution in fact exists.

If there is an optimal categorial solution, then for any two operations A and A', the intersection of the domain of A and the domain of A' will be either the domain of A, the domain of A', or $\emptyset$. This is an easy consequence of standard assumptions about the nature of categories and constituent structure, as long as it is assumed that, in an optimal categorial solution, aux-operations are defined over categories and aux-elements belong to exactly one category.

Suppose, however, that no such optimal categorial solution exists. In principle, it is possible to salvage a categorial solution by revising the inventory of aux-elements. There is no reason to think that a given symbol identified on phonetic grounds will act the same way in all environments, and obvious counterexamples to this presumption exist: <u>need</u> is an example of a form which can behave systematically in either of two distinct ways, and it is thus possible to revise the inventory of elements to include two instances of <u>need</u>, only one of which is an aux-element. But once this mechanism is exhausted--and it depends in part on the semantic plausibility of assigning one phonological form to more than one lexical element--then we are left with a variety of possibilities: we can define operations over a complex of categories and features, we can define them over the elements themselves, we can define them in relation to the domain(s) of other operations, or we can adopt some combination of these alternatives.[5]

As a result, even where no optimal categorial solution exists, the method advocated here is capable of revealing those relations between operations which any solution of the aux-phenomena--whether based purely on categories or on a mixture of categories and features (insofar as these can be distinguished)--must respect.

A.5 Verv and Ax

It is necessary to assume at the outset that we have access in some way to a list of the lexical elements of English. It is not so important that this list be free of all redundancies (that is, we can tolerate the presence of <u>will</u>, <u>not</u>, and <u>won't</u>) as that it may be assumed to exist in some form in which we can speak of the lexical elements which belong to this set. Given such a list, we can assign interesting structure to it by classifying its elements in terms of the operations which standardly apply to them.

Consider first the class of elements $\underline{e}$ which occur in good sentences of the following form:

(2)

3sg Pro e+ $\begin{Bmatrix} -s \\ -\partial z \\ -z \end{Bmatrix}$ X

(where 3sgPro stands for any one of the elements $\underline{he}$, $\underline{she}$, or $\underline{it}$; e+ $\begin{Bmatrix} -s \\ -\partial z \\ -z \end{Bmatrix}$ stands for a lexical element which can be analyzed as the concatenation of a lexical element $\underline{e}$ followed by any one of the segments indicated (crudely) by -$\underline{s}$, -$\underline{\partial z}$, or -$\underline{z}$; and X stands for any expression formed by concatenating lexical elements)

We shall refer to an element of this class by the term $\underline{verv}$.

With the exception of $\underline{need}$ and $\underline{dare}$, the set of aux-elements listed in section A.2 is disjoint from the set of vervs. For when the aux-elements manifest agreement with the subject at all, they always do it in way which departs from the criterion stated above: $\underline{has} \neq \underline{have}$ + z, $\underline{is} \neq \underline{be}$ + z, $\underline{does}$ (/dΛz/) $\neq$ $\underline{do}$ (/du/) + z. Any lexical element which is standardly taken to be a verb is a verv, with one apparent exception: $\underline{says}$ (/sϵz/) $\neq$ $\underline{say}$ (/se/) + z. If we take the phonological representation of $\underline{say}$ to be /sϵ/, however, its paradigm becomes completely regular (both in the present tense and the past, for $\underline{said}$ = /sϵd/), in line with the assumption that there exists a phonological rule which tenses all nonlow final lax vowels (cf. Chomsky and Halle (1968) for evidence supporting this assumption). No parallel assumption makes $\underline{has}$, $\underline{is}$, or $\underline{does}$ regular in the same way. Finally, if we assume in addition that the symbols $\underline{need}$ and $\underline{dare}$ each represent two lexical elements, an assumption which is easily justified on both syntactic and semantic grounds, then the bifurcation is complete: no verv is an aux-element and no aux-element is also a verv.

What is interesting about this definition of the class of vervs is that it has categorial consequences. Every verv, without exception, may occur in an infinitival construction, that is, a good sentence of the form (3),

(3)
X to v Y
(where X and Y are variables ranging over concatenations of the lexical elements of English and v stands for an arbitrary verv)

Furthermore, every verv, without exception, occurs suffixed by -ing, for example, in the construction (4):

(4)
what with 3sg.acc.Pro v+-ing X,Y

Finally, for every verv, without exception, there exists both a "present tense" form and a "past tense" form, though in contrast to the present tense form (which is, in essence, the defining characteristic of the class of vervs), the particular morphological shape of the past tense form of a given verv cannot be stated categorically.

We now define a third class of elements in addition to third person singular pronouns and vervs. The simplest definition of this class presumes that the set of aux-elements is already given: let Ax be the set of aux-elements which invert, that is, for which there are good sentences of the following two forms:

(5)
a.   3sgPro a X

b. a 3sgPro   Y

(where Pro is a nominative pronoun, a is an ax, and X and Y are anything at all)

The set ax includes the following elements: can, can't, could, couldn't, will, won't, would, wouldn't, must, mustn't, may, ?mayn't, might, ?mightn't, ought, oughtn't, shall, ?shan't, should, shouldn't, need, dare, have, has, haven't, hasn't, had, hadn't, am, is, are, ain't, isn't, aren't, was, were, wasn't, weren't, does, do, doesn't, don't, did, didn't.

It is possible to define this class without reference to the set of aux-elements. The principal difficulty is to avoid including adverbial elements. The following definition suffices for obvious cases: Let Ax be the set of elements a, for which good sentences of the following forms exist:

(6)
a.   3sgPro a X

b. a 3sgPro   Y

(where Pro is a nominative pronoun and X and Y are anything at all, but neither includes a tensed verv or any element which is itself an element of Ax)

Among the elements which satisfy this definition, we may distinguish two disjoint classes: those which manifest morphologically their agreement in some context with a pronoun to the left and those which do not. Call the first class nonmodals and the second modals. Then Ax = Modals ∪ Nonmodals. Given these distinctions, our definitions have the following categorical consequences:

(A)   No element of Ax can be negated to its left.

(Moreover, for all elements a of Ax (relative to the assumption that won't = will + n't, shan't = shall + n't) there are good sentences of the following form:

(7)
Pro a n't X

Finally, there is no element v in Verv for which the following is a good sentence:

(8)
Pro v n't X)

(B) No modals have infinitival forms.

(C) No modals have forms with -ing.

(D) No modals have past tense forms which are formed regularly, insofar as past tense forms of the modals may be identified.[6]

(E) All nonmodals occur in infinitival, past participle, and present participle constructions.[7]

(F) Finally, in sentences of the form Pro X, contraction of Pro and the first element of X is limited to cases in which the first element of X is also an element of Ax, though the particular forms in question must be specified ad hoc for each combination.

The generalizations above are categorical: they have no exceptions. Except for the complete cleavage which exists between the class Verv as defined here and the class Ax, it is fair to say that most of these regularities are well known. Nevertheless, if the union of these two classes is taken to a single homogeneous category--call it Verb--then such regularities are impossible to state unless new mechanisms are introduced.[8]

One such mechanism is to split categories into a set of features, perhaps hierarchically organized. Another is to assign a variety of syntactic features to each lexical element, which it carries in every environment in which it occurs. As Pullum and Wilson (1977, 744, n. 3) note, these are not equivalent devices. In our discussion, we have employed a third, analogous mechanism in introducing structure over the set Ax: namely, the division into modals and nonmodals. As we shall see below, this device is distinct from the other two.

Consider now whether or not there is a set Verb = Verv $\cup$ Ax over which grammatical operations are defined in English. Here we may pose two

questions. First, although it is trivial to define
such a set as the union of Verv and Ax, is it
possible to define it without reference to Verv and
Ax? Second, assuming an adequate definition of this
class on grounds independent from those already
introduced, what role does the notion Verb play in
defining the domain of various syntactic operations?
In a way, these two questions amount to the same
thing: since it is not possible to effectively
enumerate the open class of elements in Verv, some
operational procedure must be stated.

A.6 What Is the Nondifference between Main "Verbs" and Auxiliary "Verbs"?

In principle, it is possible to advance the claim
that Ax and Verv are dependent subsets of a larger
and independently specifiable category Verb on one
of two bases: equivalence in terms of categorial
assignment or equivalence in terms of constituent
structure.[9] Of these, the second is much the weaker
empirically, for it must be based solely on
theoretical assumptions about constituent structure,
particularly assumptions concerning the relation
between the categorial value of the "head" of a
phrase and the categorial value of the phrase as a
whole. Interestingly enough, it is the first of
these which is the simplest to falsify.[10]

A.7 Are Ax-elements Auxiliary Verbs?

A.7.1 Brief Review We cannot review here every
plausible contention that there are operations that
can be defined only over the union of Verv and Ax.
In many instances, they are bound to particular
assumptions. For example, Pullum and Wilson's
(1977) contend that since Affix Hopping applies both
to "auxiliaries and main verbs" they should belong
to a common "supercategory". This contention is
valid only in frameworks which contain such a rule.
Moreover, if Gapping is a rule which applies to
conjoined NPs as well as conjoined sentences, as
Jackendoff (1972) has argued, then there is as much
reason to conclude from the fact that Gapping
applies to both nouns and aux-elements that nouns

and aux-elements belong to a common "super-category", as there is to conclude from the fact that Gapping applies to both aux-elements and verbs that these items belong to a common supercategory.[11] Rather than consider every such argument, then, we will simply examine a case which involves both category and constituent structure.

A.7.2 A Case Study: "VP Deletion" Consider the rule standardly referred to as "VP Deletion", a rule in which ax-elements play a prominent role. In his comprehensive and illuminating dissertation (1976, 35), Sag suggests that this rule might more appropriately be termed Post-Auxiliary Ellipsis. This remark, based in part on work by Bresnan (cf. Bresnan (1976)), stems from the fact that "VP Deletion" may choose various targets, all of which manifest an aux-element to the left of the ellipsis site. Thus, we have both examples of the sort illustrated in (9) and those illustrated in (10)-(11):

(9)
a. Frankie will seem to want to leave St. Louis, but Johnny won't seem to want to leave St. Louis.
b. Frankie will seem to want to leave St. Louis, but Johnny won't seem to want to.
c. Frankie will seem to want to leave St. Louis, but Johnny won't seem to.
d. Frankie will seem to want to leave St. Louis, but Johnny won't.

(10)
a. Hume must have been aware of it, and Kant must have been aware of it too.
b. Hume must have been aware of it, and Kant must have been too.
c. Hume must have been aware of it, and Kant must have too.
d. Hume must have been aware of it, and Kant must too.

(11)
a. John will be there, and Max may be too.
b. John will be there and Max may too.
c. John may be there, and Max almost certainly will be.
d. John may be there and Max almost certainly will.

The fact that "VP Deletion" can have multiple outputs can be summarized by stipulating that ellipsis is possible in an environment which contains Aux to the left of the "deletion site". Sag formulates the rule as follows:

(12)
Verb Phrase Deletion (optional)

$$X - Aux - VP - Y$$

S.D.: 1   2   3   4 $\Rightarrow$
S.C.: 1   2 $\emptyset$ 4

Deletion of VP is of course constrained by the recoverability of its representation at the level of "logical form". This definition has two important properties. First, the symbol Aux is introduced under VP, as follows:

(13)
VP $\longrightarrow$ Aux VP
Aux $\longrightarrow$ tense - (M) - (have-en) [12]

Second, the "logical form" of a verb phrase is specified as an expression which involves lambda-abstraction over the subject. Thus, recoverability means that, as Sag states it,

"With respect to a sentence S, VPD can delete any VP in S whose representation at the level of logical form is a λ-expression that is an alphabetic variant of another λ-expression present in the logical form of S or in the logical form of some other sentence S', which precedes S in discourse." [13]

Consider now the hypothesis that ax-elements are categorized as [+V, +Aux, ±Tense] and that verv-elements are categorized as [+V, -Aux, ±Tense]. (This categorization is often appealed to by those who argue that ax-elements are merely verbs with the additional feature [+Aux].) What we would like to show is that such categorizations make certain generalizations difficult to state with any plausibility.

If we consider sentences which contain ordinary tensed vervs, a nontensed VP otherwise equivalent at the level of "logical form" may be omitted under appropriate conditions, as in the following example:

(14)
John knows the answer and Bill does too.

(= John knows the answer and Bill knows the answer too.)

We may describe this situation by saying that tense is transparent to VP-equivalence.

Interestingly enough, however, if the tensed element is an ax-element, tense is never transparent in this way. Consider the following cases:

(15)
John is in the next room and Bill may be too.[14]

(= John is in the next room and Bill may be in the next room too.)

(16)
*John is in the next room and Bill may too.

(= John is in the next room and Bill may be in the next room too.)

(17)
John should be in the next room, but Bill shouldn't (be).

(= John should be in the next room, but Bill shouldn't be in the next room.)

AUX in English

Note that when <u>be</u> lacks tense, it may, together with its complement, be lacking. This is adequately described by the rule if we take the structure of such sentences as (17) to be grossly as follows:

(18)
John$_{NP}$ should$_{Aux}$ (be$_{Aux}$ (in the next room)$_{PP}$)$_{?VP}$

but$_{CONJ}$ Bill$_{NP}$ shouldn't$_{Aux}$ (be$_{Aux}$)$_{?VP}$

What is crucial here is the assumption that <u>be</u> is categorized as [+Aux]: this accords with its status as "context predicate" (in the sense of Bresnan (1976)) and, if true, demonstrates that the feature [+Aux] does not in and of itself prohibit analysis as a "target predicate" (ibid.). Consequently, it is not possible to analyze the failure of "VP Deletion" in (16) as resulting from a general prohibition against the deletion of a piece marked [+Aux]. Rather, it must be a consequence of the analysis of the supposed "antecedent", the expression <u>is in the next room</u>.

One might suppose that the solution lies in requiring that the "antecedent" also be an expression of the form <u>Aux VP</u>, a position which has in fact been advanced (Bresnan (1976)). Sag demonstrates that this claim faces serious difficulties. He provides the following pair, the first of which shows that <u>seem(s)</u> is not a context predicate for "VP Deletion", the second of which shows that "VP Deletion" can apply in cases where the "antecedent" is not preceded by a context predicate for "VP Deletion", i.e. by Aux (or [+Aux]).

(19)
a. *Harry seems (to be) upset, but Bill doesn't seem.

    (= Harry seems (to be) upset, but Bill doesn't seem to be upset.)

b. Harry seems upset, but Bill doesn't seem to be.

   (= Harry seems upset, but Bill doesn't seem to be upset.)

Sag's example shows that to suppose that the trigger must be to the right of Aux (or [+Aux]) raises serious difficulties. As a result, we can conclude that the difficulty in (16) does not arise from a requirement that the trigger be to the right of Aux; even if it did, we would still need to determine why tense is transparent on certain elements (i.e. verv-elements) and not on others (i.e. ax-elements).

Another approach to the problem might consist in assuming that the representation of ax-elements is not a λ-expression. But here the same asymmetry presents itself: why do certain elements which are assumed to be categorized as [+V, +Aux] lack such representations while others have them? Thus, we are faced with the problem of stating the requisite restriction in terms of the features available: ±V, ±Aux, ±Tense. The generalization is this: no element with the combination of features [+Aux, +Tense] can be the head of the trigger of "VP Deletion". This class coincides, oddly enough, with our class Ax. In systems which do not recognize Ax as a category, however, this restriction can be stated in one of two ways: one in terms of the feature complex [+V, -[+Aux, +Tense]], or alternatively [+V, +[+Aux, +Tense]]; the second in terms of constituency (namely, ax-elements do not form a constituent with the expression to their right). On the first alternative, once again we must ask whether the feature [±V] serves any function at all in distinguishing the two classes. On the second, the obvious structure to suppose would be one having the constituent relations shown in (20) rather than (21). This tack removes the possibility of arguing that ax-elements are members of the category V because they are dominated by VP. Thus, on neither alternative is there any strong argument for supposing that ax-elements are members of a super-set Verb which can be defined independently of

(20)

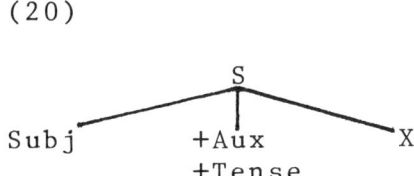

(21)

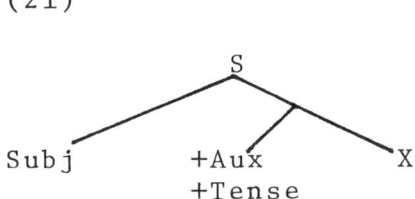

Ax and Verv and which acts as the domain of various operations.

A.8 Standard Problems with Standard Notions

Before discussing the analysis we shall propose, we would like to review certain assumptions which have guided research on this problem. First is the assumption that each lexical element should be assigned to as few categories as possible, a presumption which has as a consequence the view that if the behavior of a particular element patterns with other elements in one environment, its behavior in other environments should, in the best of all possible words, be a function of the category it belongs to relative to the first environment. If we reduce this assumption to a slogan, it becomes: once a verb, always a verb; or once an aux, always an aux. The second assumption concerns the structure assigned to a string of lexical elements: again, it is assumed that if a certain structure is motivated with respect to one rule, then this structure should always be assigned. Finally, there are assumptions about constituency: namely, movement and ellipsis operations are always to be defined over constituents, if possible.

If we consider the three aux-operations which are standardly treated under the names Inversion, Affix Hopping, and VP Deletion, there is a conflict

(22)

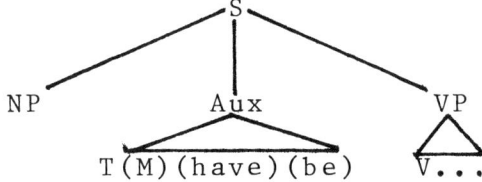

(23)

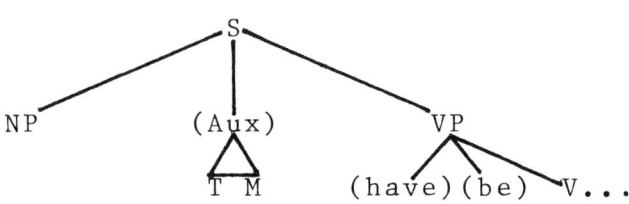

(24)

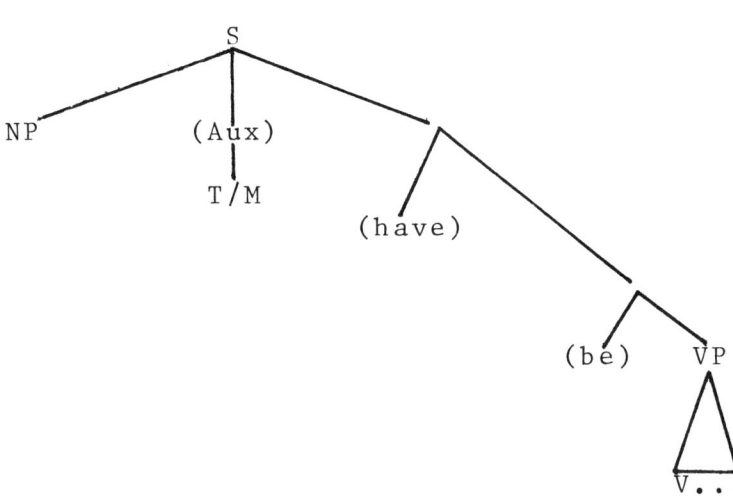

among these assumptions. Empirically, Inversion (however it is formally expressed) affects only the first of the aux-elements, namely, a modal or a tensed occurrence of (ax-element) do, be, or have (and with have there is the problem of whether it is compatible with preceding (ax-element) do or not). As is well known, this class is not homogeneous with respect to all operations: modals and ax-element do never occur in nonfinite contexts, but have and be are found there; yet have, be, and do mark subject-verb agreement while the modals never do (except in archaic forms such as the Biblical thou shalt). These differences can be expressed in terms of categories only by assuming that we allow considerable freedom in terms of domination. As a result, Inversion cannot be formulated in terms of lexical categories, but rather must be stated in terms of constituent structure or a nonlexical category. But this leads to other complications, for it is not obvious that the constituent structure necessary for the simplest statement of the Inversion rule is optimal when we consider other operations, such as "VP Deletion".

Most discussion of the aux-phenomena in English has revolved around choosing a proper constituent structure and categorization. The choices are limited by standard assumptions about constituency; the major candidates have been those in (22), (23), and (24).[15] On the first account, Inversion is notoriously messy, as it involves the structural bugaboo $T\left(\left\{\begin{array}{c}M\\ \underline{have}\\ \underline{be}\end{array}\right\}\right)$. If either of the second two structures is employed and a have/be raising rule is used, then Inversion can be stated with reference to the (position) Aux. Alternatively, if features are employed on the second analysis, then Inversion can be stated in terms of the feature [+Aux] (or the feature [+V] if "main verbs" are always preceded by the aux-element do at the level at which Inversion applies). Yet none of these structures provides an adequate basis for a definition of "VP Deletion" in terms of a single constituent, for the simple reason that tenseless have and be do not behave

AUX in English   246

homogeneously with respect to this rule. This is
illustrated in the following examples.

(25)
a.   Hume seems to have known that, and Max may have
     too.

     (= Hume seems to have known that, and Max may
        have known that too.)

b.   ?Hume seems to have known that, and Max may too.

     (?= Hume seems to have known that, and Max may
         know that too.)

     (≠ Hume seems to have known that, and Max may
        have known that too.)

(26)
a.   John seems to have been to Florence and Max
     seems to also.

     (= John is such that he seems to have been
        to Florence and Max is such that he seems to
        have been to Florence too.)

     (≠ It seems that John went to Florence and
        back and it seems that Max went to
        Florence and back too.)

b.   ?John seems to have been to Florence and
     Max seems to have also.

     (≠ John is such that he seems to have been
        to Florence and Max is such that he
        seems to have been to Florence also.)

     (?= It seems that John went to Florence and
         back and it seems that Max went to
         Florence and back also.)

(27)
a.   A praetor must be some kind of government
     official and, for all I know, a consul may

also.

(= It must be the case that a praetor is some kind of government official and, for all I know, it may be the case that a consul is some kind of government official too.)

b. ?*A praetor must be some kind of government official and, for all I know, a consul may be too.

(same interpretation as (27a))

(28)
a. A letter must be on the way, and a package may be too.

(= It must be the case that a letter is on the way and it may be the case that a package is on the way too.)

b. ?A letter must be on the way, and a package may too.

(same interpretation as (28a))

The judgments in such examples are rather subtle, but nonetheless real. What is most interesting about them is that they seem amenable to semantic analysis by which the function of have or be may be distinguished in the cases in which they behave differentially with respect to "VP Deletion".

A.9 Toward a Theory of "VP Deletion"

Let us sketch a theory rich enough to account for this fact, a theory based on the possibility of different semantic structures being assigned to a single string of elements. We shall not make specific proposals concerning the content of the various semantic elements we refer to, but we shall address below the syntactic consequences of the approach we adopt.

We shall suppose that every verv has a specifiable right domain, (rd), and that tense is an operator which both composes a (nominative) subject to its left with the result of applying the meaning of the verv to which it is attached to the verv's right domain, and provides an abstract "space" in which the result of this composition of subject and verv may be evaluated. Modals constitute a similar operator, though they are not attached inflectionally to the verv. In simple cases, they may be said to compose two elements, subject and verv (more specifically, subject and the result of composing the verv with its right domain), and to provide an abstract "space" in which the result of this composition may be evaluated. We represent these rather similar operations as follows:

(29)

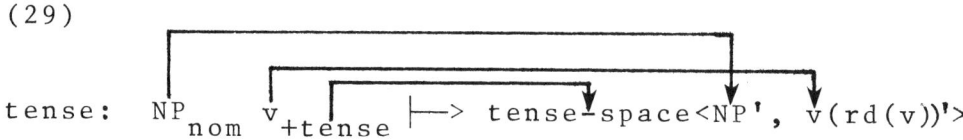

tense: NP_{nom} v_{+tense} $\longmapsto$ tense-space<NP', $v(rd(v))'$>

(where NP_{nom} denotes a nominative noun phrase, NP' denotes the intension of NP_{nom}, $(v(rd(v)))'$ denotes the intension of the result of applying the intension of v to the intension of the elements in its right domain, and NP', $v(rd(v))'$ denotes the intension of the composition of NP' and $v(rd(v))'$)

(30)

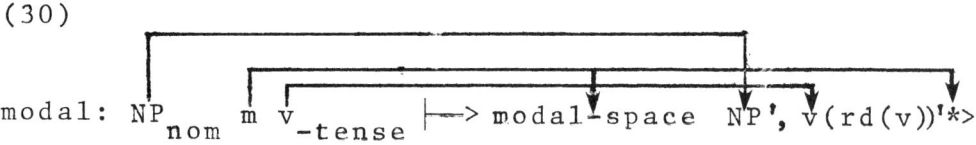

modal: NP_{nom} m v_{-tense} $\longmapsto$ modal-space NP', $v(rd(v))'*$>

(where m denotes a given modal, NP' denotes as above, and $v(rd(v))'*$ denotes the result of introducing the propositional content of the modal into the resulting composition)[16]

If modals have the same interpretation in inverted contexts, we may generalize the domain of the modal operator as follows, where parentheses to the left of the arrow indicate a domain of free order:

(31)
modal:

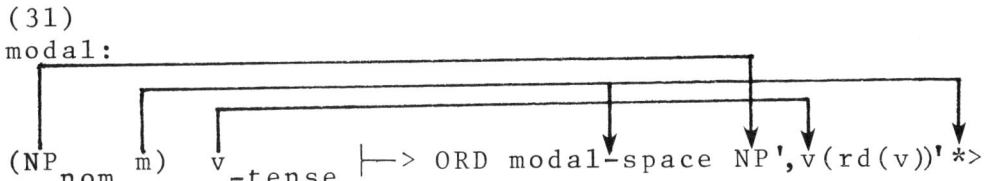

(NP$_{nom}$ m) v$_{-tense}$ $\vdash\!\!\!\rightarrow$ ORD modal-space NP',v(rd(v))'*>

(where it is assumed that this rule abbreviates two rules whose effects may be modified by general considerations of the order of modal-elements, if such exist, indicated above by the symbol ORD)

Now, suppose that a modal occurs in a context in which its right domain is either tenseless have or be, together with the right domain of (tenseless) have or be. We represent such a situation as either (32) or (33):

(32)
(NP$_{nom}$ m)   have rd(have)

(33)
(NP$_{nom}$ m)   be rd(be)

Let it be supposed that in these contexts, two distinct modes of composition are possible. We shall represent these as follows:

(34)
(NP$_{nom}$ m) have rd(have) $\vdash\!\!\!\rightarrow$
    modal (have)-space < NP', v(rd(v))'*>

(NP$_{nom}$ m) have rd(have) $\vdash\!\!\!\rightarrow$
    modal-space < NP', have(rd(have))'*>

(NP$_{nom}$ m) be rd(be) $\vdash\!\!\!\rightarrow$
    modal (be)-space < NP', rd(be)'*>

(NP$_{nom}$ m) be rd(be) $\vdash\!\!\!\rightarrow$
    modal-space < NP', be(rd(be))'*>

Although we have not mentioned the conditions under which these different modes of composition are possible, it is a useful strategy to identify the first of the have-cases with those in which have does not ordinarily delete in "VP Deletion", and the second with those in which it may delete, and similarly with the be-cases. In doing so, we may hope to refine our understanding of the interaction between aux-elements. There is independent semantic evidence that under certain conditions just this sort of reordering of scope relations between a modal and an element in its right domain is possible. One such case is the so-called can't seem to construction, in which, on the interpretation in question, a sentence such as (35) seems to be more closely paraphrased by (36) than by (37):

(35)
John can't seem to put it all together.

(36)
It seems that John can't put it all together.

(37)
It isn't possible for John to seem to put it all together.

Another case involves the interpretation of such sentences as (38),

(38)
You needn't have bothered to do that.

which is ambiguous and can be paraphrased either as (39) or as (40):

(39)
It isn't necessary that you bothered to do that.

(40)
It wasn't necessary for you to bother to do that.

Such examples provide independent evidence for the existence of rules of the sort proposed above for the composition of modals with tenseless <u>have</u> and <u>be</u>.

If "VP Deletion" is defined relative to the results of composition, as the results of Williams (1977) and Sag (1976) demonstrate on independent grounds, and if the differences which we have suggested exist in the interpretation of sequences consisting of modal and either <u>have</u> or <u>be</u>, then many of the still-extant problems concerning "VP Deletion" can be resolved. For what may be empty can be identified with the second coordinate in the domain of evaluation "space", namely, a predicate of any syntactic category. As a result, we can formulate "VP Deletion" as follows:

(41)
The second coordinate of a two-place "space operator" may be satisfied by a recoverable second coordinate of some other operator.[17]

This is rather informal, but if we construe <u>recoverable</u> as Sag (1976) does, for example, it is possible in principle to account in this way not only for his results, but also, in principle, for all the facts discussed here.[18] To fully analyze the known phenomena concerning the behavior of tenseless <u>have</u> and <u>be</u>, which constitute the crucial set of cases, would take us far beyond the confines of this book. (For a fuller discussion, see Oehrle and Shiman (1980).) Yet what is crucial to note here is that if this attempt succeeds, then we will have formulated "VP Deletion" with no reference to the category "VP" at all. This step seems necessary in any case, given the variety of syntactic categories susceptible to ellipsis on the right of tensed <u>be</u>.

A.10 Consequences for Syntax
The solution proposed here for the difficulties confronting standard assumptions about constituency rests on the possibility of referring to two "syntactic" structures: the first is a sequence of lexical elements, the second a sequence of semantic

symbols. "VP Deletion" makes reference to the relation between these two structures. Yet Inversion, for example, is defined only over the sequence of lexical elements, and in fact may be construed simply as an operation over the syntactic domains relative to which rules of composition are defined. (As pointed out above, we leave open the question of whether or not this operation over the syntactic domains in which the meaning of ax-elements is defined has a systematic effect on the rules of composition, and, if so, exactly how this effect is to be characterized and represented.) As a result, despite the fact that each of the "syntactic structures" is extremely simple, together they allow succinct expression of a variety of classical problems whose interaction is difficult to express satisfactorily in the standard phrase structure system, even allowing for the introduction of transformations and the multiplicity of distinct syntactic structures which their operation requires. A more complete comparison of the system proposed here with standard approaches to syntactic structure depends on a fuller elaboration of its properties than is possible in this book (but see Oehrle and Shiman (1980)).

A.11 AUX in English

The definition of equivalence proposed in chapter 1 rests on the notion based on "syntactic constituent". Although this definition was formulated relative to the standard ideas of constituency familiar in immediate constituent analysis and phrase structure grammars, it is still applicable to the system proposed above, although its applicability depends on how we choose to define the notion "constituent" in such a system. There are two ways of doing this, which lead to different characterizations, but both of them undoubtedly pick out constituents in English sentences which fall unambiguously under the definition of the equivalence class AUX. Under any definition of the term constituent, every lexical element is a constituent. On this view, the constituents which fall under the definition of the equivalence class coincide exactly with the class of ax-elements. A second way to define constituency refers to the structure of the second "syntactic" system, which represents the composition of lexical elements. All of the sentences we considered above have representations of the form (42):

(42)
X-space <subj, pred>

For any sentence, consider the elements which are mapped onto x to be a constituent. The various members of this constituent would be larger than the class of ax-elements and would include, in addition to them, tense, infinitival to, and certain sequences consisting of either tense or a modal followed by have or be. On this view of constituency, there is also no question that such a constituent in a sentence unambiguously conforms to the definition provided in chapter 1. Hence, it appears that under any plausible definition of constituency in this system, in sentences which provide a space of evaluation there will always be a constituent which is a member of the cross-linguistic equivalence class AUX.

Notes
1. In part, no doubt, this is because such concepts may have rather different consequences in different theories of grammatical structure.

2. For the moment we ignore subtleties which arise in defining instantiation when we consider the possible existence of a distinction between obligatory and optional aux-operations; in this case one must specify that every instantiation I of any well-formed combination of members of C to which all obligatory operations defined on I have applied is a well-formed English expression.

3. If "categories" must stand up to tests of universal cross-linguistic validity, there is no reason to exempt "features" from similar scrutiny.

4. In most discussions of this question, the necessity of the condition is neglected.

5. To any practitioner of linguistic analysis, this must sound tautological, for it is in carrying out such procedures that one arrives at what is taken to be an acceptable or interesting solution. What renders it nontautological is the fact that it is just the existence of such solutions that is being called into question: there is no guarantee that they exist.

6. <u>Dare</u> is a possible exception to this. The behavior of this form has not received the scrutiny it deserves, partly no doubt because of the uncertainty of the judgments such sentences as these elicit:

(i)
a. He dare not open his mouth.
b. He doesn't dare to open his mouth.

(ii)
a. He wouldn't dare open his mouth.
b. He wouldn't dare to open his mouth.

(iii)
He didn't dare open his mouth.

(iv)
?*He dared not open his mouth.

(v)
?*Dare he open his mouth?

(vi)
*He mustn't dare open his mouth.

(vii)
*He hasn't dared open his mouth.

If these judgments are correct, it is not clear that <u>dare</u> should count as an element of Ax at all, since it fails to clearly invert over a 3rd person singular pronoun. By the same token, then, it fails to offer a clear counterexample. In fact, it is difficult to assign the nonverv uses of dare to any category larger than itself.

7. It is obviously not the case that for every function of a nonmodal there exists the set of properties specified by (E). Do is an obvious example. Clearly, then, the impossibility of sentences such as (i)

(i)
*John tried to do go.

is not the result of any morphological deficit, as is sometimes argued. If it were, then it should be possible to find two homophonous vervs, one of which has an infinitive form and the other of which does not. To our knowledge, no such cases exist. Hence, it is the argument which is deficient, and not the form.

8. Moreover, the following interesting statements hold:

(i)
If an operation is not categorical over the domain Ax, it is not categorical over the domain Verb.

(ii)
If an operation is not categorical over the domain Verv, it is not categorical over the domain Verb.

(iii)
If an operation is defined only over the union of the elements of Ax and the elements of Verv, it may be categorical over Verv but it is never categorical over Ax.

(iv)
There are categorical operations over Ax and over Verv whose analogues are not categorical over Verb.

These observations can be summarized by saying that irregularities in the operations defined over A̲x̲ or V̲e̲r̲v̲ alone are transmitted as irregularities in the comparable operations defined over V̲e̲r̲v̲, whereas irregularities in the operations defined over V̲e̲r̲b̲ are not necessarily transmitted as irregularities in the comparable operations defined over A̲x̲ or V̲e̲r̲v̲.

9. In each of these cases, validity of the arguments advanced depends furthermore on the empirical consequences of assumed category-equivalence or constituency-equivalence in the theory within which the arguments are put forth. It is obvious that such concepts cannot be taken as given a priori, simply because it is possible to elaborate different grammatical theories in which they play different grammatical roles. For example, categories can be defined on the basis of intersubstitutability, on grounds of morphological similarity, in terms of "relational" notions such as "subject (of x)", in terms of semantic properties, in functional terms (as in categorial grammar, where VP may be equated with a function from terms to propositions), and in other ways. Not all such definitions converge, unfortunately. By the first, for instance, the nominative pronouns do not form a single category. Hence, it is not really possible to argue in detail either for or against claims concerning categorial status in the absence of explicit assumptions about the empirical consequences of categorial equivalence or nonequivalence. Similar remarks apply to the notion of constituency as well; for it may be taken to be a domain of dependency, a domain over which the possibility of distinct ordering relations is defined, or a domain of coordination. As in the case of categorial assumptions, these diagnostics do not always coincide, at least not in English. As a result, the arguments which follow are as general as possible, for we shall try to sweep into our grasp at times rather divergent notions of the fundamental, but at times cavalierly applied, concepts of category and constituency.

10. Another approach sometimes invoked is the argument that there is a continuum of cases which bridge the gap between "main verbs" and "auxiliaries" and thus that "auxiliaries" should be treated as "auxiliary verbs". This approach has the curious property of making irregularity the only characteristic that the various elements have in common. Moreover, since there exist words which share the properties of adjectives and prepositions (near, like, etc.), by the same reasoning these categories should be collapsed into a single one, say, Preposadjective, whose members are distinguished by the feature ($\pm$P). Needless to say, similar advances could be achieved regarding the categories Noun and Adjective on the basis of the mixed properties of such words as fool (enough of a fool, fool enough), fun (a fun thing to do, no fun), good (a good thing to do, no good).

11. Interestingly enough, Sag's (1976) formulation of Gapping mentions neither Verb nor Aux nor Noun.

12. This rule obviously lacks generality, for it allows "perfective" have to occur only in tensed environments, though this is merely a technical difficulty. Moreover, the meaning of the symbol 'Aux' here is that of the author quoted, and is not to be confused with the use of the term AUX earlier in this book. In what follows, we shall have occasion to refer to categories Aux and features $\pm$Aux in relation to various uses of this term in the literature. These terms are always used contextually to refer to specific previous proposals or possible extensions of them. Obviously, none of these uses is to be identified with the term Ax or such related terminology as ax-element, which depend solely on the criteria introduced in this appendix.

13. This is supplemented by the condition that such deletion is subject to what Sag called the Backward Anaphora Condition.

14. That the missing constituent need not be a VP at all raises certain difficulties for the

formulation of the rule of "VP Deletion". We presume that this is one reason why Sag suggests that the rule might better be termed <u>Post-Auxiliary Ellipsis</u>.

15. Structure (22) is similar in spirit to Chomsky's (1957) proposal, though the constituent structure of (22) differs in fact from the one Chomsky proposed; structure (23) is that of Jackendoff (1972); structure (24) is that of Akmajian, Steele, and Wasow (1979). There are many other possibilities for constituent relations among these various elements, and the number of possibilities increases dramatically when we consider the distinctions which arise from assigning different categorial symbols to various nodes or different syntactic features to various constituents. Of the other possibilities which are consistent with general conventions governing the graph-theoretical properties of phrase structure diagrams, the most important are those in which <u>T/M</u> is not adjoined directly under <u>S</u> but forms, together with the constituent to its right, a constituent which is the right daughter of <u>S</u>. Thus, a variant of (24) along these lines is:

(i)

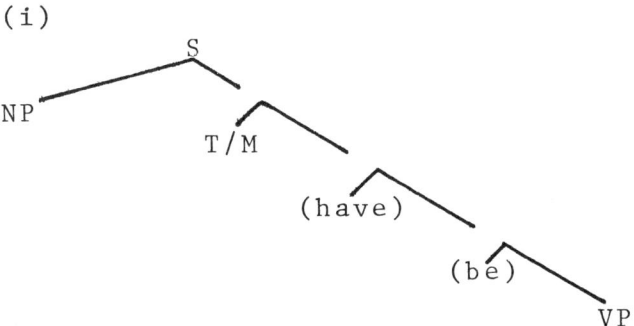

Since the arguments which follow depend only on the grouping of ax-elements, and since such possibilities do not affect the argument given here, we have, in the interests of generality, glossed over such differences.

16. This complication is prompted by the fact that the modal _can_ has an "ability" sense, whose effect is difficult to represent if we treat all modals as purely propositional operators.

17. The term _second coordinate_ as used here is a way of smuggling in the notion "predicate", without referring to the syntactic guise of that predicate.

18. In particular, we are assuming that tense and modal themselves are never the second coordinate of any operator. This accounts for the unacceptability of (16). Moreover, it may well be the case that other factors besides the range of the mappings sketched here intervene in certain cases: when the modal-spaces of two conjoined sentences coincide, for example, more radical forms of ellipsis seem to be possible, as in (17). Furthermore, it is possible that given such sequences as ...m have/be ... and ... m have/be ..., where the two modals differ and are in contrast, more radical ellipsis than we predict on the basis of the ranges of the mappings sketched here may occur. If this is correct, then the problems to which Akmajian and Wasow's (1975) rule of Auxiliary Ellipsis were addressed are governed by a complex variety of factors, including composition, redundancy, and contrast. We have not intended to provide a full treatment of these here, for we have been concerned only with the ways in which the "VP Deletion" phenomenon bears on the question of whether or not ax-elements and verv-elements belong to a common category Verb.

Appendix B

THE AUX IN GERMAN AND THE HISTORY OF ENGLISH

B.1 Introduction

There appears to be widespread agreement in the generative literature on the English auxiliary system (e.g. Ross (1967), McCawley (1975)) and echoed in work on German and the history of English (Huber and Kummer (1974), Evers and Scholten (1980), Allen (1974), Lightfoot (1974), Mitchell (1971), Wagner (1969)) that Modern German, Old English (OE), and possibly Middle English (ME) all lack some relative or precursor of the category termed in studies of Modern English (NE) Aux. Indeed, some proponents of the main verb analysis seem to consider the purported nonexistence of this category in these languages to be an argument against its existence in Modern English. We will take issue with this consensus. In so doing, we will adopt a somewhat different perspective from previous investigators. In the past, the argument concerning German, OE, or ME has been equated with the question of whether or not the cognates of NE auxiliary elements--in particular, the modals--exhibit the characteristics which distinguish NE auxiliaries from main verbs. The fact that the cognates of the NE modals are demonstrably verbs (at least in German and OE) has been taken as sufficient argument that these languages have no category comparable to NE Aux. Our concern, however, is not whether a specific, preselected class of words constitutes some syntactic category, but rather whether the languages in question have any element(s) which fall within the characterization of AUX given in chapter 3. In this appendix, we will argue that the languages in question clearly do. Further, we will present an analysis of the role of this element in the grammar of German, as well as an account of how and why the OE Aux changed into the NE Aux.

B.2 The German Aux$_G^1$

B.2.1 Arguments against the Category in German A variety of facts have led to the conclusion that German has no counterpart to the NE Aux, an issue which must be distinguished absolutely from the question that this work addresses. German cognates of English modals differ from their NE counterparts in that they exhibit clearly verbal inflections. (1) illustrates this with the conjugation for können (can):

(1)

	Present	Past
1st singular	kaan	konnte
2nd singular	kannst	konntest
3rd singular	kann	konnte
1st plural	können	konnten
2nd plural	könnt	konntet
3rd plural	können	konnten

Unlike NE modals, the German forms may also appear in nonfinite constructions:

(2)
Er scheint gehen zu müssen.
he seems go to must
'He seems to have to go.'

Further, the German cognates of English modals may iterate (see Bierwisch (1963, 68-69)).[2]

(3)
a. Weil   Fritz   kommen wollen   konnte....
   because Fritz   come   wanted:to   could
   (Huber and Kummer (1974, 141))
   'Because Fritz could (possibly) want to come....'

b. Dass du   fahren können musst ist verstanden.
   that you drive   can   must   is   understood
   'That you must be able to drive is understood.'

They are not restricted to any fixed order with

respect to each other or the perfect <u>haben</u> 'have', though, of course, the meaning is altered by a change in the order:

(4)
Weil   Fritz kommen können wollte... (cf. (3a))
because Fritz come   can   wanted:to
'Because Fritz wanted to be able to come...'

(5)
a. Weil   Hans essen müssen hat...
   because Hans eat   must   has
   (Huber and Kummer (1974, 141))
   'Because Hans had to eat...'

b. Weil   Hans gegessen haben muss...
   because Hans eaten   have   must
   (Huber and Kummer (1974, 141))[3]
   'Because Hans must have eaten...'

c. Weil   Hans essen müssen haben soll...
   because Hans eat   must   have   should
   (Huber and Kummer (1974, 141))
   'Because Hans is supposed to have had to eat...'

They may also occur in certain constructions without any other verb in the same clause:

(6)
a. Hans kann keinen Handstand.
   Hans can   no   handstand
   (Bierwisch (1963, 77))
   'Hans can't do a handstand.'

b. Fritz will/möchte,   dass Emil Paula küsst.
   Fritz wants/would:like   that Emil Paula kisses
   (Huber and Kummer (1974, 288))
   'Fritz wants/would like Emil to kiss Paula.'

c. Ich muss nach Hause.
   I   must home
   'I must go home.'

In short, the peculiarities of inflection and

cooccurrence of NE modals which create difficulties for the main verb analysis of the NE auxiliary system simply do not exist in German (but cf. section B.2.4 below).

Similarly, the processes which single out the elements of Aux in NE either do not occur in German, or apply to the cognates of English modals in the same way as to other verbs.[4] For example, while contraction can be used as a diagnostic for membership in the NE Aux, contraction does not apply to the German cognates of NE modals.

(7)
a. Er will   gehen.
   he wants:to go
   'He wants to go.'

b. *Er'll gehen.

Other tests for the English Aux do have counterparts in German, but they apply equally to all finite verbs. For example, neither the placement of negatives nor the inversion in questions distinguishes between the cognates of the NE modals and other verbs.

(8)
a. Ich kann das Bild   nicht sehen.
   I   can the picture not   see
   'I can't see the picture.'

b. Ich sehe das Bild   nicht.
   I   see the picture not
   'I don't see the picture.'

c. ...dass ich das Bild   nicht sehe.
      that I   the picture not   see
   '...that I don't see the picture.'

d. ...dass ich das Bild   nicht sehen kann.
      that I   the picture not   see   can
   '...that I can't see the picture.'

(9)
a. Kannst du Englisch (sprechen)?

can   you English   (speak)
'Can you speak English?'

b. Sprichst   du   Englisch?
   speak   you   English
   'Do you speak English?'

It seems, then, that there is no reason to assign the German cognates of these English auxiliary elements to a separate category; they are simply verbs. This has generally been taken as sufficient grounds for denying the existence of any counterpart in German to the NE Aux. In the absence of any cross-linguistic characterization of AUX, such a conclusion seemed reasonable; however, in the present context, it is obviously unwarranted. We may agree that the cognates do not constitute a separate category and still ask whether German has anything that conforms to the characterization given for the category AUX. It turns out that the answer is clearly affirmative.

B.2.2   The Finite Verb   Recall our characterization of AUX in chapter 3. Superficially, the element in German which most nearly satisfies our characterization is the finite verb.

The finite verb is marked for tense, thus expressing the requisite temporal notion. In addition and unlike NE, German has a highly productive subjunctive mood,[5] used for expressing uncertainty or counterfactuality. The verb marked for mood is always the same as the one marked for tense.

There can be little question that tense in German can reasonably be identified with what we have called tense in other languages, and we will not attempt to argue the matter in any detail here. As in other languages (e.g. English), German tense marking is one of several factors (including adverbials, aspectual verbs, and properties of the context) which interact in complex ways to express temporal notions, especially (but not exclusively) the distinctions among past, present, and future time.

Whether or not German mood can be identified with what we have been calling "modality" is perhaps somewhat problematic. Curme (1952, 215) describes mood as "a grammatical form denoting the style or manner of predication." He goes on to say that "the indicative represents something as a fact or as in close relation to reality" (216). "The subjunctive mood, however," according to Stopp (1957, 370), "expresses a discrepancy between reality and some view or attitude taken up by the speaker." In the following examples, cited by Curme, the glosses are indicative of the fact that the German subjunctive mood serves many of the same functions as NE modals.[6]

(10)
a. Der Berg   <u>sei</u> auch noch so hoch, ich
   the mountain <u>be</u>   also still so high   I

   ersteige ihn. (p.218)
   climb   it

   'The mountain may be ever so high, (but) I will
    climb it.'

b. Unser König, den   Gott <u>erhalte</u>... (p.220)
   our   king   whom God <u>keep</u>
   "Our king, whom, we pray, God may keep..."

c. Nichts ist, das   die Gewaltigen <u>hemme</u>.
   nothing is   that the powerful   restrain
   (p.222)[7]
   'There is nothing that can restrain the powerful.'

d. Er <u>sage</u>, was   er   <u>wolle</u>... (p.225)
   he say   what he   want:to
   'Say what he might...'

e. Ich wüsste wohl, was   zu tun <u>wäre</u>. (p.230)
   I   knew   well   what to do   were
   "I think I know what would be best to do."

f. Wie <u>wäre</u> es   mit   einer Partie Billard?
   how were   it   with   a   game   billiards
   "How should you like a game of billiards?" (p.231)

g. Er wäre der letzte, den ich um Rat
   he were the last whom I for advice

   fragte. (234)
   asked

   'He would be the last one I would ask for advice.'

h. Kaufe dir, was du gern hättest.
   buy yourself what you happily had (234)
   'Buy yourself what you would like to have.'

Of course, not all German subjunctives are best translated by English modals.[8] As is the case with temporal notions, modality in both languages is expressed through the interaction of several factors. Our characterization of AUX does not require that the elements of an instantiation of AUX in one language always correspond one-to-one to members of an instantiation of AUX in another language. Rather, we claim that the notions expressed by members of AUX in every language will fall within a certain range. The point of the above examples is to illustrate that there is a great deal of overlap between the uses of the German subjunctive and of NE modals. Further, the function of the subjunctive in German is evidently to express possibility, doubt, or counterfactuality. This is fully in accord with our characterization of AUX.

In addition to marking the criterial notions of tense and modality, the finite verb in German has a role in questions and subject agreement. Finally, it is restricted to precisely the three positions in which AUX can appear: final position in subordinate clauses, sentential second position in declarative main clauses, and initial position in interrogative and imperative main clauses. (11) through (13) illustrate the fact that the verb must occur in first, second, or last position, depending on the type of clause it is in.

(11)
a. Sieht er dich?
   sees he you
   'Does he see you?'

b. *Er sieht dich? (except as an echo question)

c. *Er dich sieht?

(12)
a. Er sieht dich.
   he sees you
   'He sees you.'

b. *Sieht er dich.

c. *Er dich sieht.

(13)
a. ...dass er dich sieht
      that he you sees
   '...that he sees you.'

b. *...dass sieht er dich...

c. *...dass er sieht dich...

(14) illustrates the further point that whereas almost any major constituent may occupy initial position in declarative main clauses, the finite verb is quite rigidly restricted to second position.

(14)
a. Ich lernte letzte Woche von Boris Schach
   I learned last week from Boris chess

   spielen.
   play

   'I learned to play chess last week from Boris.'

b. Letzte Woche lernte ich von Boris Schach spielen.

c. Von Boris lernte ich letzte Woche Schach spielen.

d. Schach spielen lernte ich letzte Woche von Boris.

Thus, while declarative main clauses exhibit a good deal of variety in their word order (including some patterns not illustrated in (14), for example, changing the orders of letzte Woche and von Boris), the finite verb in such a clause has no freedom of order at all.

The characteristics discussed above do not exhaust the properties which an instantiation of the category AUX will exhibit. Most important, assuming that the finite verb is a single constituent, it does not contain a fixed and small set of elements; the set of verbs in German is an open class. There is an analysis of German, however, which captures all the properties of the finite verb discussed above and which provides an element the characteristics of which are precisely those expected of an instantiation of AUX.

B.2.3 An Analysis The above observations can be incorporated into a transformational grammar of German as follows. The base rules include those listed in (15).

(15)
S ———> NP   VP Aux_G

VP ———> ... V

Aux_G ———> Tense   M[9]

Tense in German, as in English, is either Present or Past; M in German, unlike NE, is either Indicative, Subjunctive, or Imperative.[10] Aux_G obligatorily attaches to V, the last element of VP. There is an obligatory root transformation (in the sense of Emonds (1976)) which moves Aux_G (and whatever it is attached to) to the immediate right of the first major constituent in the sentence. This transformation applies after various preposing rules. Whether there is also a transformation moving Aux_G into initial position in yes-no questions and imperatives, or whether instead there are abstract markers for questions and imperatives that are treated by the Aux-Second rule as the first major constituent, is a question that we will leave open.

In short, Aux_G is a constituent which contains a specified set of elements, the membership of which includes both tense and modality; the rules given in (15) satisfy properties (a), (d), and (f) in the list of properties in (7) of chapter 3. Further, Aux_G must be treated as obligatorily attaching to some adjacent element and will be positioned in, at least, second and final positions; that is, it exhibits properties consistent with (b) and (c) in the same list. Aux_G will also contain elements marking subject agreement, the mechanism for which is not specified in the analysis sketched above; thus, its notional membership is consistent with property (g) in list (7). (Aux_G is involved, as well, in the mechanism by which questions are marked; a fact which is consonant with the same property, but which is not obviously specified by it, as it stands.)[11] Finally, as mentioned in footnote 9, tense and modality can be marked by a single morphological element; therefore, the property that elements occur in a fixed order, property (e), and the property that the relative order of elements does not follow from other general principles, property (h), apply, though trivially. In sum, all of the properties which hold for AUX are true of Aux_G.

B.2.4 **Three Remarks** A few comments are in order here. First of all, we will not discuss directly the controversial assumption made above, that German is underlyingly verb-final. There is a considerable literature on this subject (for example, Bach (1962), Bierwisch (1963), Maling (1972), Ross (1970; 1973)), to which the interested reader is referred; a clear exposition of the arguments for verb-final order (albeit applied to Dutch, not German) is provided by Koster (1975). Our main point in this section--namely, that the properties of German Aux_G are included in the specifications for AUX--is orthogonal to the issue of underlying word order.

Second, the rules in (15) ignore certain cooccurrence restrictions analogous to those which have played a major role in discussions of the English auxiliary system (especially Akmajian,

Steele, and Wasow (1979)). Specifically, perfectives are impossible in imperatives and in complements to verbs of perception, verbs of temporal aspect, and <u>lassen</u> 'let', as the contrast between (16) and (17) shows.

(16)
a. Trinken Sie das Bier!
   drink you the beer
   'Drink the beer!'

b. Er spürte seine Augen feucht werden.
   he sensed his eyes damp become
   (Curme (1952, 277))
   'He felt his eyes becoming damp.'

c. Die Zigarre blieb brennen.
   the cigar remained burn
   (Curme (1952, 275))
   'The cigar continued burning.'

d. Der Oberst liess die Soldaten zwei
   the colonel let the soldiers two

   Stunden ruhen.
   hours rest

   (Curme (1952, 276))

   'The colonel let the soldiers rest for two hours.'

(17)
a. *Haben Sie das Bier getrunken!
   have you the beer drunk

b. *Er spürte seine Augen feucht geworden sein.
   he sensed his eyes damp become be

   (cf. Er spürte, dass seine Augen Feucht
       he felt that his eyes damp

```
           geworden    waren.
           become      were
```

'He felt that his eyes had become damp.')

```
c. *Die    Zigarre   blieb       gebrannt   haben.
    the    cigar     remained    burned     have

d. *Der    Oberst    liess    die    Soldaten    zwei
    the    colonel   let      the    soldiers    two

   Stunden    geruht    haben.
   hours      rested    have
```

These facts suggest that a more elaborate analysis of the German verbal phrase is called for. However, since this question appears to have no bearing on our main concern, we will not pursue it here.

Third, we have also ignored certain other features of the German verbal system that a more thorough treatment would have to address. Among these is the fact that the modal verbs of German have what appear to be two distinct (and noninterchangeable) perfect participles, one morphologically regular, the other homophonous with the infinitive.

(18)
```
a. Ich    habe    Bäume    fällen    gekonnt.
   I      have    trees    fell      could
```
   'I knew how to fell trees.'

```
b. Ich    habe    Bäume    fällen    können.
```
   'I was able to fell trees.'

Further, while there are a number of verbs in German which may take infinitival complements without zu (cf. (14)), the modal verbs are unusual[12] in prohibiting zu:

(19)
```
a. Ich    lernte     Schach    (zu)    spielen.
   I      learned    chess     (to)    play
```
   'I learned to play chess.'

b. Ich möchte   Schach (*zu) spielen.
   I   would:like chess   (to)   play
   'I would like to play chess.'

Finally, there is a reordering rule in German which, under complex and dialect-dependent conditions, moves the finite verb in a subordinate clause to the left of the other (nonfinite) verbs (see Edmondson (1980) for extensive discussion). This is illustrated in (20).

(20)
a. Ich weiss, dass er hat singen wollen.
   I   know   that he has sing   wanted:to
   'I know that he wanted to sing.'

b. *Ich weiss, dass er singen wollen   hat.
    I   know   that he sing   wanted:to has

c. *Ich weiss, dass er singen gelernt.
    I   know   that he sing   learned

d. Ich weiss, dass er singen gelernt hat.
   I   know   that he sing   learned has
   'I know that he has learned to sing.'

e. Ich weiss nicht, ob   er ihn hat
   I   know not   whether he him has

   nach Hause kommen hören.
   home   come   heard

   (Bierwisch (1963, 108))

   'I don't know whether he has heard him come home.'

f. Ich weiss nicht, ob   er ihn nach Hause
   I   know not   whether he him home

   kommen gehört hat.
   come   heard has

(Bierwisch (1963, 108))

'I don't know whether he has heard him come home.'

Incidentally, (20e) and (20f) also illustrate the fact that the modal verbs are not the only ones with two different past participles. The correlation between the form of the participle and the position of hat in these two examples suggests that there may be a single factor responsible for both.

B.2.5 Why Aux_G It is natural at this point to ask whether there is any reason to prefer the analysis of German sketched above over one which makes no use of the category Aux_G. More specifically, would it make any difference in the analysis we have just outlined if the category Aux_G were dropped from the base rules altogether and all occurrences of it in transformational rules were replaced by something like [V, [+finite]]? If not, one might argue that, all else being equal, the grammar without the extra category is to be preferred on grounds of parsimony.

It is immediately evident that there will be little or no basis for choosing between these alternatives strictly on descriptive grounds. Since Aux_G, at least in derived structure, is always attached to a verb, it is clear that we will achieve the same results whether we formulate our rules in terms of [V, [+finite]] or in terms of Aux_G. There may, however, be a difference at the level of explanation. The analysis without Aux_G provides no principled reason for the properties given in section B.2.2. The various singularities of the finite verb (for example, its role in subject marking and questioning, and its positional constraints) must be treated as an arbitrary collection of properties. In contrast, our analysis in terms of Aux_G, together with our characterization of AUX, provides a principled basis for the observed behavior of the finite verb in German. Introducing the category Aux_G was a way of building into our theory of grammar the claim that certain syntactic and semantic properties would tend to cluster together. Thus, the analysis making use of Aux_G

makes stronger claims and hence provides a more explanatory account than the alternative. It is therefore to be preferred.

It is worth mentioning, by the way, that this advantage of the Aux_G analysis cannot be overcome by claiming (along the lines of Evers and Scholten (1980)) that the properties in question universally characterize finite verbs, for this would simply be false. Brief reflection on the instantiations of AUX in Luiseño, Lummi, or Japanese, languages which formed the critical basis for the properties given in chapter 3, will illustrate this point. Thus, the explanatory advantage of the Aux_G analysis does depend crucially on the more general claims about the cross-linguistic equivalence class AUX.

B.3 AUX in the History of English

Assuming the analysis of English in appendix A and the above analysis of German, we have shown that, while both have elements fitting our characterization of AUX, it is not in general the case that related lexical items play the same role in the two auxiliary systems. This sort of nonparallelism comes through even more strikingly when we look at Old English, for OE appears to have been very much like modern German with respect to all of the phenomena we have been discussing (see, for example, Allen (1974, 93), Closs (1969, 398-401), and Lightfoot (1974, 233-234)). It appears, then, that our analysis commits us to the claim that the historical antecedents of some of our NE Aux-elements (specifically the modals) were not themselves generated under Aux. If this is the case, then it is natural to ask how and why the auxiliary system of OE changed into that of NE. This is the concern of the present section.

There are, of course, dissimilarities between the structure of OE and that of modern German, but they are generally not relevant to our concerns.[13] However, Allen (1974) discusses one difference which is of interest in the present context, namely, that OE permitted NPs and PPs to appear postverbally in subordinate clauses. Allen's analysis of this phenomenon is based on the idea that the rule shifting verbs into second position in main clauses could optionally apply in subordinate clauses as well. Quite apart from the substantial descriptive problems this approach leads to (Allen ends up positing two additional movement transformations involving NPs and PPs), it serves to obscure what in our view is a central fact about OE word order, namely, that only <u>finite</u> verbs appear in second position. In Allen's analysis, the "Verb-Second" rule must be applied to nonfinite verbs, but, as Andrew (1940, 2) observes, in a discussion of the differences between OE main clauses and subordinate clauses, "it is the position of the finite verb which matters." From our perspective, this is a crucial fact, and we therefore reject Allen's analysis. Instead, we propose that OE had an optional rule postposing (nonsubject) NPs and PPs to the end of the clause. This may have been a "stylistic" rule applicable only to "heavy" phrases. Aside from this, we analyze OE exactly as we did modern German, except for the fact that we label the category in question Aux_{OE} and the fact that the Aux_{OE}-Second rule in OE did not apply to all coordinate clauses (cf. footnote 13). Therefore, OE, like German, NE, and the languages discussed in the body of this work, has an instantiation of the category AUX.

B.3.1 <u>Lightfoot's Analysis</u> There is a considerable literature on the history of the English auxiliary system. One particularly relevant study, in the present context, is Lightfoot (1974). Although we disagree with Lightfoot's analysis of OE, much of what he says about the change from OE to NE can be elegantly incorporated into our framework. Lightfoot begins with the argument (which we rejected above) that the verbal character of the OE cognates of NE modals (which he calls the <u>pre-modals</u>) shows that OE lacked some equivalent of NE Aux, our Aux_{OE}.[14] He proceeds to argue that a series of accidental changes during the ME period led to isolation of the pre-modals as a distinct grammatical category, resulting in their reanalysis as modals and the introduction of a new syntactic category. This change in the grammar, he suggests, precipitated several further changes in the language. After presenting Lightfoot's argument in greater detail, we will show that our analysis of OE, together with our thesis about the cross-linguistically identifiable category AUX, can provide a principled account of the changes Lightfoot documents, including several he labels "accidental". We will also show how these changes might have been instrumental in bringing about other changes in the history of English.

Lightfoot (1974, 240) summarizes "the first stage of the story" as follows:[15]

"Four independent changes took place which had the effect of isolating the pre-modals as a distinct class:

(a) loss of all the direct object constructions with pre-modals,
(b) loss of all the preterite-presents except the pre-modals, thereby isolating the pre-modals as a unique inflexional class,
(c) increased opacity of the past tense pre-modals might, could, should, would and must,
(d) the development of to infinitives with almost all verbs except the pre-modals [footnote omitted].

In early Old English the pre-modals had no characteristics peculiar to themselves, but by the end of the Middle English period they had become identifiable as a unique class by virtue of these four independent changes in various parts of the grammar...."

He continues (pp. 240-241):[16]

"These changes seem to have taken effect by the end of the fifteenth century...The pre-modals were now firmly established as a unique class inflexionally, syntactically and semantically...Evidence suggests that at this time they were re-analyzed as a new category, 'Modal', being derived as part of an S containing the verb they govern; the grammar did not continue treating them as verbs and piling up more and more 'exception features'. The evidence is a whole series of changes taking place in the sixteenth century...

(e) The old pre-modals could no longer appear in infinitive constructions....
(f) The old pre-modals could no longer occur with -ing affixes....
(g) As from the mid-sixteenth century there could be only one modal in any clause....
(h) The old pre-modals could no longer occur with have and an -en affix."

These changes in the language follow automatically from Lightfoot's hypothesis that the pre-modals changed categories and came to be introduced by the rule $Aux_{OE} \longrightarrow$ Tense (M). Changes (e), (f), and (h) would follow from the requirement that modals be introduced next to Tense, and (g) would be a consequence of the fact that each clause has only one Aux_{OE}.

We paraphrase Lightfoot's remaining three claims about how the language changed as a result of the reanalysis of pre-modals into modals:

(i) The pattern for negative sentences changed. Earlier "the negative particle occurred immediately after the first verb, whether or not it was a pre-modal" (p. 241).[17] While not continued to follow modals, Lightfoot (p. 242) claims that in "clauses containing just one verb two patterns developed in the early sixteenth century": not preceded the verb, either by itself or following the appropriate form of do.[18] In the late seventeenth century, the form with do became standard.
(j) The NE pattern for questions, in which only auxiliaries precede the subject, began to replace the OE pattern, in which any finite verb could precede the subject.
(k) The "quasi-modal" verbs be going to, have to, and be able to, which are very close semantically to the true modals, entered the language.

Lightfoot claims that (i) and (j) resulted from modifications in the Negative Placement and Inversion transformations, brought about indirectly by the postulated reanalysis. We will discuss these in detail below. Change (k) took place because "the reanalysis...created a vacuum, which the grammar immediately filled by creating a new set of semantically equivalent verbs" (p. 243).

B.3.2   A Reanalysis of Lightfoot's Observations We will assume that Lightfoot's factual claims about the language are correct. We refer the interested reader to Lightfoot's paper for supporting data. However, we believe that a more satisfactory account of the mechanisms of these changes can be achieved within the framework we have been advocating.

On our account, both OE and NE have an instantiation of the category AUX, Tense and M. In OE, however, the elements of the category M are not the pre-modals, but the moods. We believe that the sequence of changes Lightfoot discusses began with the gradual loss of mood distinctions in OE. The erosion of mood distinctions is noted by Lightfoot (p. 247, footnote 18), Traugott (1972, 148-149), and Visser (1969, section 836). According to Visser, the loss of the subjunctive "was in the first place due to the phonological changes the language underwent in the course of time." He goes on to summarize the "gradual decay" of the subjunctive in English, continuing into the present. Abstracting away from the gradual nature of this change, let us suppose that the use of the subjunctive at some point became sufficiently unusual that children learning the language were unable to recognize mood as the instantiation of the notional category M. Since an instantiation of AUX must contain at least either tense or modality, OE retained an instantiation of the category under this change. Since an instantiation of AUX may include both tense and modality and since, in the case at hand, the language already contained a set of irregular verbs expressing modal notions (i.e. a subset of the so-called "preterite-presents") to which the category Aux_{OE} attached, the reanalysis of these into the category is a particularly natural change. This account receives support from Traugott (1972, 148-149):

"During OE the inflectional distinctions between indicative and subjunctive came...to be obscured by the tendency of unstressed vowels to be pronounced [ə]. With the loss of the contrast, the segmentalized auxiliary phrases with scul- and will- that had already been used sporadically as alternates for the subjunctive came to be used more and more and to be generalized to more and more contexts...By ENE the original inflectional subjunctives had been largely taken over by phrases with auxiliaries like should, would, might, may."[19]

We suspect that a subtle semantic shift accompanied the change from pre-modal verb to modal. While we have no direct evidence of this hypothesis, we have observed a phenomenon in modern English and German which lends it plausibility. Consider the following examples:

(21)
a. Alcoholics don't need to drink.
b. Alcoholics need not drink.

(21a) may mean either that alcoholics have no physical need to drink (that is, they can get by without it), or that it is not a necessary property of alcoholics that they be drinkers (that is, it is not part of the meaning of the word). In contrast, (21b) has only the latter meaning; it tells us who may count as an alcoholic, not what the physical needs of alcoholics are. In (21b) need is a modal, whereas in (21a) it is a verb. The reading which is semantically nonmodal is not available when need is syntactically a modal. Similarly, in German we have a semantic contrast between (22a) and (22b).

(22)
a. Ein   Schüler muss in die Schule gehen.
   a   student must in the school go

b. Ein   Schüler muss in die Schule.

        a   student   must   in   the   school

(22a) can mean either that students are required to go to school or that going to school is, by definition, a property of students. (22b) has only the former reading: it cannot be interpreted as a claim about defining properties of students. Though muss is not a modal in either example, it cannot be coincidence that it is the alethic interpretation which is impossible when muss is blatantly nonauxiliary (by virtue of being the only verb in the sentence). The point of these examples is to argue that there is a connection between the syntactic and semantic properties of these elements, alethic interpretations being correlated with the syntactic behavior of modals. If this is correct, then it is surely reasonable to speculate that the pre-modals, in turning into modals, narrowed their ranges of interpretation.

Thus, we claim, the decay of mood distinctions in OE led language learners to reanalyze the pre-modals as members of the category M, quite possibly with accompanying modification of their interpretations, where M is part of Aux_{OE}. Let us now go back and reexamine Lightfoot's claims in terms of this hypothesis.

(a) The fact that the pre-modals "lost the ability to take direct objects" becomes an automatic consequence of the reanalysis, rather than being an accidental factor contributing to it.

(b) The loss of the other members of the preterite-present inflectional class may likewise be viewed as a consequence rather than a cause of the reanalysis of the pre-modals. When the pre-modals became modals, only six preterite-present verbs remained. Of these, according to Lightfoot (pp. 236-237), three dropped out of the language altogether, one developed a more regular inflectional paradigm before disappearing, one survived as a modal in some dialects, and one survived, at least for a time, both as a modal and as a regular verb. This looks far less peculiar on our account than on Lightfoot's: when the most common members of a highly irregular inflectional class are reanalyzed as members of another category, it seems quite natural that the remaining members would either disappear from the language or regularize their inflections. It is no accident on our account that those members of the class which survived (i.e. the pre-modals) form a semantically coherent set, for the fact that they express modality is a central factor leading to their reanalysis.

   (c) Semantic factors are also relevant to the loss of genuine tense distinctions in modals. One (perhaps the) fundamental function of the category of modals is to express alethic notions. Obviously, what is logically necessary (or possible) at one time is necessarily logically necessary (or possible) at all times. This makes tense marking on modals at least partially superfluous, and indeed we find, across languages, that modals are generally not marked for tense. Thus, when OE pre-modals were reanalyzed (with concomitant loss of some nonmodal interpretations), the relationship between former present/past pairs was lost. This was undoubtedly facilitated by the morphological irregularity of tense marking on the pre-modals.

   (d) We suspect that the development of to-infinitives has little or nothing to do with the category change of the pre-modals. Even in NE, a substantial number of true verbs are followed by infinitives without to (for example, verbs of perception, let, make, and help). Moreover, the modal ought requires a following to. Hence, we see little reason to believe that the spread of to-infinitives was either a cause or a consequence of the reanalysis of the pre-modals.

   (e)-(h), (k) Our analysis accounts for these precisely as Lightfoot's does.

   (i), (j) These changes require a bit more exposition. Lightfoot claims (without argument) that ME contained transformations of Negative Placement and Inversion, which made crucial mention of the category V. When the pre-modals were reanalyzed, the category V was split. Here Lightfoot's discussion becomes somewhat metaphorical: the split of the category V meant that "the grammar had to decide" (p. 242) how these phenomena should be affected. In both cases, apparently, the decision was to substitute Aux for V in the rule. Clearly, on Lightfoot's account, the decision could just as easily have been different; in fact, he remarks in a footnote, "Logically it is possible that the grammar could have elected to invert only on the V, but this would have given very strange cross-over phenomena: take John could the bread?" (p. 247). Talking "about grammars anthropomorphically" (p. 242) in this way obscures a problem in this discussion: on Lightfoot's analysis, one change in the grammar precipitated another one, but no (nonmetaphorical) account is given of the connection between the two changes. The latter change does not serve to "maintain the old patterns" (p. 242) in the language; indeed, they are altered at least as much as if it had not taken place. In short, Lightfoot's hypothesis about the reanalysis of pre-modals does not in any way account for the changes cited in (i) and (j).

Under our theory, the reanalysis of the pre-modals would not by itself affect the patterns of negatives or questions. The relevant rules would always be formulated in terms of Aux and, so long as the rule attaching Aux to the immediately preceding verb existed, the old pattern was maintained. We attribute the changes given here as (i) and (j) not directly to the reanalysis of the pre-modals, but rather to the loss of the obligatory attachment of Aux. It may very well be that the creation of independent modals was a cause of the weakening of this rule, for it no longer applied to every instance of the category. Rather, it was now confined to situations where Aux lacked a modal. In any event, we claim that, in the early ME period, the attachment rule began to apply optionally, rather than obligatorily. When it failed to apply--and Aux contained only tense--the tense marker would be stranded. It was necessary, therefore, for some "dummy" verb to be introduced to carry the tense. This, of course, was do.[20] We will return below to the development of the "periphrastic do". For the present, we will simply regard its emergence as evidence that the obligatory attachment of all instances of Aux to verb was no longer necessary. The changes noted in (i) and (j) follow as immediate consequences of this hypothesis.[21] If the loss of the rule was gradual, then the change from ME patterns of negation and questioning to the NE patterns would likewise be gradual. Ellegård (1953, part 2) presents considerable evidence that this was indeed the case.

Our account of (i) and (j) has at least two advantages over Lightfoot's. First, it is more easily reconciled with the rather gradual nature of the change in the patterns of negation and questioning from ME to NE. Second, it leaves the Inversion and Negation rules unchanged. Hence, on our account, it is no accident that it is an instantiation of AUX, rather than the verb, which was operative in negation and questioning: in the history of the language, Aux plays a central role in the processes that are commonly associated with AUX. The "logical possibility" that Lightfoot entertains in his footnote (that is, that only main verbs would be fronted in questions) would be unmotivated and unexpected on our theory.

In summary, we argue that Lightfoot's proposal concerning the reanalysis of the pre-modals is on the right track, but incomplete. The changes he documents (including both those he views as causes and those he regards as effects) can be traced back to a single initial change: the erosion of the subjunctive mood in OE, which triggered the reanalysis of pre-modals as modals in Aux. Given our claims about the role of the cross-linguistically justified category AUX in the grammars of various languages, the entire sequence of changes receives an extremely natural explanation.

One final point about Lightfoot's proposal needs to be addressed, namely, the chronology. He claims that there is a clear division, with changes (a)-(d) occurring before 1500 and the remainder after that date. If this is indeed the case, then something is missing from our analysis. However, we find his argument for the existence of such a sharp break in the history of the language unconvincing. Evidence for all of the changes he documents can be found both before and after 1500, and no compelling case has been made for regarding them as sequential rather than contemporaneous. For example, by Lightfoot's own evidence, change (a) was not complete for all pre-modals until the seventeenth or eighteenth century, but changes (e)-(h) were complete well before the end of the sixteenth. Thus, we place little weight on this aspect of Lightfoot's argument.

B.3.3 Further Changes Lightfoot says little about the history of do, but we would like to pursue the matter briefly. There are a great many works on the development of the periphrastic do in English, and a number of theories regarding its origin have been proposed and debated (see Ellegård (1953, part 1) or Visser (1969, sections 1411-1422) for some discussion). One attractive proposal in the present context is the suggestion of Hausmann (1974) that the use of do as an auxiliary was an outgrowth of its use as a "substitute verb" in examples like (23) (cited by Hausmann, pp. 164-165).

(23)
a. Al-walda þec   gode forgylde, swa he nu
   almighty you   good repay   as   he now

   gyt   dyde!
   still did

   'May the Almighty reward you with good, as He just now has done.'

b. ondrædende   þæt   Læcedemonie   ofer hie
   dreading   that Lacedaemonians over them

   ricsian mehten swa hie   ær   dydon
   rule   might   as   they earlier did

   '...dreading that the Lacedæmonians might rule over them as they had done before.'

Hausmann distinguishes this use from the

periphrastic do on the grounds that the former can appear in the perfective,[22] whereas the latter cannot. It is evident that our account of the changes occurring in the Aux, combined with Hausmann's observations, make the introduction of do as a dummy tense carrier a natural result. Since do already served as a substitute for verbs in one situation (namely, anaphoric constructions like (23)), it was a natural choice when a substitute became necessary in order to rescue a stranded tense.

The changes that we have discussed so far had another interesting effect. While the OE Aux had consisted entirely of verbal inflections, the reanalysis of the pre-modals introduced independent elements into the category. The use of do as a tense carrier further reduced its dependence on the verb. As a result, the grammar of English now had the machinery necessary to permit Aux to be generated in a position not adjacent to a verb. We believe that this in fact happened. Specifically, we propose that in the ME period the grammar of English was simplified by the elimination of the Aux-Second rule, and that the Aux was then base-generated in second position. Thus, on our account, English went from an underlyingly S O V Aux language to an S Aux O V language. (A later change, which we will discuss below, turned it into an S Aux V O language.) We have two reasons for positing this change in the grammar.

First, though ME appears to have exhibited a good deal of variability in word order, the order we posit as basic seems to have been common. Thus, Mossé (1952, 129) claims, "In the compound and periphrastic tenses the object or the adjunct was generally found between the inflected auxiliary verb and the participle or infinitive."[23] Among the examples he uses to illustrate this claim are the following:

(24)
a. pryed   God   he   wulde   hym   ɣeve
   prayed   God   he   would   him   give
   "prayed God that He would give him"

b. the houndes... were on a defaute   y-falle
   the hounds   were on a false:scent fallen
   "The dogs had fallen on a false scent."

c. he hath a thousand slayn
   he has a thousand slain
   "He has killed a thousand."

According to Mossé (p. 130), Aux-final constructions were found only in poetry. Hence, it seems reasonable to conclude that Aux was no longer generated in final position.

Our second argument for claiming that Aux was now generated in second position concerns the use of the periphrastic do. It is well known that there was a marked increase in the use of do at the end of the ME period, reaching a peak in the middle of the sixteenth century (see, for example, Ellegård (1953, 157-163), Traugott (1972,138), or Visser (1969, sections 1418-1420)). In the words of Jespersen (1931, V25.6), "the exuberant use of do, chiefly unstressed, and having no real grammatical value, was reached in the 16th c. ...but from the 17th c. a reaction set in and gradually restricted the use of do." Such an upsurge in the frequency of periphrastic do is one predictable consequence of the changes we have posited. Our analysis claims that do occurs when Tense is stranded; it further claims that, in ME, Tense and the verb were not, in general, generated adjacent to one another. Hence, it follows that do would be required in a great many contexts. Specifically, in addition to negative, inverted, and elliptical constructions, sentences with transitive verbs or preverbal adverbs would result in the stranding of Tense. Ellegård (1953, part 2, chapter 6) documents the fact that the frequency of do in these constructions was indeed higher than in others.[24] It is interesting that no other analysis has been able to account for the widespread use of do in this period in terms of independently motivated changes.

The "reaction" to the "exuberant use of do" that Jespersen mentions, resulting in the present more restricted use of that form, can be attributed to a second change in the basic word order. Specifically, we claim that, in the seventeenth century, the underlying order of the English verb phrase changed from verb-final to verb-initial, that is, that English changed from S Aux O V to S Aux V O. This had the effect of placing the verb adjacent to Tense once again, with the further consequence that the need for periphrastic do was greatly reduced. Of course, the fact that English already had an optional rule postposing objects makes it difficult to verify when the basic word order changed. However, our hypothesis that it occurred in the seventeenth century provides a natural account of the oft-noted and puzzling decline in the use of do.

B.3.4 Summary (I) and (II) summarize the main features of our analysis of the history of the English Aux:

(I) Relevant Aspects of OE Grammar

S ———> NP VP Aux

VP ———> V

Aux ———> Tense M

M is a mood marker

Aux_{OE} is obligatorily attached to the immediately preceding V.

Aux_{OE} is moved to second position in declarative main clauses.

(Aux_{OE} is moved to initial position in questions and imperatives.)

Nonsubject NPs and PPs may be optionally postposed.

Of course, our account is only a very rough sketch. It is both inexplicit and incomplete in

(II) | Changes in Grammar[25] | Results in Language | Approximate Time

	Changes in Grammar[25]	Results in Language	Approximate Time
A.	Erosion of mood distinctions		OE to the present
B.	Reanalysis of pre-modals into the category M	No direct objects with modals	By 14th century
		No modals in infinitive	
		No modals with -ing	
		No modals in perfective	
		Only one modal per clause	
		Loss of preterite-presents	
		Loss of tense in modals	
		Creation of quasi-modals	
C.	Gradual loss of the attachment rule	Emergence of periphrastic do	Early ME to present
		Development of NE patterns for negatives and questions	
D.	Aux-Second rule eliminated and base order changes to S ⟶ NP Aux VP	"Exuberant use of do"	16th century
		S Aux O V order standard	
E.	Base order changes from O V to V O	Use of do subsides	17th century

many places. However, it provides an analysis of the major developments in the English auxiliary system over the last millenium, and it does so within the framework of a substantive universal theory of AUX. This has made it possible to provide a more motivated account of the changes in the language than had previously been available.

B.4 The Changeable AUX

We have seen that the English auxiliary system underwent considerable change during a relatively short period. On reflection, it is clear that the general properties of the AUX that we have discussed make its instantiations diachronically rather unstable. One key property is the propensity of AUX to attach to something else. Elements which do not appear independently would naturally be harder for language learners to recognize as separate entities. Hence, they would tend to be reanalyzed as parts of something else, and thereby lose their original identity. In the case of AUX, if it is necessary that every language have some category which instantiates it, then, when such reanalysis occurs, something else must be reanalyzed as a member of the set AUX. Thus, we might expect that auxiliary elements across languages would exhibit a high turnover rate. It does in fact appear to be the case that languages frequently change the elements of the category which instantiates AUX. This is revealed most clearly in Steele's work on the Uto-Aztecan auxiliary system; cf. Steele (1978a). Binnick (1976) documents changes in the tense and aspectual systems of several languages which also fit the pattern we have sketched.

In addition, there are signs of ongoing change in the auxiliary systems of modern English and German. _Shall_ is not part of the active vocabulary of many Americans, presumably because, in its contracted form, it is indistinguishable from _will_. Some other speakers use _shall_ only in questions (Shall I get the car?), where contraction is impossible. We conjecture that _shall_ is on its way out of English. Other modals appear to be on the way in. For instance, the adjectives _better_ and _best_ can be used as modals in some contexts (You better (not) eat that), but not in others (*Better I eat that?). The widespread use of don't with third person singular subjects may indicate that many speakers have reanalyzed don't as a modal.

Other ongoing changes in the English auxiliary system are even more interesting from our point of view. For example, consider the process of contraction illustrated in (25).

(25)
a. What's he done? (= What has he done?)
b. What's he doing? (= What is he doing?)
c. What's he do? (= What does he do?)

Present tense auxiliaries which end in the phonological segment /s/ are all contracted as /s/ (orthographic 's). As far as we know, the standard view is that this contraction is a synchronic process. However, there is a very simple generalization that cannot be stated if one takes that view: namely, that 's simply represents third person present tense. The aspectual distinctions of (25a-c) are in fact reflected in the morphological form of the main verbs (perfective done, progressive doing, and infinitive do), and 's contributes nothing more than an indication of third person present tense. If we view 's as being formed by a synchronic rule of contraction, then there is no single source for it: it derives from the particular morphemes has, is, or does, and the simple generalization about 's cannot be stated.

If we turn to declarative sentences, we see that 's functions in the same way, except for the gap shown by (26c):

(26)
a. He's done something wrong.
b. He's doing something about it.
c. *He's do a lot of things. (cf. He does a lot of things.)

In other words, 's functions to mark third person present tense whenever the main verb of the sentence is nontensed (a participle or infinitive); when the main verb is tensed, 's may not appear. Thus, in certain respects we can say that English resembles Luiseno, in that 's is a second position clitic which expresses person and tense, attached to the first element in a sentence (the wh-words in (25) and the subject pronoun in (26)). That is, 's has properties otherwise expected for members of the set AUX.

While we have no doubt that contraction is a genuine diachronic process, we have raised doubts about its status as a synchronic process which derives 's. Another phenomenon in English for which the synchronic contraction hypothesis for 's is dubious is shown in (27) and (28).

(27)
a. There's three cars in the garage.
b. *There is three cars in the garage.
c. There are three cars in the garage.

(28)
a. There's been three men here.
b. *There has been three men here.
c. There have been three men here.

In general informal American English, sentences such as (27a) and (28a) are widely used and are perfectly natural. But if 's derives from is or has by contraction, we immediately run into problems of number agreement, which is obligatory for these full verbs, as (27b,c) and (28b,c) show. It appears as though there's has become a single unanalyzable unit, no longer (synchronically) derived by contraction, representing a present tense existential.

However, other evidence suggests that contraction must still be posited as a synchronic process of English. Consider the examples in (29):

(29)
a. He's a nice man. (He is a nice man.)
b. *He's a lot of money. (He has a lot of money.)
c. *He's a lot of things. (He does a lot of things.)

These cases show that 's can stand for main verb is,
but not main verbs has and does. But this is just
what we would expect if contraction of auxiliaries
were a synchronic process. It is well known that
main verb be exhibits auxiliary characteristics,
main verb have shows some auxiliary-like behavior
(but is highly erratic in this regard in American
English), and main verb do has no auxiliary
properties whatever. If 's were analyzed in these
cases as having nothing to do with the morphemes is,
has, and does, the ungrammatical examples in (29)
would simply be a mystery: after all, why should 's
represent has and does in questions (cf. (25)), but
not in simple declarative sentences? Obviously, has
and does are auxiliaries in (25) but not in (29),
and only the synchronic contraction hypothesis links
's with auxiliary has and does.

Thus, an intriguing situation arises: on the one
hand, a simple generalization--namely, that 's
stands for third person present tense--cannot be
stated if contraction is a synchronic process; on
the other hand, the obvious relation of 's to its
parent verbs cannot be captured if we do not posit a
synchronic contraction process. This kind of
paradox is what we might well expect when a language
is in an intermediate state, where certain changes
have begun but have not become so pervasive as to
cause the older system to restructure.

Another interesting aspect of so-called
contraction processes can be seen in questions in
which the inverted auxiliary is said to contract
with the subject:

(30)
a. Did you leave yesterday?
b. Djou leave yesterday?

(31)
a. Didn't you like this?
b. Dintcha like this?

(32)
a. What do you want to do?
b. Waddaya want to do?

Forms such as djou, dintcha, waddaya, and numerous others are in fact single phonological words occurring at the beginning of questions. Assume for the moment that these forms have indeed become single lexical items: how would we analyze them lexically?

Notice first that a word such as dintcha cannot be assigned to any English lexical category: it is neither a noun nor a verb, and in fact does not assimilate to any existing lexical category in English. Second, the position of the word is sentence-initial. Third, this word and others like it express the following notions:

(33)
a. Tense (e.g. dintcha is past tense)
b. Modality (e.g. wouldja)
c. Negation (e.g. dintcha)
d. Person Marking (e.g. dintcha is second person)
e. All such forms mark questions.

It is striking that the sentence-initial words ("contractions") under consideration exhibit properties specified for AUX; questions such as (30b), (31b), (32b) are most naturally viewed as a new English instantiation of the category.

We might view these sentence-initial forms as the result of a synchronic contraction process; but then, as before, certain surface generalizations are missed. For example, consider the following three sentences:

(34)
a. Watcha been doing? (What have you been doing?)
b. Watcha doing? (What are you doing?)
c. Watcha do on Saturdays? (What do you do on Saturdays?)

The form watcha, as a lexical item, is a wh-word (hence marking a question that we know will contain an internal "gap") that expresses second person present tense. This simple characterization of watcha is not possible on the contraction hypothesis, which entails that watcha arises from three entirely different sources: what have you, what are you, and what do you. In addition, the phonological form watcha shows no indication, or phonological trace, of the verbs have, are, or do. If watcha is the result of synchronic contraction, then it is the contraction of the combination of what + ya, with no intervening verb form. The aspectual distinctions among the sentences of (34) do not force us to postulate have, are, or do, since these semantic distinctions are again attributable to the inflections on the other verbs in the sentence. It appears that English is developing a set of initial particles that are becoming lexicalized in certain cases and for which a contraction analysis is increasingly implausible, particles which are reasonable candidates for membership in AUX.

That we cannot discount the synchronic contraction hypothesis is shown by forms similar to watcha, namely, what'vya, what'rya, and what'dya, which in fact do show the traces of have (v), are (r), and do (d). One could claim that if v, r, and d are subject to deletion, then this would leave the sequence what + ya, thereby giving rise to watcha in all three cases. Once again, English seems to be in an intermediate state, when certain contractions are beginning to be lexicalized, but are still closely enough tied to more transparent forms as to require the contraction analysis.

Even if we are forced to posit contraction as a synchronic rule for the cases we have been discussing, an important point remains. Namely, it is striking that a synchronic process should create sentence-initial particles with the cluster of properties outlined in (33). For example, notice that no contraction of what plus the following elements takes place in (35).

(35)
a. What used up the gas? (*Watchused up the gas?)
b. What yanked the door open? (*Watchanked the door open?)

Even though the words following *what* begin with the phonological segment /y/, which we might expect to serve as a trigger for the same palatalization that occurs when *what* is followed by *you*, no such palatalization or contraction occurs in these cases. Certainly we can always stipulate, as a blunt fact, what words can contract in initial position, and what words cannot. However, this simple stipulation explains nothing, and seems to describe just a set of accidental properties of one language. On the other hand, if we say that contraction of the subject with other elements--whether diachronic or synchronic contraction--creates an instantiation of AUX, then it automatically follows that the units that result from contraction must have the cluster of properties that characterizes AUX, of which the properties in (33) are a subset. With respect to (35), the verbs *use* and *yank* do not have properties of AUX, and we would thus never expect them to be contractible. In this way, we can see that the postulation of a category AUX can serve to constrain rules, as well as to explain why certain language-particular rules operate the way they do and why certain historical changes occur.

The signs of change in modern German are also interesting, for they resemble closely what we have posited as the early stages of the change from OE to NE. First, it seems that the use of the subjunctive in German is on the decline. Thus, Diekhoff (1914, 297-298) notes that "on the whole,...the use of the subjunctive has been constantly waning as time goes on." This tendency has evidently not yet reached the point where it would trigger a reanalysis, but our discussion of the history of English suggests that this is a likely consequence. Second, it has been observed by Curme (1952, 278), Erben (1969), and Hausmann (1974, 171-173) that many dialects of German make a periphrastic use of *tun* 'do'. Among the many examples cited are those in (36):

(36)
a. I   tat   essen, wenn es regnen tat.
   I   did   eat   if   it rain   did
   'I would eat if it rained.'

b. Tut euch nicht bekleckern!
   do yourselves not mess:up
   'Don't mess yourselves up!'

c. Wer tutt sich hier firchten....?
   who does himself here fear
   'Who here is afraid?'

d. Tun tut er mer emende nischt, aber
   do does he me in:the:end nothing but

   ich tu mich ferchten.
   I do myself fear

   'In the end he won't do anything to me, but I'm afraid.'

These examples suggest that the rule attaching Aux_G to Verb is optional in some German dialects. Hausmann (1974, 173) argues persuasively that <u>tun</u> was chosen as a tense carrier for the same reason that <u>do</u> was: both are used as substitute verbs in anaphoric constructions. Thus, two of the changes we posited in OE appear to be well under way in modern German.

B.5 Conclusion
Within our theory of AUX, the observable differences between the auxiliary systems of English and German are not a random collection of accidents; nor are the historical changes in the English auxiliary. Rather, the range of possibilities permitted by our universal characterization of AUX is sufficiently narrow that much of the apparent arbitrariness can be explained. Thus, far from being counterexamples to our main thesis, German and the history of English provide strong support for it.

Notes
1. We will use the subscripted labels $\underline{Aux}_G$ and $\underline{Aux}_{OE}$ to refer to the German and Old English categories under consideration. The discussion of this aspect of the languages in this section has

used the label <u>Aux</u> and, since we are addressing issues raised in the literature, we maintain a reasonable continuity with it by using this label. However, we must reiterate the point of the first chapter: we could give any label to the German or Old English categories under consideration--insofar as we can give an analysis which reasonably establishes them as syntactic constituents--and still ask whether they are to be included in the set AUX. The subscripts, therefore, are meant to distinguish them from one another and from the label <u>Aux</u> which is reserved for modern English.

2. Bierwisch (1963, 174) points out that there are dialects which also allow iteration of the perfect <u>haben</u>: <u>Ich habe gegessen gehabt</u>.

3. This example is in fact unacceptable as given in most dialects of German, which require that <u>hat</u> precede <u>essen</u>. The existence of a rule effecting the necessary reordering is alluded to below. See Edmondson (1980) for a detailed discussion of this phenomenon.

4. One possible counterexample is Verb Phrase Deletion. Evers and Scholten (1980, 91) claim that "VP Deletion is impossible...in German." Curme (1952, 287) and Grosu (1977), on the other hand, discuss examples of Verb Phrase Deletion in German, but do not specify the conditions under which it applies. All of their examples involve leaving behind a cognate of an English auxiliary element, but we do not know whether this is coincidental or not. Evidently, Verb Phrase Deletion in German is far more restricted than in English, as indicated by (i):

(i)
a. *Er wird nicht geschlafen haben, aber ich
   he   will not   slept   have   but   I

   werde.
   will

   'He will not have slept, but I will.'

b. *Ich singe, wenn sie (tut).
   I   sing   when she (does)

c. *Er scheint zornig zu sein, und sie
   he seems angry to be   and she

   scheint zu sein, auch.
   seems   to be   too

   'He seems to be angry, and she seems to be, too.'

Whether such observations can in fact be used to drive a wedge between the cognates of the elements of the English Aux and other German verbs cannot be determined in the absence of a careful analysis of German Verb Phrase Deletion, which is beyond the scope of this work.

5. There appear to be at least two distinct constructions in NE which are called subjunctives. One is the use of were with singular subjects in counterfactual conditionals:

(i)
If my grandmother were a bicycle, she would have wheels.

The other is the use of nonfinite verbs in certain that-complements:

(ii)
I insisted that he make amends.

It seems that the former construction is being replaced (at least in American English) by the use of were with all types of if-clauses. For a treatment of the latter, see chapter 4.

6. In what follows, the verb in the subjunctive is underlined, the numbers in parentheses refer to pages in Curme (1952), and glosses in double quotation marks are taken directly from Curme. It

should be mentioned that several native speakers of German have remarked that some of the examples in (10) seem rather antiquated to them.

7. Curme presents this as an example of a use of the subjunctive which is "in English usually rendered by <u>may</u> or <u>can</u>."

8. It is interesting to note that most of the examples of subjunctives that Curme gives would be translated most naturally into English with the use of some tenseless construction e.g. a particle or gerund, an infinitive, or a modal. Cf. footnote 5.

9. Tense and M are listed here is a specific order, but as Elizabeth Traugott has pointed out to us, there does not appear to be any evidence for this (or the opposite) ordering in German, since it is not obviously possible to identify some single morpheme with each. That is, a single morphological element may mark both.

10. Traditional grammars of German treat the imperative form of verbs as a separate mood. We have accepted this analysis without trying to justify it. Nothing in what follows depends crucially on this assumption.

11. Aux_G, as we have analyzed it above, also marks the imperative. This is outside the list of notional categories specified in chapter 3. However, footnote 4 of that chapter discussed the possibility that it be included.

12. However, verbs of perception and <u>lassen</u> also seem to prohibit <u>zu</u>:

(i)
Ich sah/lasse ihn Schach (*zu) spielen.
I   saw/let   him chess (to)   play
'I saw/let him play chess.'

13. Two that have appeared in the transformational literature are these: (i) the finite verb often

appeared in final position in coordinate clauses as well as subordinates (Closs (1969, 400)); and (ii) there appear to have been some additional cooccurrence restrictions on verbal sequences (Closs (1969, 399)).

14. Aux_{OE} is of course our designation, not Lightfoot's.

15. Lightfoot (1979), which was published after this appendix was written, adds a fifth change to the list. He argues that if the pre-modals, at least on their epistemic reading, were verbs with a sentential subject, they should, once the word order of OE had changed to the word order of ME, have allowed the following sequence: SVOM. However, this order is exceedingly rare; thus, "...following the SOV-to-SVO base change some special mechanism would be needed to distinguish the epistemic pre-modals from other one-place predicates, avoiding the expected SVOM or it M[NP...]$_S$ structures..." (p. 108). As Lightfoot himself notes, this argument assumes an analysis of epistemic pre-modals which is not obviously correct; if it is not, there is no reason to posit a fifth change which isolated the pre-modals from other verbs. In any case, we see no major obstacle to incorporating the fact that SMVO was the standard order for early ME into the analysis which we will propose below.

16. What we designate as (e)-(h) here Lightfoot calls (a)-(d). We have changed his indexing to avoid confusion between these changes and the ones listed in the earlier quotation.

17. In OE, the pattern was different, with the negative particle preceding the verb (see, for example, Traugott (1972, 107)). The pattern Lightfoot describes was established in "the middle of the fourteenth century", according to Mosse (1952, 112).

18. Lightfoot gives no examples of _not_ preceding the verb and not following _do_. No other source we

have consulted mentions this pattern. Our discussion assumes the accuracy of Lightfoot's claims, but it would not be substantially affected if he is in error on this point.

19. If, in OE, the markings for tense and mood were not obviously distinct morphological elements, as appears to be the case in German, the erosion of mood distinctions does not require the absolute loss of the (set of) morpheme(s) which previously marked both. Rather, as the distinction between indicative and subjunctive moods was lost, the tense distinction became primary.

20. Ellegård (1953, 209), Hausmann (1974, 168-171), and Traugott (1972, 138,199) all date the use of do as a tense carrier from early ME. Visser (1969, 1498) disagrees, claiming that it "was already in use in pre-conquest times in the spoken language."

21. Actually, only one of the two patterns of negation Lightfoot mentions would follow automatically. Which of the two it would be depends on how one introduces the periphrastic do at this stage of the language. Cf. footnote 18.

22. Hausmann cites (23b) as an example of do in the perfective; however, as Elizabeth Traugott has pointed out to us, (23b) is not syntactically perfective.

23. Mossé also gives many examples in both main and subordinate clauses of main verbs preceding their objects. This might seem to conflict with our proposal. However, O V order was common as well. See the discussion below.

24. The existence of the periphrastic do immediately preceding the verb in this period is not clear counterevidence to this account, since such examples might be emphatics, or might result from postposing the object after the rule responsible for the appearance of do. What would be a problem for our analysis would be evidence that there were O V

constructions in which the V was finite, in this period.

25. The analysis of NE presented in Akmajian, Steele, and Wasow (1979) suggests that, at some point in the history of English, Tense and Modal ceased to cooccur in Aux. This change is not specified in the chart.

LIST OF ABBREVIATIONS

acc	accusative
act part	active participle
adj	adjective
dat	dative
f	feminine
imperf	imperfect
m	masculine
neg	negative
nom	nominative
obj	object
prt	particle
Prt Com	Particle Complex
prt seq	particle sequence
pass part	passive participle
perf	perfect
pl	plural
sg	singular
subj mark	subject marking

REFERENCES

Abdel-Massih, T., Z. N. Abdel-Malek, and E. M. Badawi (1979) <u>A Comprehensive Study of Egyptian Arabic</u>, Center for Near Eastern and North African Studies, The University of Michigan, Ann Arbor.

Akmajian, A., S. Steele, and T. Wasow (1979) "The Category AUX in Universal Grammar," <u>Linguistic Inquiry</u> 10, 1-64.

Akmajian, A. and T. Wasow (1975) "The Constituent Structure of VP and AUX and the Position of the Verb BE," <u>Linguistic Analysis</u> 1, 205-245.

Allen, C. (1974) "Old English Modals," in J. Grimshaw, ed., <u>Papers in the History and Structure of English</u>, UMass Occasional Papers in Linguistics, Department of Linguistics, University of Massachusetts, Amherst.

Andrew, W. O. (1940) <u>Syntax and Style in Old English</u>, Cambridge University Press, Cambridge.

Bach, E. (1962) "The Order of Elements in a Transformational Grammar of German," <u>Language</u> 38, 263-269.

Bierwisch, M. (1963) <u>Grammatik des Deutschen Verbs</u>, Studia Grammatica II, Berlin.

Binnick, R. (1976) "How Aspect Languages Get Tense," in S. Steever, C. Walker, and S. Mufwene, eds., <u>Diachronic Syntax</u>, Chicago Linguistic Society, University of Chicago, Chicago, Illinois, 40-49.

Bresnan, J. (1971) "Contraction and the Transformational Cycle in English," unpublished paper, MIT, Cambridge, Massachusetts.

Bresnan, J. W. (1976) "On the Form and Functioning of Transformations," <u>Linguistic Inquiry</u> 7, 3-40.

Chomsky, N. (1957) *Syntactic Structures*, Mouton, The Hague.

Chomsky, N. (1965) *Aspects of the Theory of Syntax*, MIT Press, Cambridge, Massachusetts.

Chomsky, N. (1970) "Remarks on Nominalization," in R. Jacobs and P. Rosenbaum, eds., *Readings in English Transformational Grammar*, Ginn, Waltham, Massachusetts.

Chomsky, N. and M. Halle (1968) *The Sound Pattern of English*, Harper and Row, New York.

Chomsky, N. and H. Lasnik (1977) "Filters and Control," *Linguistic Inquiry* 8, 425-504.

Closs, E. (1969) "Diachronic Syntax and Generative Grammar," in D. Reibel and S. Schane, eds., *Modern Studies in English*, Prentice-Hall, Englewood Cliffs, New Jersey.

Culicover, P. (1976) *Syntax*, Academic Press, New York.

Curme, G. (1952) *A Grammar of the German Language*, Macmillan, New York.

Diekhoff, T. (1914) *The German Language*, Oxford University Press, New York.

Edmondson, J. (1980) "Gradienz und die doppelte infinitivkonstruktion im Deutschen," *Papiere zur Linguistik* 22.1.

Ellegård, A. (1953) *The Auxiliary Do*, Almqvist and Wiksell, Stockholm.

Emonds, J. (1976) *A Transformational Approach to English Syntax*, Academic Press, New York.

Erben, J. (1969) "*Tun* als Hilfsverb im heutigen Deutsch," in U. Engel, P. Grebe, and H. Rupp, eds., *Festschrift für Hugo Moser*, Pädagogischer Verlag

References

Schwann, Düsseldorf.

Evers, A. and T. Scholten (1980) "A Dutch Answer to the Luiseño Argument," _Utrecht Working Papers in Linguistics_ 9.

Fillmore, C. (1971) _Santa Cruz Lectures on Deixis_, reproduced and distributed by the Indiana University Linguistics Club, Bloomington, Indiana, November, 1975.

Fodor, J. A. (1975) _The Language of Thought_, Thomas J. Crowell, New York.

Gazdar, G., G. Pullum, and I. Sag (1980) "A Phrase-Structure Grammar of the English Auxiliary System," paper presented at the Fourth Groningen Round Table.

Greenberg, J. (1963) "Some Universals of Grammar with Particular Reference to the Order of Meaningful Elements," in J. Greenberg, ed., _Universals of Language_, MIT Press, Cambridge, Massachusetts.

Grimshaw, J. (1979) "Complement Selection and the Lexicon," _Linguistic Inquiry_ 10, 279-326.

Grosu, A. (1977) "On the Status of Positionally Defined Constraints in Syntax," _Theoretical Linguistics_ 4.1/2.

Hale, K. (1980) "The Problem of Free Word Order in a Theory of Grammar: The Case of Walbiri," presentation given at the University of Arizona, Tucson, Arizona.

Hausmann, R. (1974) "The Origin and Development of Modern English Periphrastic _Do_," in J. M. Anderson and C. Jones, eds., _Historical Linguistics I_, North Holland, Amsterdam.

Heny, F. and B. Richards, eds. (to appear) _Proceedings from the Fourth Groningen Round Table_.

Higgins, R. (1973) The Pseudo-Cleft Construction in English, Doctoral dissertation, MIT, Cambridge, Massachusetts.

Huber, W. and W. Kummer (1974) Transformationelle Syntax des Deutschen I, Wilhelm Fink Verlag, Munich.

Hyde, V. (1971) An Introduction to the Luiseño Language, Malki Museum Press, Banning, California.

Jackendoff, R. (1972) Semantic Interpretation in Generative Grammar, MIT Press, Cambridge, Massachusetts.

Jackendoff, R. (1977a) "Constraints on Phrase Structure Rules," in P. Culicover, T. Wasow, and A. Akmajian, eds., Formal Syntax, Academic Press, New York, 249-284.

Jackendoff, R. (1977b) $\bar{X}$ Syntax, Linguistic Inquiry Monograph 2, MIT Press, Cambridge, Massachusetts.

Jacobs, R. (1975) Syntactic Change, University of California Publications in Linguistics 79, University of California, Berkeley and Los Angeles.

Jacobsen, W. (1976) "Noun and Verb in Nootka," in B. Efrat, ed., The Victoria Conference on Northwestern Languages, Heritage Record No. 4, British Columbia Provincial Museum, Victoria, B. C.

Jelinek, E. (1980) On Defining Categories: Verb, AUX, and PREDICATE in Colloquial Egyptian Arabic, Doctoral dissertation, University of Arizona, Tucson, Arizona.

Jespersen, O. (1931) A Modern English Grammar on Historical Principles, George Allen and Unwin, London.

Kaisse, E. (1981) "Luiseño Particles and the Universal Behavior of Clitics," Linguistic Inquiry 12.

References

Kajita, M. (1968) <u>A Generative-Transformational Study of Semi-Auxiliaries in Present-Day American English</u>, Sanseido, Tokyo.

Kitagawa, C. (1973) "Adverbial Clauses of Contrast and Reason," <u>Papers in Japanese Linguistics</u> 2, 75-101.

Klima, E. S. (1964) "Negation in English," in J. A. Fodor and J. J. Katz, eds., <u>The Structure of Language</u>, Prentice-Hall, Englewood Cliffs, New Jersey, 246-323.

Koster, J. (1975) "Dutch as an SOV Language," <u>Linguistic Analysis</u> 1, 111-136.

Koster, J. (1978) "Conditions, Empty Nodes, and Markedness," <u>Linguistic Inquiry</u> 9, 551-594.

Kuipers, A. (1968) "The Categories Verb-Noun and Transitive-Intransitive in English and Squamish," <u>Lingua</u> 21, 610-626.

Kuno, S. (1972) "Pronominalization, Reflexivization, and Direct Discourse," <u>Linguistic Inquiry</u> 3, 161-195.

Kuroda, S.-Y. (1965) <u>Generative Grammatical Studies in the Japanese Language</u>, Doctoral dissertation, MIT, Cambridge, Massachusetts.

Kuroda, S.-Y. (1973) "Where Epistemology, Style and Grammar Meet--A Case Study from Japanese," in S. Anderson and P. Kiparsky, eds., <u>A Festschrift for Morris Halle</u>, Holt, Rinehart and Winston, New York, 377-391.

Lakoff, R. (1972) "Language in Context," <u>Language</u> 48, 907-927.

Liberman, M. Y. (1974) "On Conditioning the Rule of Subj.-Aux. Inversion," in E. Kaisse and J. Hankamer, eds., <u>Papers from the Fifth Annual Meeting, North Eastern Linguistic Society</u>, Harvard

University, Cambridge, Massachusetts, 77-91.

Lightfoot, D. (1974) "The Diachronic Analysis of English Modals," in J. M. Anderson and C. Jones, eds., *Historical Linguistics I*, North Holland, Amsterdam.

Lightfoot, D. (1979) *Principles of Diachronic Syntax*, Cambridge University Press, Cambridge.

McCawley, J. (1975) "The Category Status of English Modals," *Foundations of Language* 12.

Maling, J. (1972) "On Gapping and the Order of Constituents," *Linguistic Inquiry* 3, 101-108.

Martin, S. E. (1975) *A Reference Grammar of Japanese*, Yale University Press, New Haven, Connecticut.

Mitchell, J. (1971) *A Study in Diachronic Syntax: The Auxiliary from Old English to Modern English*, Doctoral dissertation, University of Iowa, Iowa City, Iowa.

Mossé, F. (1952) *A Handbook of Middle English*, translated by J. A. Walker, Johns Hopkins Press, Baltimore, Maryland.

Oehrle, R. (1979) "A Theoretical Consequence of Constituent Structure in *Tough* Movement," *Linguistic Inquiry* 10, 583-593.

Oehrle, R. T. and L. G. Shiman (1977) "An Analytic Grammar for Vision and Natural Languages," unpublished manuscript.

Oehrle, R. T. and L. G. Shiman (1979) "Some Properties of the English AUX and their Grammatical Consequences," paper presented at the Salzburg AUX Festival, Salzburg, Austria.

Oehrle, R. T. and L. G. Shiman (1980) "The AUX Analyzed by Natural Categories," paper presented at the Groningen AUX Conference, Groningen, The Netherlands.

Perlmutter, D. and P. M. Postal (1977) "Toward a Universal Characterization of Passivization," in K. Whistler et al., eds., *Proceedings of the Third Annual Meeting of the Berkeley Linguistics Society*, 394-417.

Pullum, G. K. (1981) "Evidence against the 'AUX' Node in Luiseño and English," *Linguistic Inquiry* 12.

Pullum, G. and D. Wilson (1977) "Autonomous Syntax and the Analysis of Auxiliaries," *Language* 53, 741-788.

Ross, J. (1967) "Auxiliaries as Main Verbs," *Studies in Philosophical Linguistics*, Series 1, W. Todd, ed., Great Expectations Press, Evanston, Illinois.

Ross, J. (1970) "Gapping and the Order of Constituents," in M. Bierwisch and K. E. Heidolph, eds., *Progress in Linguistics*, Mouton, The Hague.

Ross, J. (1973) "The Penthouse Principle and the Order of Constituents," in *You Take the High Node and I'll Take the Low Node*, Chicago Linguistics Society, University of Chicago, Chicago, Illinois.

Sag, I. (1976) *Deletion and Logical Form*, Doctoral dissertation, MIT, Cambridge, Massachusetts.

Sapir, E. (1921) *Language: An Introduction to the Study of Speech*, Harcourt, Brace, New York.

Selkirk, E. (1978) "On Prosodic Structure and Its Relationship to Syntactic Structure," paper presented to the Conference on Mental Representation in Phonology.

Steele, S. (1975) "Past and Irrealis: Just What Does It All Mean?" *IJAL* 41, 200-217.

Steele, S. (1977) "On the Count of One," in A. Juilland, ed., *Linguistic Studies Offered to Joseph Greenberg*, Vol. 3, Anma Libri, Saratoga, California, 591-613.

Steele, S. (1978a) *The AUX in Uto-Aztecan: A Historical Study*, manuscript.

Steele, S. (1978b) "The Category AUX as a Language Universal," in J. Greenberg, C. Ferguson, and E. Moravcsik, eds., *Universals of Human Language*, Vol. IV, Stanford University Press, Stanford, California.

Steele, S. (1980) "Four Syntactic Affixes in Luiseño," paper presented at the Symposium on Uto-Aztecan Historical Linguistics, Albuquerque, New Mexico.

Steele, S. (1981) "The Luiseño Absolutive, and the Other Syntactic Operators," manuscript.

Stopp, F. (1957) *A Manual of Modern German*, University Tutorial Press, London.

Thompson, L. and M. Terry Thompson (1971) "Clallan: A Preview," in J. Sawyer, ed., *Studies in American Indian Languages*, University of California Publications in Linguistics 65, University of California Press, Berkeley and Los Angeles, 251-294.

Traugott, E. (1972) *A History of English Syntax*, Holt, Rinehart and Winston, New York.

Uyeno, T. (1971) *A Study of Japanese Modality--A Performative Analysis of Sentence Particles*, Doctoral dissertation, University of Michigan, Ann Arbor, Michigan.

Visser, F. (1969) *An Historical Study of the English Language*, E. J. Brill, Leiden.

Wagner, K. (1969) *Generative Grammatical Studies in the Old English Language*, Julius Gross Verlag, Heidelberg.

References

Williams, E. S. (1977) "Discourse and Logical Form," *Linguistic Inquiry* 8, 101-139.

INDEX

Abdel-Malek,N.,80
Abdel-Massih,T.,80
Absolute time,21
Absolutive,176-177,178,180,
  184,185,214,215,219n3,220n6,
  221n9
Abstract markers,268
Abstractness,22
Action-infinitival
  complements,201
Active participles,76
Additive function,223n11
Adverbials,235,264
Adverbial clause,103,106
Adverbs,10,99,100,227
Affixes,62,68,69,70,98,102,
  108,113,115,139n44,143,148,
  155,158,184,219n3,222n10
Affective element,193,194
Adjectives,10,11,66,84,206,
  257n10,289
 of feeling,109
Adjuncts,41,132n22,182,184,
  185,285
 absolutive marked,222n10
Affix hopping,237,243-245
Agentive propositions,204
Agentive NP's,205
Agents,223n14
Agglutinative language,97
Agreement,102,227
Akmajian,A.,14,15,16,24,25,33,
  98,99,116n1,117n5,118n7,
  119n8,120n8,121n8,124n8,
  129n17,133n23,165n5,258n15,
  259n18,269-270,302n25
Alethic interpretation,280
Alethic notions,281
Allen,C.,260,274,275
American English,292

Anaphoric constructions,285,
  296
Andrew, W.,275
Antecedent,241
Arguments,66,199
 of verbs,205
Article,60
Aspect,14,76,79,115,127n13,
  135n27,146,156,159,173,175,
  177,178,180,181,182,184,
  185,219n3
Aspectual distinctions,290,
  294
Aspectual notions,41
Aspectual reference,43
Aspectual suffixes,219n5,
  220n6
Aspectual verbs,264
Aspects of the Theory of
  Syntax,1,8
Assertions,27,45,49,169,175,
  178,190,191,195,196
Attachment,143-145,269,289
Attachment properties,164n1
Attachment rule,288
Autonomous syntactic
  constituent,62
AUX,2,3,13,15,16,21,115,
  119n8,120n8,143,143,144,
  145,146,147,150,153,154,
  157,158,160,161,162,163,
  164n1,166n7,167n11,168,169,
  188,211,212,213,214,215,
  217,252,253,260,264,266,
  268,269,274,275,276,278,
  289,293,295,296
 absolute properties of,
  149-155
 in the history of English,
  274-295

Index 314

AUX controversy,13-17
Aux,239,245,257n11
  as feature,240,241,242,
    257n11,260,263
  as main verb,14
  as syntactic category,13-14
  in German,261-273,296-297n1,
    298n11
  in OE,274-288,296-297n1,
    300n14
Aux-elements,5,188,210,237-238
  invertible,194
Aux-final constructions,286
Aux-operator,210,243-245,253n2
Aux-phenomena
  in English,227-228,245
  finite character of,230-232
Aux-second rule,268,275,285,
  288
Auxiliary ellipsis,259n18
Auxiliary verbs,237-243,
  257n10,277
Available grammars,230
Ax,232-237,242,243,254-255n6,
  255-256n8,257n12
Ax-elements,240,242,250,252,
  253,257n12,258n15,259n18
Ax-element,tensed
  occurrence of,245

Bach,E.,268
Backward anaphora condition,
  257n13
Badawi,E.,80
Base rules,268,273
Bierwisch,M.,269,272-273,
  297n2
Bi-imperfect,74,83,138n39
Binding condition,202
Binding relation,199
Binnick,R.,289
Bound affixes,83
Bound pronominal affix,96

Bound pronominal subject
  markers,60
Bound subject,203,207
Boundary properties,120n8
Boundaries,133n23
Bresnan,J.,238,241

Case labels,18n1
Casual speech,71
Categorial labels,8
Categorial grammar,256n9
Categorial symbol,12,228
Categorical distinctions,7,
  66
Categorical operations,255n8
Categories in Universal
  Grammar,15
Categorization,245
Category,2,4,6,7,8,9,13,16,
  18n3,19n6,120n8,155,212,
  217,226,227,228-230,231,
  232,238,243,245,253n3
Category-equivalence,256n9
Causal agents,224n14
Certainty,21
ch→sh rule,129n17
Charles,A.,136n29
Chomsky,N.,1,4,7,11,12,13,14,
  15,21,67,202,229,233,258n15
Chomsky-adjunction,121n8,
  123n8,124n8
Classical Nahuatl,154
Clause,106
Clause type,79
Clitic complex,17
Clitic elements,59
Clitic particles,62,63
Clitic pronouns,118n7
Clitic sequence,68,73,118n8,
  119n8
Clitic types,60
Clitics,16,63,66,67,68,72,
  120n8,158

transformational treatment of,119n8
Cliticization,158
Closs,E.,274,300n13
Conjoined NP,237
Collective action,209
Colloquial Eqyptian Arabic, *see Egyptian Arabic*
Command relations,107
Commands,192
Common categorial solution, 228
Comp,5
Comparative grammar,226
Complementation,201
Complementizer,64,196,197,200
Complements,41,100,106,132n22, 182,184,201
 absolutive-marked,222n10
 of predicates,80
Complement-types,196
Complete utterances,173
Composition,142,154,157,251
 of AUX,149
 of elements,147
 of lexical elements,253
 of subject and verv,248
 rules of,252
Compositionality,62
Compound tense,285
Compound words,68
Concessive connectives,103
Conditional sentences,138n40
Conjectives,190
Conjuncts,102
Constituency,43,62,71-73,97, 116,117n3,121n8,126n8, 128n16,242,243,245,251-252, 253,256n9
Constituency-equivalence,256n9
Constituent,21,22,24,25,26,33, 39,58,59,72,73,95,97,98,113, 114,115,119n8,120n8,145,155, 161,212,217,227,268,269

Constituent boundaries,121n8
Constituent structure,22,231- 232,238,245,258n15
Contained tense,107
Containment phenomenon,103
Context predicate,241
Continuative,102
Contraction,227,263,289,290, 291,293-294,295
 of auxiliaries,292
Copular sentences,65,89,158
Copular verb,66,76
Coordinate clause,275
Coordinate conjunction,106
Cooccurrence,113,263
Cooccurrence restrictions,31, 269-270,300n13
Core grammar,7,11,12,13,19n7
Counterfactual conditionals, 298n5
Counterfactuality,264
Criterial notional categories,161
Criterial properties,163
Cross-linguistic categories, 156-157
Cross-linguistic comparison, 2,3,6,12,21
Cross-linguistic equivalence, 3,141,155,163,168,217
Cross-linguistic identification,18n2
Cross-linguistic investigation,23
Cross-linguistic similarity, 4,8
Culicover,P.,14
Curme,G.,265,270,295,297n4, 298n6,299n7,299n8

Declarative main clauses,267, 287
Declaratives,169,175,178,181, 212,227,266,290,292

Decomposition of AUX,160
Deep structures,14
Definitional properties,8,17,
  162
Deictic orientation,44
Deletion site,239
Denotation,205
Deontic space of modals,195
Dependent clauses,137n35
Desiderative expressions,172
Determiner,5,10,11
Detransitivizing suffix,69
Diachronic contraction,295
Diekhoff,T.A.,295
Direct quotation,44,172
Direct object,18n2,288
Discourse context,111
Distant nonfuture,28,48
Do mapping,189
Do support,188
Dominating tense,107
Dummy tense carrier,285
Dummy verb,282
Dutch,269

Echo questions,49,191
Edmondson,J.,272,297n3
Egyptian Arabic,23,73-97,114,
  115,138n38,139n42,141,143-
  144, 145,146,154,155,166n10
Elicitation questions,191
Ellegård,A.,283,284,286,301n20
Ellipsis,189,227,243,259n18,
  286
El Rakhawy, T., 138n38
Embedded clauses,80,201,209
Embedded clause types,79
Embedded infinitival proposi-
  tional complement,201,206
Embedded infinitive phrase,
  202
Embedded propositions,206
Embedding clause,209
Embedding predicate,201

Emonds,J.,14,194,268
Emotive,136n27
Emotive adjective,109
Emphasis,146,156,159,187,189,
  223n11,227
Enclitic particles,61,66,69,
  70,71,137n36
Enclitic sequence,72,73,114,
  143,155,156
English,5,13,15,16,18,21,22,
  71,98,102,116,127n11,165n7,
  ,166n7,173,186-211,212,213,
  214,215,218n1,268,278,279,
  291,293,294,296,299n8
English auxiliary system,151,
  153,260,269-279,275,289,
  297n4
English complementation,198
English modals,266
English passive,69
English propositional
  structures,210
English syntax,211
English verb phrase,287
English verbs,17
Epistemic interpretation,
  224n15
Epistemic pre-modals,300n15
Equi,14,204
  obligatory,201
Equivalence,3-7,13,212
Equivalence class,see also
  AUX,17,19n6,19n9,155-156,
  226,252-253
Erben,J.,295
Essential invariance,13
Evers,A.,260,274,297n4
Evidential,156,159
Evidential markers,145-146
Exclamation,191-192,193
Existential sentences,139n42

Failed obligation,138n40
Falling intonation,190,191

Features,232,253n3
Fillmore,C.,223n13
Final conjunct,102
Final past tense,102
Final position,147,148,155,
  157,158,159,165n7,166-
  167n11,266,269,286,300n13
Finite sentence,83,91,94,95,
  97
Finite verbs,266,267,268,273,
  274,275,299-300n13,302n24
of German,264-268
First person plural,129n17,
  130n17,131n21
First person possessive prefix,137n35
First person pronoun,64
First person singular,131n21
First person singular pronoun,
  44
First person singular subject,
  36
First person singular subject
  marker,130n19
First person subject,109
First position,127n13,147,148,
  155,157,158,159,165n7,166-
  167n11,188,189,194
Fixed internal order,160
Fixed order,269
Fixed order of elements,155
Fixed universal inventory,15
Focus,65
Fodor,J.A.,199,200,201
Formality marker,111
Free propositions,204
Free VP's,205
Free word order,161
Full verbs,291
Function,205,255n7,256n9
  semantically additive,171
  syntactically nonadditive,171
Functional structure,170
Future,28,29,61,129n16,174,
  206,264-265
Future tense,83,88
Future tense,negative form of,
  87
Future tense sentences,90
Futureness,30

Gamal,A.S.,138n38
Gamal,Suad,138n38
Gap,293
Gapping,237,257n11
Gazdar,G.,14,16,17
Gender,76,79
Genetic endowment,7
German,18,165n7,166n7,260,279,
  289,296,296n1,297n1,n3,
  298n4,299n6,n9,301n19
German Aux,261-274
German verb phrase deletion,
  298n4
German verbal phrase,271
Gerund,102,196,298w8
Gerundive,100
Grammar of Luiseño,44,54,55,
  57,58,285
Grammatical property,226
Grammatical relations,65
Grammatical roles,256n9
Greenberg,J.,4
Grosu,A.,297n4

Ha-imperfect,76,83,138n39
Hale,K.,58,160
Halle,M.,233
Hausmann,R.,284-285,295-296,
  301n20,n22
Have/be raising rule,245
Head of the predicate,178,
  184,185,219n5,220,221n7
Head of relative clause,184
Headed structures,154
Heavy phrases,275
Higgins,R.,202
Higher clause,208

Higher predicates,166n9,201
History of English,260,302n25
Huber,W.,260
Hyde,V.,117n5,117n6

Imperative,41,43,66,79,80,91,
 95,138n40,147,148,164n4,169,
 175,181,187,192,212,227,266,
 268,270,287,299n10,n11
Imperfective aspect,74
Ich-Spaltung,200
Independent clauses,66
Independent subjunctive
 clause,80
Independent subject,92,95,
 164n3
Indicative,268,301n19
Indicative that-clauses,194
Indices,195
Infinitival clauses,209
Infinitival complement,209,210
Infinitival expressions,200
Infinitival constructions,234,
 236
Infinitival markers,210
Infinitival phrase,203
 intrinsically bound,208
Infinitival proposition,202,
 206
Infinitive,100,196,201,207,
 209-210,255n7,271,281,285,
 288,290,291,299n8
Infinitive-embedding pre-
 dicates,206
Infinitive VP,202
Inflection,281,262-263,294
Inflected auxiliary verb,285
Informal American English,291
Initial particles,294
Initial position,266,267,287,
 295,*see also First position
 and Position 1*
Innateness,8
Instructions,192

Instrumental agent,203
Instrumental nouns,66
Instrumental propositions,204
Instrumental VP's,205
Instruments,203,224n14
Internal order of AUX,142,149,
 150,154,157,161
Interpretation,227
Interrogative,169,175,227,266
Intersubstitutability,256n9
Intonation,31,71,190,192,215
Intonation break,71,147
Intonation contours,213,214
Intransitive sentences,203
Inventory of categories,229,
 230
Inversion,191,227,243-245,
 252,263,278,281,283,286,292
Irrealis,138n40
Irregular verbs,278

Jackendoff,R.,4,5,10,14,151,
 152,153,237,258n15
Jacobs,R.,129n16
Jacobsen,W.,137n31
Japanese,97-114,115,117n4,
 139n43,141,143,146,147,148,
 150,155,158,164n4,165n6,
 274
Japanese affixes,144,164n2
Jelinek, E.,90
Jespersen,O.,286

Kaisse,E.,16,25,118n8,119n8,
 120n8
Kajita,M.,202,203
Kitagawa,C.,103
Klima,E.,193
Koster,J.,12,269
Kuipers,A.,66
Kummer,W.,260
Kuno,S.,109
Kuroda,S.-Y.,109

Lakoff,R.,111
Lambda-abstraction,239
Lambda-expression,242
Language faculty,1
Language families of the Northwest,137n31
Language-internal categories, 3,5,6,9,12
Language-internal properties, 167
Language-particular grammars, 13
Language-particular rules,295
Language-specific categorial labels,7,19n9
Lasnik,H.,7,11,12,67
Layered analysis of S,99-114
Layered-S system,98,99,109
Lexical analysis,55,56,57,58
Lexical category,67,68,154, 245
Lexical elements,229,232,234, 236,243,251-252
Lexical entries,56,66
Lexical items,293
Lexical specification,222n10
Lexicon,57,38
Liberman,M.,193
Linguistic change,58
Lightfoot,D.,260,274,275-284, 300n15,n16,n17,n18,201n21
Logical form,19n8,239,240
Logical necessity,33
Logical type,196
Lower clause,208
Low-level phonetic rules,71
Luiseño,15,16,17,23-59,97,114, 115,116,117n5,118n7,118n8, 119n8,120n8,121n8,127n11, 131n20,132n22,136n27,141, 143,144,145,146,147,149, 150,154,155,165n5,173-186, 211,212,213,214,215,218n2, 219n3,221n9,222n10,274,291

Luiseño clitics,16
Luiseño Particle Sequence, 122n8,126n8,151,165n5, 166n10,175
Luiseño suffixes,28
Luiseño syntax,58
Lummi,23,59-73,97,114,115, 116,117n4,136n29,141,143, 150,151,155,156,158,165n5 274
Lummi clitic particles,61
Lummi Enclitic Sequence,144, 145,165n5,166n8
Lummi predicates,64
Lummi sentence,59,64
Lummi Sentence Well-Formedness Condition,66-67,73
Lummi syntax,67

McCawley,J.,260

Main clause,81,135n24,184, 222n10,275,301n23
Main verb,97,166n9,237,245 257n10,283,290-291,292, 301n23
Main verb analysis,229,260-263
Main verb stem,100
Major constituent breaks,71
Maling,J.,269
Martin,S.,139n44
Matrix subject,209
Matrix tense,106
Matrix variable,209
Maximal scope,193
Meaning relationships,(unpredictability of),66
Middle English (ME),260,275-276,281,282,283,285,286, 288,300n15,301n20
Middle position,25,*see also Second position and Position 2*

Minimal Interaction Condition, 62,68-70
Mitchell,J.,260
Modal,5,13,153,188,195,210, 224n15,235,236,245,248,249, 250,251,253,258n15,259n16, 259n18,261,263,274,275,277, 279,280,281,282,283,288,289, 290,299n8,302n25
 syntactic behavior of,279-280
Modal affixes,107-110
Modal assertion,27,30,32,33, 47,54,128n15,151,178,179
Modal Auxiliaries,17
Modal constructions,138n40
Modal elements,order of,249
Modal force,151
Modal-spaces,259n18
Modal statements,31
Modal verbs,271,273
Modality,14,21,22,24,33,34,59, 61,72,73,98,113,115,116n2, 135n27,145,146,149,150,151, 154,156,159,161,165n6,194, 196,217,227,265,266,269,293
Modality element,108
Modern English(NE),260,263, 265,277,278,281,284,288,289, 295,298n5,302n25
Modern German, 260,274,275, 295,*see also German*
Modes of composition,249-250
Mood,264,265,268,278,280,287, 288,299n9,299n10,301n19
Morpheme boundary,143
Morphology,19n8
Morphological component,57
Morphological dependency,227
Morphological elements,301n19
Morphological irregularity,281
Morphological properties,4
Morphological rule,67
Morphological similarity,256n9
Morphological unit,70

Mossé,F.,285,286,300n17, 301n23
Move α,19n8
Movement,243
Movement rules in English,99

Near future,127n13
Near nonfuture,28,34,127n12
Near past,127-128n13
Near time,31,39,40
Negation,97,111,114,145,146, 156,159,189,227,283,288, 293,301n21
Negative,98,121n8,144,263, 277,282,286
Negative element,165n5
Negative imperatives,181,182
Negative particle,88,89,90, 91,94,95,300n17
Negative Placement,278,281
Negative present tense sentences,94
Negative pronouns,89,90,91, 92,93,95
Node,82,83,90
Nominalizer,64,137n32
Nominative pronouns,235,256n9
Non-core grammar,12
Non-present tense sentences, 95
Nonassertion,27,47,54
Nonconfigurational languages, 58
Nonconstituency position,32
Noncriterial notional categories,161
Nondefinitional properties,6, 7,8,17,19n6,141,142-149,162
Nondistinctness,208
Nonfinite clause types,79
Nonfinite contexts,245
Nonfinite constructions,261
Nonfinite embedded clause type,80

Nonfinite sentence types,79, 81
Nonfinite verbs,275,298n5
Nonfuture,28,29,174
  distant,46
Nonintersecting categories,10
Nonlexical category,153,245
Nonmodal assertions,27,39,40, 52,54,174,178,179
Nonmodals,235,236,255n7,279
Nonquotative speech,48,50,51, 52,178
Nonreportive speech,109
Nonrepresentational form,191
Nonverbal predicates,76
Nonvolitional agents,223n14
Northwest languages,64
Notional categories,60,73,145, 150,154,159,299n11
Notional criteria,4
Notional types,142,148,150, 160
Noun,3,10,11,59,66,83,84, 117n4,237,257n10,n11,293
Noun Phrase,10,11,112,248, 274,275,287
Number,23,35,40,52,76,79, 118n7,164n3
Number agreement,291
Number distinction,26

Obligation,21,33
Obligatory bound particles,62
Object,5,59,170,285,287, 301n23,n24
Object agreement,146,159,169n3
Object marking,146,156,159, 161,164n3
Occam's Razor,3
Oehrle,R.,117n2,225n15,231, 251,252
Old English (OE),260,274, 275,276,277,278,283,285, 295,296,296n1,300n15,n17, 301n19

OE categories,297n1
OE Grammar,287
OE word order,275
Optative,61
Optimal Categorial Solutions, 228-229
Ordering relationships,151
Overt subject,91

Palatalization,295
Partial function,223n11
Particle boundaries,124n8
Particle Complex,43,44-45,46, 47,50,53,54,55,56,57,58,59, 114,143,144,147,148,154, 155,174,178,179,181,182, 214,221n7
  nonquotative,149
  semantics of,56
Particle 1 position,149
Particle sequence,24,25,30, 31,32,33,34,35,37,39,43,45, 46,47,48,49,50,51,52,54,56, 58,118n6,121n8,123n8,124n8, 126n8,128n14,129n17,131n20, 133n23,134n23,180,181
  as a Semantic unit,24-43
Particle 2 position,149
Particle 3 position,149
Particles,23,24,26,27,38,41, 83,94,117n6,145,174,175, 179
Participle,76,77,84,196,285, 291,299n8
Passive,18n2,67
Passive participles,76
Past,61,83,87,90,102,103,106, 129n16,195,234,236,264-265, 268,281
Past continuous,46
Past habitual,46
Past participles,236,273
Pastness,30
Penultimate position,158

Perception verbs,184
Perfect,74,83
Perfect participles,271
Perfect verb paradims,76
Perfective,76,77,285,288,290,
    301n22
Periphrastic do,288
Periphrastic tense,285
Perlmutter,D.,18n2
Permission,21
Person,23,35,36,40,52,76,79,
    118n7,164n3,291
Person marking,293
Person subjects,61,83,84,85,
    90,92,95,97
Phantom syntactic variable,
    198
Phantom variable expression
    197
Phonological properties,4
 of particle sequence,25
Phonological independence,70
Phonological interaction,
    129n17
Phonological properties,62-63
Phonological regularity,72
Phonological sequences,71
Phonological unit,62,70
Phrasal categories,151-152
Phrase marker,13,14
Phrase structure,252
Phrase structure grammars,252
Phrase structure rules,14,55,
    98,108,113,114,139n45,153
Plural,28,34
Plural imperative,181
Plural/nonplural distinction,
    40
Plural subject,36
Position,145,147,154,166n7
Position of modals,194
Position 1,26,27,31,33,38,53,
    54,124,126n10,146,175,179
Position 2,26,43,51,66,146

Position 3,26,33,51,53,54,
    126n9,146,174,175,179
Positional constraints,273
Positional properties,157
Positive imperatives,182
Possessive,180,184,185,214,
    215,219n3,221n9
Possessive marked form,135n27
Possessive prefix,51,53,176,
    177,184,220n6,222n10
Possessive pronoun,64,137n35
Possessive pronoun affixes,66
Possible grammar,9,10
Possibility,21,116n2
Postal,P.,18n2
Post-Auxiliary Ellipsis,238,
    258n14
Postposition,221n9
Predicate,60,64,65,66,76,77,
    80,81,82,84,90,91,92,93,94,
    95,96,97,139n42,144,205,
    251,259n7
Predicate head,59
Predicate nouns,76
 definite,89
Predicational adjectives,76,
    111
Pre-modal verb,279
Pre-modals,275,277,280,278,
    281,282,283,285,288,300n15
Preposing rules,268
Prepositions,83,257n10
Prepositional phrase,10,76,
    274,275,287
Present participle,236
Present tense,83,88,90,91,95,
    103,106,234,264-265,268,281
Present tense auxiliaries,290
Present tense existential,291
Present tense sentences,89,
    93,94
Present time,127n12
Preterite-present,278,288

Preterite-present inflect-
   ional class,280
Preverbal adverbs,286
Primary stress,70
Probability,21,116n2
Proclitic,158
Progressive,290
Pronominal enclitics,60
Pronoun of separation,89,90,
   91,95,97
Pronoun subject,90
Pronoun,59,90,235
Proposition,205
Propositional arguments,170
Propositional basis of
 assertions,170,174
 imperatives,170,182
 orders,170
 questions,170,174
Propositional constituents,204
Propositional content,206,248
Propositional radical,206
Propositional representations,
  198
Propositional satisfaction
   conditions,169,175
Propositional structure,201,
   209,210
Prosodic phrasing,137n37
Prospective aspect,76
Pullum,G.14,16,17,25,116n1,
     118n8,120n8,121n8,122n8,
     123n8,124n8,126n8,236,237
Purposive construction,67

Qualified knowledge,61
Quantifiers,227
Quasi-modal,277,288
Question marking,72,145,146
Questioning,273,283
Questions,30,32,49,50,127n11,
     156,159,169,175,178,181,190,
     191,193,194,195,212,263,266,
     268,277,282,288,292,293

Quotative speech,26,44,45,47,
   48,127n11,145,151

Raising,14,201,204
Raising verbs,203
Recoverability,239,251
Referential differences,199
Referential distinctions,198
Reflexive pronoun,198,199,200
Regressive assimilation,72-73
Relational notions,256n9
Relations,226
Relationship to adjacent
   elements,142
Relative clauses,41,132n22,
   182,184,222n10
Relative order,156
Relative scope,150
Relative time,21
Relativization,194
Reordering,297n3
Representational vs nonrepre-
   sentational,190
Requests,169
Requirement,21
Responsibility,137n34
Restricted control,69
Right domain,247-248,249,250
Rigid word order,158
Rising intonation,190,191
Root operations,194,194
Root transformation,
   obligatory,268
Ross,J.R.,14,260,269

S-layer,98,99,100
Sag,I.,14,16,17,238,239,241,
   242,251,257n11,257n13,
   258n14
Salish languages,66,136n29
Scope of tense,103
Scope relations,151,250
Scholten,T.,260,274,297n4
Second coordinate,259n17

Second person object suffix,69
Second person present tense, 293
Second person singular,76
Second person singular subjects,52
Second position,123n8,147, 148,155,157,158,159,161, 165n7,166-167n11,189,194, 267,269,275,285,286,287, see also Sentential second position, Position 2
Second Position Condition,62, 63-67
Second-position enclitics,116, 291
Second-position particles,58, 59,115
Selectional restrictions,203, 209
Selkirk,E.,137n37
Sentence,3,18n1,112,168,169, 173,175,212
  of possession,51-52,135n27
Sentence conjunction,106
Sentence operator,102
Sentence parsing,22
Sentence particles,111,113
Sentence types,27,30,32,33, 39,40,41,43,45,52,54,55,56, 79,83,91,93,127n11,174,227
Sentence structure,96
Sentence-final position,65,98, 147,158,165n6
Sentence-initial particles, 294
Sentence-initial constituent, 63
Sentence-initial element,68, 137n35
Sentence-initial position,65, 121n8,132n23,137n36,293
Sentence-level condition,62, 67-68

Sentential access,159,166-167n11
Sentential complements,14,100, 170
Sentential negation,83,94,95
Sentential properties and relations,227
Sentential second position, 24,58,121n8,134n23,266,see also Second position
Sentential scope,148,159,160, 167n11
Sentential subject,300n15
Semantic additivity,218n1
Semantic analysis,247
Semantic categories,189
Semantic characterization,162
Semantic classification,168, 213
Semantic composition,205
Semantic criteria,4,18n5,212
Semantic decomposition,160
Semantic distinctions,294
Semantic field,116n2
Semantic function,171
Semantic interfependence,25, 32
Semantic interpretation of tense,102
Sentential negation,91
Semantic object,222n10
Semantic properties,256n9, 273,280
  of particle sequence,25
Semantic relations,150,196
Semantic shift,279
Semantic specification,56
Semantic structures,247
Semantic symbols,251-252
Semantic unit,25,26
Semantic variables,204
Semantically additive mapping,184
Sequence of clitics,64

Sequence of tense rule,195
Shiman,L.,225n15,231,251,252
Singular imperatives,181
Singular subjects,298n5
Space operator,251
Speaker assessment,44
Speaker attitude,164n4
Speaker attitude affixes,148
Speaker attitude marker,147
Speaker desire,33
Speaker attitude particle, 164n2
Speaker's report,44,49
Speaker supposition,29,128n15
Specifier,153
Speech acts,157,169,175
Statements,31,49,50,128n14
Steele,S.,15,16,24,25,33,58, 98,99,116n1,117n5,118n7, 119n8,120n8,121n8,124n8, 129n7,130n18,131n20,133n23 136n27,141,154,165n5,177, 184,222n10,258n15,170,289, 302n25
Stem,184,219n3,222n10
Stopp,R.,265
Stranded tense,285
Stress contours,71
Strong probability,61
Structural context,112
Structural description,229
Stylistic rules,275
Subcategorization,99,110,106-107,108,113,202
Subject,5,18n2,23,52,59,60,67, 69,82,91,92,93,94,95,96, 131n20,139n42,151,164n3, 170,184,188,194,196,197, 198,199,200,201,202,203, 206,209,222n10,248,256n9, 277
 intrinsically bound,201,202
Subject agreement,146,156,159, 164n3,266,269

Subject marking,23,25,26,27, 30,32,35,36,37,38,39,40,41, 45,46,47,48,51,52,54,83, 118n7,129n17,130n18,131n20, 137n34,145,146,156,159,161, 164n3,222n10,273
Subject of a complement,200
Subject person marking,73
Subject position,200
Subject pronouns,291
Subject-binding,201
Subject-containing complements,197
Subject-verb agreement,245
Subjective Doubt,190,191
Subjective Nondoubt,190
Subjectless complements,198, 199
Subjectless infinitival complements,197
Subjectless VP-complements, 198
Subjunctive verb inflection, 80,95,264,265,266,268,278, 283,295,298n5,n6,299n7, 301n19
Subjunctive clause types,79
Subordinate clause,18n1,168, 170,173,182,184,186,187, 196,225n15,227,266,274, 301n23
 absolutive-marked,222n10
 syntactic form of,194
Subordinate constructions,41, 43,128n13
Subordinate present tense,195
Subordination,64,132n22,210
Substitute verbs,284,296
Suffixes,43,47,97,127n12, 128n13,176,220n5
Surface filter,67
Surface structure,14
Supercategory,237,238
Superficial structure,81

Suppositions,33,190
 from general knowledge,30
 with external verification,30
Synchronic contraction,295
Synchronic contraction hypothesis,294
Syntactic additivity,218n1
Syntactic analysis,55,58,162
Syntactic categorial label,115
Syntactic category,1,2,4,251
Syntactic constituency,25
Syntactic constituents,71,115,252,297n1
Syntactic decomposition,160
Syntactic features,5,229,236
Syntactic function,171,188
Syntactic layering,99
Syntactic mode,14
Syntactic properties,4,230,273,280
 and particle sequence,25
Syntactic relations,196
Syntactic representation,102
Syntactic rule,19n8
Syntactic specification,56
<u>Syntactic Structures</u>,13,22
Syntactic structures,137n37,251-252
Syntactic subject,198
Syntactic subordination,173
Syntactic theory,22
Syntactic type,196
Syntactic variable,67
Syntactically additive mapping,180
Syntax of infinitival complements,205
Syntax (of Luiseño)24,55,177

Tags,192,214,215,223n12,227
Target predicate,241

Temporal coordinates,207,208,209,210,224n15
Temporal notions,41,266,264-265
Temporal properties,224n15
Temporal reference,21,22,43,176,182,184
Temporal relations,201,205
Temporal restriction,185,206
Temporal variable,206
Tense,13,14,21,22,24,28,33,34,46,47,59,61,72,73,79,81,83,89,90,91,95,97,98,106,114,115,127n13,145,146,150,151,153,154,155,159,161,165n6,166n7,170n173,174,175,177,178,180,181,182,185,187-188,194,195,196,210,217,219n3,227,228,240,241,242,247-248,253,258n15,259n18,264,266,268,269,276,278,282,286,287,288,291,293,299n9,301n19,302n25
 grammatical status of,21-22
Tense affixes,99-107
Tense carrier,296,301n20
Tense distinctions in modals,281
Tense elements,165n7
Tense mapping,189
Tense marking,281
Tense morphemes,100
Tense suffixes,34,220n6
Tense/aspect suffixes,41
Tensed complement,100
Tensed environments,257n12
Tensed verbs,102
Tensed vervs,240
Tenseless complements,99
Tenseless constructions,299n8
Tenseless forms,102
Tenseless sentences,106
Tenseless <u>that</u>-clause,186,193,196

Tenseless verbs,100,102
That-complements,298n5
That-relatives,194
Thematic relations,205,206
Thematic role,201,203,206
Theory of grammar,229,273
Third person present tense, 290,293
Third person singular,76
Third person singular pronoun, 234,254,255n6
Third person singular subject, 52,290
Third position,45,127n12,*see also Position 3*
Thompson,L.,68
Thompson,M.,68
Time reference,106
Topic,165n7
Topic marker,109
Topicalized element,147,148
Transitive infinitival complements,202,203
Transitive predicates,83
Transitive sentences,59,198
Transitivizing suffix,69
Transitive verbs,286
Transformations,14,252,273, 275,281
Transformational grammar of German,268
Traugott,E.,278,279,286, 299n9,300n17,301n20,n22
True modals,277
Truth value,157,158,160,161, 163,167n11,168,205,212
Typological considerations, 158,216

Uniform Three-Level Hypothesis,152-153
Universal cross-linguistic validity,253n3
Universal inventory,1,2,9,11

Universal Grammar,2,7-13, 19n7,226
Universal grammatical properties,226
Uncertainty,264
Unverifiability,30
Unverified,129n16
Uto-Aztecan,176
Uto-Aztecan auxiliary system,289
Uyeno,T.,111

V_n,14,16,17
Variable,222n10
  intrinsically bound,202
Verb,3,5,10,11,14,16,17,27, 31,41,59,62,65,66,67,68,69, 70,72,76,79,80,81,95,115, 117n4,137n34,143,158,164n2, 165n7,175,181,193,195,199, 200,201,202,203,205,206, 208,222n10,229,230,236,240, 242,243,255n8,257n11, 259n18,263,264,266,268,273, 280,281,282,283,285,293, 294,296,298n4,n6,299n10, 300n15
Verb phrase (VP),10,11,112, 198,205,22n10,239,256n9, 257-258n14
  nontensed,240
  transitive,203
Verb phrase-equivalence,240
Verb Phrase-Fronting,227
Verb phrase complements,199
Verb Phrase Deletion,227, 238-245,247-251,252,259n18, 297n4
Verb stem,97,166n7
Verb-final language,97,287
  German as,269
Verb-initial language,151, 287
Verb-Second rule,275

Verbal affixes,70
Verbal inflection,285
Verbs of perception,281,
  299n12
 complements to,270
Verbs of temporal aspect,270
Verifiability,30,40
Verified,129n16
Verb,232-237,243,247-248
  255n7,256n8
Verb-elements,259n18
Visser,F.,278,284,286,301n20
Voice,76
Volitional agent,201,202,203,
  206,207,223n14
Vowel apocope,129n17
Vowel deletion,143

W* language,58
Wagner,K.,260
Walbiri,161
Wasow,T.,14,15,16,23,25,33,
  98,99,116n1,117n5,118n7,
  119n8,120n8,121n8,124n8,
  129n17,133n23,165n5,258n15,
  259n18,270,302n25
Wh-complements,193
  tensed,194
  movement,194
  questions,128n14
Wh-words,291,293
Willful control,69
Williams,E.,251
Wilson,D.,14,236,237
Word order,55,64,227,267-268
Word-internal phonological
  processes,24

X° Readjustment,124n8
X-bar convention,120n8,151,
  152,153,166n10
X-bar syntax,10

Yes/no questions,31,61,190
  268

Younes,Nagwa,138n38

OHIO UNIVERSITY LIBRARY

turn this book as soon as you
In order to avoid a
by the latest date